THE
LAST
MOGUL

THE
LAST
MOGUL

*The Unauthorized Biography
of Jack Kent Cooke*

ADRIAN HAVILL

ST. MARTIN'S PRESS ▪ NEW YORK

Design by Robert Bull Design

Library of Congress Cataloging-in-Publication Data
Havill, Adrian.
The last mogul : the unauthorized biography of Jack Kent Cooke.
p.   cm.
ISBN 0-312-07013-6
1. Cooke, Jack Kent.   2. Businessmen—United States—
Biography.   I. Title.
HC102.5.C57H39 1992
338'.04'092—dc20
[B]   91-36089

First Edition: January 1992

10 9 8 7 6 5 4 3 2 1

This book is for
David and Amanda
and especially,
"Mike"

On Predestination

I believe in predestination. I believe that we are going to be what some power has decided we're going to be. As Shakespeare wrote, "There's a destiny that decides our ends rough hewn though they may . . ." —I've forgotten the verb he used. But I've always believed I would reap the good things of life.

On Optimism

Two small boys are brought into a room where the floor is covered with horse manure. The first little boy couldn't take the smell and ran out. The second little boy looks at the floor and said, "Oh boy, Where's the pony?"
That second little boy is me.

JACK KENT COOKE
on his philosophy of life

CONTENTS

Acknowledgments xi
General Notes xiii
Preface xv

PART ONE: WASHINGTON

Chapter 1: Opening Day, 1987 3

PART TWO: TORONTO

Chapter 2: Opening Day, 1912 23
Chapter 3: Jack Be Quick 38
Chapter 4: Jack Jumps Over 44
Chapter 5: Radio Days 53
Chapter 6: Literary Ways 67
Chapter 7: A Major in the Minors 87
Chapter 8: Citizen Cooke 102

PART THREE: LOS ANGELES

Chapter 9: Contests and Indians 117
Chapter 10: Cable Fights 126
Chapter 11: Hoops and Hoopla 142

CONTENTS

Chapter 12: Six Kings and A Jack 153
Chapter 13: The Unraveling 168
Chapter 14: Cooke vs. Cooke 178

PART FOUR: WASHINGTON

Chapter 15: Life Three 199
Chapter 16: Acquisitions for the Modern Mogul 213
Chapter 17: Suzanne/Susan 229
Chapter 18: Cooke vs. Cooke, II 244
Chapter 19: Marlene/Marlena et al. 257
Chapter 20: Coming Home 270
            Afterword 281
            Sources 284
            Bibliography 290
            Index 293

ACKNOWLEDGMENTS

No book like this could be written without the help of many people. Besides researchers in Washington, Los Angeles, Toronto, New York City, Lexington, Kentucky, and Alderson, West Virginia, I would like to thank Chris Friedenberg in Los Angeles and Lincoln Richman in New York City. My editorial assistant, Brenda Nicely Atkins, was always there when I needed her.

I wish I could acknowledge everyone who provided information or helped me on this book. However, many enthusiastically spoke to me only on the basis of anonymity; those sources will have to always remain confidential. Those who assisted me by giving me information or extending other courtesies should be recognized. They include my editor, Bob Weil, whose guidance and counsel will never be forgotten. Also: Brian Henley, Lyn Dale, Jerry Ormond, Jack Welch, Eddy Perkovic, Norman and Edna Tarver, Larry King, Carol Doumani, Bill and Susan Dalton, Al Dubin, Vera and Bill Brady, Brenda Webb, Bob Duckman, Lt. Cdr. Gary Durham, Kathleen O'Brien, Don Kowet, Richard Romano, Chuck Conconi, Kathleen Maxa, Diane Martin, Julie Martin, Suzanne Martin Cooke, Jim Gustafson, Florence Effie Sessoms, Gary Lautens, Norm Perry, Alex Barris, Tom Jakobek, Paul Frick, Gloria Shan, Rabbi David Monson, Margo Reid, Mary Pollock, Art Rose, Harry Markson, Mark Feldstein, Jerry Berns, C. Stanley Allen, Pamela Czapla, Blake Spraggins, Michael Keller, G. Allen Dale, Dick Beddoes, Faye Pollard, David Schwartz, Larry Anthony, Jack Limpert, Fraser Sutherland, Stephanie Petrewski, Arthur Crowley,

ACKNOWLEDGMENTS

Esq., Angel Miguens-Oller, John Fraser, Joe Blair, Agnes Williams, Scott Wycoff, Annett Madison, Ken "Jiggs" McDonald, Walter Friedenberg, David Sands, Harry Bluestone, Gloria Daniels, Cathy Gilder, Ginger Fox, Benno Gerson, Marjorie Havill, Angela Kilkenny, Barbara Donahue, Sam Wood, Bill Murphy, Rudy Maxa, Shang Patterson, Barbara Pepelko, Robert Nelson, Ph.D., Susan Williams, and Gwen Harrell Swinburne.

GENERAL NOTES

The author contacted and interviewed 152 people for this book. Many were interviewed several times and for as long as four hours at a sitting.

This book makes use of police records, court proceedings, data provided by the Securities and Exchange Commission, letters, diaries, newspaper, and magazine articles which span seventy-eight years, books, photographs, documents supplied under the Freedom of Information Act, public papers supplied by individuals to the Cable Television Museum at Pennsylvania State University, school yearbooks, video tapes, and confidential information supplied by individuals.

In researching this biography, the author and/or a researcher visited Hamilton and Toronto, Ontario, Canada, several times, as well as New York City, Los Angeles, and Lexington, Kentucky; the women's Federal Correctional Institute in Alderson, West Virginia; the cable television museum in College Station, Pennsylvania; Washington, D.C.; and Middleburg, Virginia.

The author is extremely grateful for the assistance provided by the special collections department of the library of Hamilton, Ontario, the Metro Reference Library and the Robarts Reference Library in Toronto, the Library of Congress, the library of the Embassy of Canada, McMasters University in Hamilton, Ontario, the city library of Lexington, Kentucky, and the courts of the County of Los Angeles as well as other public libraries in the cities mentioned above.

While everything in this book is true, it is written at times in a novelistic style. If the author describes the weather a certain way, climatic conditions were checked through newspapers of the day. If an interior or exterior setting is depicted, the reader can be assured that the author was either there himself or had the setting described to him in detail by someone intimate with the surroundings.

The author's interviewing method was to hold conversations with the subject, jotting down notes as unobtrusively as possible. At the end of each hour of conversation, the author would retire out of sight of the subject and quickly summarize the conversations by speaking into a tape recorder.

The author also kept a daily journal in which he detailed the events that related to this book. The journal was kept on a seven-day-a-week basis.

Some dialogue has been reconstructed. The reader should not assume that the indicated speaker necessarily said those words at that exact point in time, but should believe that the speaker said those or substantially similar phrases close to the time given.

When interviewing people in their seventies, about events which took place in the 1920s and 1930s, the author was aware that the subjects' recall could be mistaken due to the passage of so many decades of time. The subjects' recollections were checked against newspapers and other records of the era whenever those sources were available.

Specific sources for each chapter are listed at the end of the book; they can be consulted for more detailed documentation.

PREFACE

How does one capsulize Jack Kent Cooke? One doesn't. Jack Kent Cooke is a paradox. He can be ruthless, tough, and seemingly uncaring, firing an employee for speaking out of turn. He can also be capable of great kindness, quietly putting funds into someone's bank account to pay for a funeral. He will speak knowledgeably about fine wines and great literature and then spend the evening listening to big band popular music with a cheese sandwich or a hot dog in his hand. He will buy a second, third, or fourth home for millions of dollars, and the next day turn in a receipt for the purchase of a candy bar while on company business. Courtly and cruel, extravagant and frugal, Jack Kent Cooke fits no mold. He is truly unique, a mogul who has made his fortune by living life by his own rules, giving no quarter, never letting down. Witness what happened when I decided to write this biography.

After receiving word from my agent, Jane Dystel, on July 5, 1990, that St. Martin's Press had agreed to a proposal from me and wanted to publish the biography of Jack Kent Cooke, I made plans to visit Canada. Jack grew up in Toronto and has spent the majority of his life in that country. I knew that any biography about him would need a lot of cooperation from the people in his native province of Ontario. Fortunately, that was never a problem in writing this book.

When I returned to my home in the Washington, D.C., area, I wrote a letter to Jack Kent Cooke on September 4, 1990. In the letter I told him that I was writing a book on his life and that I considered him one of this century's pioneers in radio and cable television, and one of the visionaries of professional sports. However, I wrote, my research would be complete and thorough and no aspect of his life would be overlooked. I told him that if he wished I would grant him fact-checking privileges. I also requested an interview or a series of interviews, and asked for a list of people with whom he thought I should talk.

Jack Kent Cooke's reaction was instantaneous. Within days I began hearing from people from all over North America to say that Jack had telephoned. They told me, "He's asked me not to talk to you. He says you're out to do a hatchet job." Many of these people had already spoken to me and were still willing to talk to me. Unfortunately, others stopped talking to me. And still others would not consent to an interview when I called them, citing his wishes. One person who did talk hadn't seen Jack in nearly thirty years. He told me that Jack Kent Cooke had telephoned at nearly midnight, and without asking about his health or his family, simply told him, "You were my employee. You are not allowed to talk to this Adrian fellow. He's out to do a hatchet job on me."

I have a great deal of admiration for our "last mogul." He is one terrific entrepreneur. If this book comes through to the reader as being written by someone who has a negative viewpoint of Jack or conversely, is his cheerleader, I would be greatly disappointed. The facts speak for themselves.

I also feel an affinity with Jack. I, too, was a firstborn and grew up in Canada, arriving there after World War II with my British mother, the son of an English father who instead settled in Zimbabwe, next to Jack's mother's homeland of South Africa. Two years after Jack obtained his American citizenship through a special congressional bill, I became one also, while serving in the 82d Airborne Division. Later in my life, also with no family money or help, I too owned a number of businesses, albeit less successful ones than Jack's, but in allied fields. Like him, I was once very active in Variety Club charities. Because of our similar backgrounds, and my admiration for him, I wrote to Jack a second time, shortly before his seventy-eighth birthday. In my letter, I repeated the offers contained in my first letter. As a birthday tribute, I enclosed a product of my research, a custom-framed reproduction of an ad he had run in his high school yearbook advertising an orchestra he had formed under his name. This time I did get a response, but not directly. His attorney, Milton Gould, wrote to my publisher and advised it that Jack had "not given his permission" for his biography to be written. There were other words as well.

Jack's next step was to subpoena me in an attempt to link me with an outstanding lawsuit he had initiated months earlier against *Washingtonian* magazine. Three attorneys questioned me for nearly three hours. The majority of those questions were about this book, which at the time had yet to be written.

Some of them were very curious. For instance, on page 76 of the deposition, this exchange took place between Jack's attorneys and me:

Q. Has Susan [*sic*] Martin Cooke ever made any comments to you about drug usage by Marlena Cooke at any time?
A. Not that I recall.
Q. Has Susan [*sic*] Martin Cooke ever made any statements to you, either in person or over the telephone, regarding prostitution on the part of Marlena Cooke?
A. Prostitution?
Q. Yes, as in selling sex for money?
A. Marlena Cooke, prostitution.
Q. In any conversation that you have ever had, with Susan [*sic*] Martin Cooke, has she ever said anything to you about Marlena Cooke and prostitution?
A. No.
Q. Has she ever asked you for any information about Marlena Cooke and prostitution?
A. No, that's news to me.
Q. Had you ever heard it said that you had such records?
A. That I have such records?
Q. Have you heard anyone—
A. I just said it was news to me. No.

Even some of the media took sides. The Washington ABC-TV outlet, WJLA, refused to respond to two letters and countless phone calls for a request to view or purchase a tape of a series of 1984 interviews it broadcast of a local anchor talking with Jack.

When I did get through to the station's Communications department, two weeks after my letter was received, I was told "we're still processing that request." (They still are.) The anchor has been a frequent guest of Jack Kent Cooke in his private box and has been with him to at least one Super Bowl game.

Jack Kent Cooke is the last of a breed. He is a totally self-made individual who earned his riches without benefit of inheritance or formal education.

While Jack could be compared to the motion picture pioneer, Louis B. Mayer, or journalism's William Randolph Hearst, he would bristle at such an effort. He once upbraided a writer who dared to suggest he was similar to cable tycoon Ted Turner. And Jack was insulted when a writer wanted to include him as one of the five best salesmen of the world. "Sir, I am not one of five anything," he said. There won't be another like Jack Kent Cooke. He, indeed, is the last mogul.

WASHINGTON

1

OPENING DAY, 1987

**"If there were one thing Jack Kent Cooke
hated above all else, it was to lose."**

The old blue limousine, washed and polished, its gleaming
color matching the owner's eyes, glided silently through the city
like a great shark. Harry Turner, the blond, overgrown country
cherub who was its driver, was taking no chances. Even though
it was early on a Sunday morning, with the District of Columbia
virtually empty of traffic, he still took special care to ease the 1975
Cadillac through each intersection stop light, as if the occupant on
the cracked leather rear seat were an egg.

The day before he had burnished the Fleetwood to a silicone
shine, even going so far as to wash each window the way the
owner liked—with old newspapers and a mixture of vinegar and
ammonia. It was messy, and the ink from the paper blackened his
hands, but the old man hated for him to use Windex. Too expensive.

"That's the way I have them do each window in the Chrysler
Building," his boss had told him. Harry doubted they actually did
it that way, considering those powerful unions up north. But the
boss owned it and he could say what he wanted. He owned the
skyscraper, the building around the corner, and Harry, too, for
that matter. And true or not—Harry would give him this—the old
man could pinch pennies better than he'd ever thought possible.
The limo, for example, was nearly thirteen years old and the boss
had brought it with him from California. He was too tight to get
a new one. And when the decision was made to switch to blackout
windows, instead of doing it right, the boss drove to an auto supply

store in Manassas, Virginia, and bought two rolls of dark plastic for $6.95 each. Then he took it to Rick Hunt Ford in Warrenton and had it glued on by the boys in the shop.

The old man asked the manager how he should pay. "Whatever you think is right, Mr. Cooke," he was told.

"You boys don't want just money," the Squire of Middleburg had told them. "I'll get you something better." So he telephoned Redskin Park and had a messenger bring a box of trinkets—old Redskins hats, press guides, and bumper stickers for the young mechanics. Now the plastic was slowly starting to peel, like runny cellophane.

But Harry wouldn't question anything right now. The boss had a burr up his butt and his driver wasn't about to rile him.

Cocooned in the backseat was the source of his fear, a short, white-haired old man in his seventies, eighty pounds lighter and nearly five inches shorter than the chauffeur. And today he was unhappy. Alone, in the back of the limousine, Jack Kent Cooke, the Squire of Middleburg, who had begun as a dirt-poor door-to-door encyclopedia salesman in the Great Depression and now, a half-century later, was the billionaire owner of the Washington Redskins, muttered the words again as if chanting a mantra.

"The bitch," he said quietly. "The bitch."

Hell, Harry thought. Mr. Cooke should be happy as a clam from what he could see. The man was just back from his honeymoon with a blonde nearly fifty years younger. He had picked up $25 million in spare change in greenmail money when the Multimedia deal fell through. And earlier this year he had coughed up nearly a billion dollars for a cable network out west and never blinked an eye.

"I need another $25 million like I need the plague," the boss had growled to the press. But that was for the press. Harry was certain that secretly the boss was pleased.

Most of all he must have been overjoyed about the Redskins. They had just gone 3–1 in the preseason and even the coaches, the biggest worry warts on the team, were thinking Super Bowl, 1988.

"Bitch, the bitch."

The trophy wife, his new thirty-year-old bride, Suzanne Elizabeth Szabados Martin Cooke, wasn't in the limousine this morning. Harry assumed she would be coming by herself or was already at the stadium. But something was wrong. Mrs. Cooke should be here in the car with her husband.

With or without her, he knew the boss wouldn't miss this one. The old man had never missed a home game since he'd moved to Middleburg. Particularly the season opener against the Philadelphia Eagles on this second Sunday in September 1987. The Las Vegas line had his team favored by 9½ points and the billionaire had been looking forward to beating up on Buddy Ryan's boys.

Harry remembered when Prince Charles and Lady Diana were in town in 1985. Jack's neighbor, the "old money" philanthropist Paul Mellon, was having the future king and his bride out to lunch at his farm that Sunday. Jack Kent Cooke was one of those invited. He declined and Mellon had called to ask his neighbor why he wouldn't be there.

"And miss the Dallas game?" Jack answered. "You must be insane." The young royals would have to meet the Squire of Middleburg another day.

No, with or without his new bride, Jack would be at his regular post in the owner's box. Harry moved the wheel to the right and edged the limo onto North Carolina Avenue. For the first time that day, he could see Robert F. Kennedy Stadium.

That stadium was a chicken bone caught in Jack Kent Cooke's throat. Built as D.C. Stadium in 1959 for baseball (the now defunct Washington Senators), the old sports complex was the third smallest in the National Football League. The Redskins had sold out every game for more than a decade and the ticket office had a waiting list of season-subscriber hopefuls in the computer that numbered more than 26,000. Jack could have filled stands twice the size. It was bad enough it was named for a Kennedy, and other teams had revenue-boosting sky boxes, not to mention plusher owner's quarters. He wanted that income, the added cash that would come by having 20,000 more seats for the faithful. And sky boxes—you didn't have to share that money with anyone. Thank God the Redskins' lease would run out after the 1990 football season.

"I'll build a new stadium myself," Jack had told his friends.

5

"With my own money, just like I did in Los Angeles with the Forum. And if Marion Barry and the D.C. government won't co-operate, then I'll build it in Virginia."

Then he had asked the mayor to give him a portion of the land used for the Langston golf course, the oldest black golf club in town, asserting that his proposal would not prevent Langston from remaining an eighteen-hole course. D.C. Mayor Marion Barry had come back with a speech in which he said, "People in hell need ice water too." The billionaire then spoke to the Redskin faithful at a luncheon, where he said he didn't want ice water and he wasn't going anywhere either. Marion Barry caved and Jack Kent Cooke got his corner of Langston thrown in a few weeks later.

If a visitor to Washington stands on the steps of the Lincoln Memorial and looks due east along the mall he first sees the Washington monument, then, the seat of power—the U.S. Capitol. And, if he could periscope up above Capitol Hill, three miles further in a straight line he would see RFK Stadium. On a Sunday in the last quarter of any year, it too is a seat of power.

Anyone who is someone in Washington tries to be present for a Redskins game. Divorces have been fought in the courts over custody of season passes. Wills have been contested over the inheritance of tickets. For the fervent Redskins fans at home, it was seats in front of the TV set. The team sometimes approached an amazing 70 percent Nielsen share locally, with two large movie theaters projecting the games free in exchange for food and drink revenues. But to have entry to a prime seat at a Washington Redskins game on a Sunday in Washington was for many of the rich and powerful more important than an invitation to the White House itself.

And being in the box, the owner's box—that was Nirvana, the glory of glories. Chuck and Lynda Bird Robb never refused. The glitterati of the press corps—Ted Koppel, Lesley Stahl, George F. Will, William Safire, Carl Rowan—were nearly always there. On a Sunday afternoon there were usually more potential or former presidential candidates on hand—Edmund Muskie, George McGovern, Paul Laxalt, Eugene McCarthy—than anywhere else in the nation. Jack Kent Cooke, a conservative Republican, even got away with playfully calling liberal Democrats Muskie, Mc-Govern, and McCarthy his "communists." And if he had wanted, the old man could have placed the pols on one side of the box and the press corps on the other and had his own all-star *Meet the Press* on any given Sunday.

To his credit, the Squire of Middleburg never used the power of his RFK box to swing a business deal directly. Not that it didn't help to invite certain people. The box was social—an ego trip to be sure—but strictly for fun.

"I've never used my influence with anyone," he once told a reporter for the *New York Times,* his voice rising with indignation. "Never, not with any club I've owned."

One of the very few celebrities to ever decline an invitation to see a football game, Jack Kent Cooke style, was Larry King, the TV and radio talk show raconteur. The Squire of Middleburg, per-haps thinking it would be neat to seat Larry King, the electronic journalist, next to box-regular Larry L. King, the author of *Best Little Whorehouse in Texas,* was furious.

"What do you mean you won't come?" he asked in an in-credulous rage.

King had gotten back at Jack by calling him "a horse's ass" in his book, *Tell It to The King.* It was strange, the way Larry and Jack had met. There was Larry, digging into the brisket at Wash-ington's top power eatery, Duke Zeibert's, and Jack had spotted him and purposely strode over. "You take Lovastatin," Jack said. It was a statement, not a question and Larry answered that he did indeed take the cholesterol-lowering drug.

"A dollar a pill, a dollar a pill!" Jack had yelled and stalked off. That was the extent of the entire conversation. So scratch the Cooke name from Larry's interview list and Larry King's name from Jack's guest list.

The billionaire kept tight control over who was invited to the fifty-four-seat enclosure. Tickets were sent out as scripted invita-tions each week by mail or could be picked up at the VIP entrance in Parking Lot 5, where the invitee also got close-in parking priv-ileges. And even though you had been asked to twenty or thirty games in a row and considered yourself a regular, you could be inexplicably, cruelly, dropped without warning.

7

Washington's high and mighty lived in fear of that day. A Washington socialite, Betty Schulman, the wife of Jack Kent Cooke's tax attorney, who had represented him for decades and who had been a regular in the box for years, had slipped and fallen on a step in the enclave, spilling her wine glass and creating a stir.[1] The fact that she injured her wrist and had to go to the hospital to have it treated drew no sympathy from Jack. She had "upset" the tone of the enclosure, and worst of all, had drawn attention away from the game. After her husband Robert died, the woman fretted and worried that the billionaire would not have her back the next year. Friends lobbied with Jack on her behalf. Jack finally reissued the invitation, but her seat was moved from a favored position in the second row to a place in "Siberia," the section furthest away from the Squire of Middleburg. "I can't look after all the widows and orphans in this world," Jack told one of Betty's lobbyists.

This morning, as the limousine neared the stadium, it was picked up by a police escort. Lights flashing, as if Jack were a visiting head of state (in many respects he was), the cop on the motorcycle led Harry around the circle, into Parking Lot 5 and up to the VIP entrance. D.C. Mayor Marion Barry had called the police escort "a professional courtesy." He had also given the billionaire a "To Whom It May Concern" letter that asked the recipient to extend "all courtesies" to the limousine. When asked about it, the billionaire just shrugged. "It makes my life happier," he said.

Once a young cop had pulled the limousine over as Harry was leaving the stadium by an unauthorized, illegal route. There was a dispute as to whether Jack yelled at the policeman. The policeman said he did, but Jack remembered otherwise.

Not that he always reciprocated with His Honor. Sure, he had coughed up Super Bowl tickets and had given the mayor a plane ride to and from the game, but that was it. Mayor Barry didn't sit in the box of Jack Kent Cooke. Barry was not, however, without nerve. When the Redskins beat the Miami Dolphins in the 1983 Super Bowl, an aide of the mayor called to ask the P.R. department if the mayor could have a Super Bowl ring too. The team's front office had some good yuks over that one.

Now, Harry grabbed the binocular case from the front seat.

He handed Jack, the Squire of Middleburg, the Emperor of RFK, his dark glasses so that he could alight from the limousine in proper film star fashion. Then he slid his giant body off the bench seat and out the door into the glare of a full sun, hurrying around to open the rear door for the billionaire. It was nearly eleven in the morning, with more than two hours before the kickoff.

Jack was early, but by design. If he were to play the role of host to the rich and powerful, he would, by God, play it well. He prided himself on his outwardly impeccable manners. But today, his etiquette failed him.

Usually Harry would get an ultrapolite "Thank you" when he handed Jack his dark glasses. Today, the glasses were taken quickly, and instead of "Thank you" he got an impatient snarl. The old man quickly put them on and then adjusted his trademark houndstooth Brooks Brothers hat made by Locke of London, England. He was wearing his lucky Bally shoes, lucky socks, and lucky knit tie. Superstitious to be sure, but very few knew. Now, he was ready.

Jack was through the opened door of the stadium and inside before the chauffeur had a chance to back the car into parking slot number one. Fuming, pacing, he stood in front of the VIP elevator, waiting for Harry.

One of the billionaire's small secrets was that he was claustrophobic. He particularly hated elevators and avoided them at all costs. Once he had gritted his teeth and ridden to the executive office on the thirty-ninth floor of the seventy-seven-story Chrysler Building he owned in New York City, and it had taken him hours to calm down. "If the elevator had stopped, had broken down," he confided, "I don't know what I would have done. I hope I never know."

He would have liked to have skipped the elevator and walk up the ramps but the public would have mobbed him. Or so he thought.

"Let's go," he told his just-arrived chauffeur and valet, pointing to the open elevator doors, an attendant inside waiting to push the buttons for them. "Lead on, lead on."

The three-story ride up seemed like miles, but in reality it took about fifteen seconds. The doors opened and the two men entered

9

the VIP lounge and the entrance to Jack Kent Cooke's Sunday pied-a-terre.

On the walls were two elaborately framed color photographs. One was of Mayor Marion Barry with Michael Jackson. The other was of Jack Kent Cooke. There were other small pictures of rock stars who had played RFK, but the photos of Cooke, and Barry and Jackson dominated the room.

Jack moved quickly down the hall, into the private party room named after NFL legend Vincent Lombardi. The Lombardi Room would be a disappointment to most at first glance. Small and dark, the only window covered by dark shutters, with a bar to the right as one enters, it is paneled in cheap wood and the floor is covered by a worn, nondescript carpet. The size of the room is scarcely larger than an average tract house dining area, about twenty feet square. But the Lombardi is the place where presidents and rulers have gathered prior to and after RFK events. And during every Redskins game the room is at the disposal of the owner of Washington's NFL team.

Jack checked it to the smallest detail. Official Redskins book matches on the ashtrays. Jumbo shrimp, very fresh. Lox, bagels, and cream cheese. Danish pastry on silver trays. Hamburgers and hot dogs served from elegant covered chafing dishes. Only French wine. *Vin ordinaire,* but good *ordinaire,* so you didn't have to be ashamed of the label. It was in bottles, not carafes, and would be served in clear crystal glasses—no plastic. Fresh strawberries. Jack glanced quickly at the waiters and waitresses. The men were in burgundy jackets and dark trousers, the women in black and white, projecting the image of French maids. The waiters weren't even waiters. They were dentists and professionals from the suburbs who took the jobs for an opportunity to see the famous at play and bits of a sold-out game on the side.

The billionaire crossed the catwalk that led from the Lombardi Room to the owner's box. It looked right. There were fifty-four seats in the box—twenty-four in the front row, eighteen in the second, and twelve in the third. Each guest got a bowl of nuts and a bowl of miniature pretzels. A *Gameday* magazine ("The Official Magazine of the NFL") was on each seat, and a gift for everyone. Today, it was a faux-leather attaché case with the NFL logo on the flap. All four color TV monitors were on. They had been placed in each corner of the box and angled on platforms held up by chains. The billionaire picked up the old black metal dial phone that connected the booth with the coaches on the field. It worked. He gazed at the vivid green rectangle below. The best natural grass field in the league. It was "prescription athletic turf, number 419 Bermuda overseeded with a blend of rye grasses," he would tell anyone who asked, and it had a verdant aura like no other, particularly just before the first game of the year, when it was in a near-pristine state. Raising his eyes, he saw his own name, Jack Kent Cooke. Two years before it had been placed directly in one of the end zones, part of an oval sphere of famous names that surrounded the mezzanine boxes and known as the Washington Hall of Stars. When a point-after was kicked, his name was caught by the TV cameras. He was listed right between the coach who had led the team to its first Super Bowl, George Allen, and North Carolina/Redskins running legend Charlie "Choo Choo" Justice. It was no accident—Jack Kent Cooke had never been a shrinking violet.

The only thing missing was Susan.

It was time to call the bitch.

Suzanne Elizabeth Szabados Martin Cooke, the woman he had married less than two months before, was still at his Watergate apartment. She was nearly five months pregnant and showing. The billionaire had asked her to have the child aborted. She had already had two abortions on his behalf; what was another? Besides, he had promised to marry her if she would go through with it and he had married her, but then Susan (the Squire of Middleburg wouldn't address her as Suzanne—he thought the name sounded "affected, pretentious") hadn't kept her end of the bargain. Still, he hadn't given up. Just last week he had offered to send her and her mother to a hospital in Switzerland that specialized in advanced pregnancy terminations. How much more thoughtful could one get?

God, it was like asking for a date.

"Susan, pet, you aren't here."

"Jack, I told you I wasn't coming. I'm not catching a cab and I'm not driving myself.[2] You could have picked me up on the way

11

in from Middleburg. Why didn't you? You are my husband. And I'm carrying your child."

She didn't have to remind him.

A pause.

"Okay, Susan. If I send Harry with a police escort, you'll be here by kickoff time. Is that acceptable?"

"That's acceptable, Jack."

Time to greet the guests.

"George, so good to have you here. And Jonathan. Why you two look more alike each year."

George F. Will, the columnist, had shown up with his fourteen-year-old son, Jonathan. Jonathan, a Down syndrome child, was dressed in the same northeastern WASP style as his father. They looked cloned, identical down to their striped rep ties and wool herringbone jackets. Even the haircuts. The conservative part to one side, the front just falling onto the forehead New England prep-school style, were exact and on the mark. Will's look came from years spent in Ivy academia, although his roots began in the center of Illinois.

It was one of the old man's great pluses, the way he had with children. Something came from within, and now he talked with George Will's son as animatedly as if talking about the bloodlines of a horse with one of his trainers. The Squire of Middleburg was a huge supporter of kids' causes. He was on the board of the Little League foundation. And years ago, he was a major benefactor for the Variety Club of Ontario, a children's charity. A Canadian magazine, *Maclean's*, once quoted a friend of his as saying, "He'd rather write a check for $500 for a child with no legs than visit the kid at the hospital because he couldn't take the suffering."

"I'd cry," Jack had said to his friend at the time.

All the regulars were here now. Lesley Stahl would sit next to him in case Suzanne/Susan was a no-show. George Will and Carl Rowan would sit in front with Gene McCarthy. Jack's son, John, who had added Kent as his middle name to please his father—deleting Peter—was down on his right, next to Rowan, who was seated next to John "What's My Line" Daly. It would make for a powerful picture when the TV cameras panned the owner's box. And they always did, several times a game, particularly just after a touchdown. When Joe Theismann, his former quarterback, had asked that his girlfriend Cathy Lee Crosby, the actress, be allowed to sit in the box during visits to Washington, the old billionaire sat her in the third row—Siberia. But when he found out about her celebrity—she told him she was about to play the Marilyn Monroe part in a revival of Arthur Miller's *After the Fall* on Broadway—he moved her front and center.[3]

At the door, *Washington Times* sports columnist Morris Siegel, who served as the Emperor of RFK's chief confidant (he and Jack were both active in trying to get a major league baseball team for the city), motioned guests over and whispered his raffish one-liners in their ears. It was apparent to everyone that the host's new wife was absent.

"The morning odds are that she's gone by the Giants game," he whispered in a throaty rasp. "Like to wager?"

Siegel was one of the last great Damon Runyon characters alive. Often playing the role of sidekick to the billionaire, Siegel had joined Jack and Suzanne for their wedding dinner at Washington's Palm restaurant on Friday, July 24, 1987.[4] And while Suzanne/Susan seethed and raged silently, the two men had talked sports for hours. Siegel was a lone eagle these days. He was the same age as the billionaire, divorced, with time on his hands.

Siegel had worked for all four Washington major daily newspapers over the past forty years and many of the major radio and television stations in town as well. Cantankerous to a fault, he usually left after quarrels with management. When Warner Wolf, the CBS sports announcer, had worked in Washington, Siegel had called him "wiener" several times, which infuriated the 5'4" sportscaster. Siegel didn't get along with Larry King either.

But Siegel could be obsequious as well. Once caught wearing a new pair of expensive cowboy boots, he had admitted that he was indeed "breaking them in for Jack Kent Cooke." A year later, he denied it, saying, "That's a good story. I wish I had made it up." The relationship was beneficial for both men. Jack had a companion he could talk to in his lonely hours, and Siegel had an inside pipeline to the Redskins.

The guests were all in the box just before the singing of the national anthem. To Jack's right was Lesley Stahl, directly behind

13

him was Larry L. King. Larry had recently offered him a chance to invest in his newest play, *The Night Hank Williams Died*. Jack had read it, found the script wanting and passed.[5] Next to King was Bobby Beathard, the team's general manager, and his wife, Christine.[6] And behind King, in the far left corner of the box was Siegel. The dentist began to slide the doors to the enclave closed.

Below, like gladiators waiting to go into battle, forty-five burgundy-and-gold uniformed warriors of the Washington Redskins prepared for Sunday afternoon battle with the green-and-white clad Philadelphia Eagles by standing at attention, waiting for the singing of the national anthem. An equal number of Redskinettes, cheerleaders for the team, stood rigidly, their gold pompons placed on their hearts. They were wearing their latest look: red jug-wine colored go-go costumes trimmed in metallic yellow, with white patent leather boots.[7] When the team had decided to give the cheerleaders new uniforms, the billionaire had taken keen interest.

"Get me Halston," was his battle cry until he found out the designer's fee. Then he and his son John designed the new outfits themselves.

Siegel was the last to his seat. His place was directly behind Larry L. King, who sat just behind Jack. With a wall directly to his left, it was the worst seat in the box.

"Jack, Jack, I can't see," he yelled at the billionaire above the noise of the crowd. It was his standard pregame complaint and it never failed to get a chuckle out of the old man. Satisfied, he had been noticed, Siegel sat down.

Just as the doors to the box were about to close, with the Redskins singers standing on the fifty-yard line singing the first verse of the Star Spangled Banner, Suzanne Cooke rushed in. She was wearing maternity clothing, but nobody seemed to notice. She and her husband kissed like newlyweds while the older women in the box murmured approvingly and their husbands momentarily fantasized about affairs with younger women. It was a scene worthy of a prime time TV soap opera.

The Emperor beamed at his consort, mouthing the words silently, "I love you."

Maybe, thought Suzanne Cooke, maybe everything will be all right.

14

But now there was a game to be played and the billionaire focused totally on the war that was taking place on the field. This was going to be his year, the Redskins' third trip to the Super Bowl of the decade.

When the Redskins' kicker Jess Atkinson drew first blood by booting a field goal to take a 3–0 lead, Jack Kent Cooke and his bride stood and embraced while the guests in the box clapped, although a casual observer couldn't be sure whether the polite applause was for the couple's kiss or the field goal. Unlike the crowd around them, which caused the volume in the stadium to hover around the 100-decibel level, the guests in the owner's enclosure did not yell, stomp their feet, or do the wave. Their polite applause was more indicative of a lukewarm ballet reception or the opening rounds at Wimbledon.

Tight-lipped, buttoned-up to the tops of their long necks, the aristocrats of the box kept their emotions within. While the mob outside the enclave let every degree of pain and torment show on a long Philadelphia drive downfield and exploded with orgasmic screams at the moment of a Washington touchdown, the gathering around the owner preferred to keep whatever passion they felt inside. Cerebral always, the women would toast a player who scored by raising a glass of white wine, the subtle move of a species whose lives revolved around manners and understatement.

Not Jack Kent Cooke. The Squire showed his passion on the outside. Every play was the big one, every score a victory or defeat. He lived the game as he lived his life—every Sunday afternoon of warfare in the NFL was just as important as his next big deal. There was a hug or kiss for Susan after every Redskins score. That was tradition. The woman closest to his side always received a Jack Kent Cooke hug and kiss after a touchdown. And after every long pass or run, he would stand, his hands placed on the back of his hips, thrust out his chest like a bantam rooster, and walk over to another man in the box and comment on the play.

"That Art Monk! No finer receiver in the league!"

"The defense really held on that series."

His passion for the game was so great he would spout poetry apropos of the moment. "I'm a little wounded, but I am not slain," he once quoted from John Dryden after his quarterback, Joe Theismann, had had his leg broken by the New York Giant's Lawrence Taylor.[8] "I will lay down for to bleed a while; then I'll rise to fight with you again."

But when his team fell far behind, the Squire would go into a deep funk which only a Redskin reversal of fortune could erase. Silent, his lips pursed and white, he would walk the length of the box speaking to no one. With the TV cameras picking up his pacing between plays, he was the cynosure of millions. It was Jack Kent Cooke being beaten down there and if there was one thing Jack Kent Cooke hated above all else, it was to lose.

"The young man's a mortgage banker," Jack told Gene McCarthy, referring to Jess Atkinson. "A University of Maryland graduate, I believe."

On the field, Jay Schroeder, the Redskins' first-string quarterback, was down. A Philadelphia player had landed on his shoulder and he was out for the game, maybe the season. The black metal phone rang continuously. Jack let it ring. It was a call from an assistant coach down on the field who would tell him the extent of Schroeder's injury. Jack knew Schroeder was injured and that his next two hours had been jeopardized.

"You feel good about this Doug Williams, do you?" he asked Bobby Beathard.

Responsibility on the field now was in the hands of Doug Williams, a veteran quarterback picked from among the few remnants of the United States Football League who were good enough to play in the NFL.

Beathard, perhaps the league's best judge of player talent, nodded. Williams always had a rifle for an arm, but when he had played for Tampa in the NFL he threw too deep for many of his receivers. The joke among the Tampa Cuban community had been, "Let Doug lead us against Castro, he can overthrow anybody." But Beathard had noticed a maturing of Williams and a new, pinpoint accuracy. Williams would serve the team well. Jack Kent Cooke had insisted they keep Williams when a possible trade for him was dangled.

Both men were rewarded when, minutes later, Williams

passed the ball into the corner of the end zone to All-Pro wide receiver Art Monk to give the Redskins a 10–0 lead. The new bride, noticing the CBS camera just outside the booth pointing directly at her, rose to the occasion. She stood up and with a pirouette worthy of a professional dancer, turned and embraced the billionaire as he returned from a little aisle back-slapping. This time her face was on camera.

Although the Redskins were never behind, Philadelphia managed to make the game interesting and even dramatic. The Eagles tied it up in the third quarter and broke the leg of the young mortgage banker as well.[9] But for Washington, the clincher that ended the day was a thirty-nine-yard pass from Williams to Monk in the end zone during the fourth quarter, and then punter Steve Cox, substituting for Atkinson, iced the game with a forty-yard field goal. The billionaire accepted congratulations and handshakes all around, as if he had just married off a daughter.

The show was over. Harry had reappeared. He gathered his master's binoculars and his glass case. Then he carried them with the flowers from the Lombardi room out to the limousine and put them in the trunk. The leftover food and wine had been taken out after halftime. The flowers would be reused later in the mansion and the leftovers would make for a fine late supper.

Harry drove Suzanne and the billionaire back to the Cooke Watergate apartment in near silence.

Jack Kent Cooke did not get out.

"Goodbye, Susan," he said.

His limousine quickly pulled away, leaving his bride standing on the circular drive of the luxurious Watergate apartment building, next to the Kennedy Center.

He called later that evening.

"I wanted to say good night. I'm very busy, but I wanted to call."

Suzanne Cooke began crying.

"What's going on. What are we doing?"

"Susan, you lied to me. I can't stay with you."

She had become "the bitch" who had refused to terminate her third pregnancy.[10]

17

He maintained control by hanging up on her. He was, as usual, very, very busy. There were deals to make and money to be made.

Notes

1. Bob Schulman, her late husband, represented many of the famous, including Howard Cosell, Frank Sinatra, Merv Griffin, Lesley Stahl, Jackie Gleason, Steve Lawrence, and Eydie Gorme. He was also active in NFL affairs and represented Alex Spanos when the construction tycoon purchased the San Diego Chargers from Gene Klein. Schulman also represented four other NFL teams.
2. After Suzanne Martin Cooke married the Squire of Middleburg, she began "to put on airs," according to critics. A few days before the first Redskins home game in 1987, two women friends took her to one of Washington's best restaurants, the Jockey Club. The maitre d' tried to seat them in a rear room, and Suzanne told him, "Mrs. Jack Cooke doesn't sit in the back." The maitre d' found them a better table.
3. When general manager Bobby Beathard, who was allotted four tickets to the box as part of his contract, invited Sir Wallace Rowling, the ambassador to the U.S. from New Zealand (they had met in, of all places, a marathon-running clinic where the fifty-two-year-old former prime minister was preparing to run the New York City Marathon), Jack Kent Cooke was impressed enough to remove two regulars from the front row for Sir Wallace and his wife.
4. Washington's Palm restaurant is similar to New York's Palm, sans the sawdust on the floor. There are cartoons of the famous on nearly every wall. Jack Kent Cooke's caricature is prominent.
5. Jack was right. The play got both lukewarm reviews and box office.
6. Christine Beathard was a favorite of Jack Kent Cooke's. Just before Suzanne and Jack were married, Cooke took her and his future wife to lunch and attempted to get the two women to go into business together. Since Christine Beathard always brought a box of her home-made chocolate chip cookies to every game, he suggested that they commercially bake the cookies and sell them through Giant Food, a local supermarket chain.

    "Susan will market them, you can supervise the baking, and I'll put up $100,000 seed money," he told Mrs. Beathard, offering a three-way profit split. He had even brought a contract.

    "And what will we call them?" Christine Beathard innocently asked.

"Why 'Rich Cookies'," the billionaire chortled.

After thinking it over for a few days, Christine Beathard declined Jack Kent Cooke's offer.

7. The Washington Redskins are the only team in the NFL to have both cheerleaders and their own marching band. Jack got Tiffany's—the New York-headquartered jeweler—to design and make the Redskins' Super Bowl ring for the 1988 win. It was the first time Tiffany's was involved in an NFL Super Bowl.

8. Students of the Cooke psyche would do well to read the British seventeenth-century poet who served Oliver Cromwell in his youth. One epic poem, "Alexander's Feast," could well be a credo for Jack. A few lines:

> Never ending, still beginning,
> Fighting still and still destroying;
> If the world be worth the winning,
> Think, O think, it worth enjoying.

9. The resourceful Beathard replaced Jess Atkinson the next week with an Iranian soccer-style kicker by the name of Ali Haji Sheikh. "The Sheik," as he was known, did so poorly that he was soon nicknamed Ali Haji "Shank" by disgruntled fans. He was cut a year later. Jess Atkinson never played in a regular season NFL game again.

10. After Jack Kent Cooke learned of his third wife's refusal to abort her pregnancy, he no longer let her live with him at his Middleburg estate (actually located in nearby Upperville, but Jack prefers the Middleburg address), beginning August 21, 1987. It climaxed with a legendary argument that took place in his limousine on a country road near Middleburg. Jack told his pregnant bride to leave the car and then left her on the road at dusk. Suzanne Cooke walked four miles to the mansion in a new pair of low-heeled shoes. She arrived, her feet blistered and bleeding. According to Mrs. Cooke, her husband locked her out of the house, and although she banged with her fists on his bedroom window, he ignored her. Suzanne Cooke said she slept in a deserted guest house "full of crawling insects" that night. The next morning, her mother arrived, summoned by Jack Kent Cooke. Another fight broke out, this time physical, with his mother-in-law, a terrified Diane Martin, seeming to both observe and officiate. Suzanne Cooke claimed later that her husband pushed at her stomach in an attempt to destroy the unborn child. In return, she smashed his glasses, rendering him virtually sightless. She left the mansion with her mother, never to return. But they still continued to see each

19

other and appear together at public functions such as the Redskins' opening game. Suzanne Cooke lived for a time at Jack's fifth-floor "in-town" Watergate co-op apartment overlooking the Potomac River, until she moved to a small estate called "Eagle's Nest," eight miles away from him. Her move back to Middleburg was an attempt to save the marriage and persuade JKC to halt divorce proceedings.

TORONTO

2

OPENING DAY, 1912

"He was . . . the maestro of young Toronto."

A light rain cleansed the sooty streets of Hamilton, Ontario, on Sunday, October 26, 1912. At 48°F, it was a balmy day for late October. The city of Hamilton, which many considered a poor cousin to Toronto, was a growing metropolis forty miles to the southwest of Canda's major English-speaking city. Not that Hamilton was tiny. In the fall of 1912 its population had just been counted—82,095—and the town was booming.

Although it had been so labeled, it would not be fair to call Hamilton "the armpit of Canada," then or now.[1] Certainly manufacturing, steel or otherwise, dominates the city even today. The two giants, Stelco and Dofasco, have provided the lifeblood for this city on Lake Ontario for decades and now employ nearly 20,000 workers. Steel is so integral to the economic vitality of Hamilton that the local brewery used to put out a brew called Steeler Beer. In 1912, though, steel was just one of several industries whose factories dotted the city. Textiles and farm-implement manufacturing were the other two big employers.

But then and today, the organization that is even more powerful than steel for bonding the city together is Hamilton's one major league sports team, the Hamilton Tiger Cats.

The Tiger Cats club, the perennial scourge of the Canadian Football League, has been around since the turn of the century. Once simply called the Tigers, it first operated as an amateur team, then semipro, then professional. Finally it merged with another pro team called the Wildcats, thus becoming the Tiger Cats and has made twenty-seven Grey Cup appearances in this century, the Canadian equivalent of the Super Bowl.[2]

The Ti-Cats were scheduled to play their big city rival, the Toronto Argonauts, on the last weekend of October, 1912.[3] But one newcomer to Hamiliton, Ralph Ercil Cooke, didn't have his mind on the game. His wife, Nancy, was about to give birth for the first time.

Ralph Cooke had only lived in Hamilton for a short time. He was a recent emigré from Melbourne, Australia. Nancy Marion Jacobs, his wife, had arrived a few years before from Johannesburg, South Africa. They had reached Hamilton by Canadian National rail, from Quebec City, the final destination of their steamship on the St. Lawrence Seaway.

Ralph and Nancy Cooke were newlyweds. They had married on May 27, 1911, and Nancy, a vibrant, boisterous bride, had conceived six months later. The couple lived in a small brick house, at 174 King William Street, three blocks from the statue of Queen Victoria, which marks the center of the city, known today as Jackson Square.

Ralph Cooke's occupation had nothing to do with steel or manufacturing. He was a salesman, plain and simple. And what he sold in 1912 were picture frames. The Canadian Fine Arts Company outlet for which he was an agent, was operated out of his house. City Hospital, on Barton Avenue, where Nancy would deliver the firstborn of the Cooke family, was two miles away.[4]

The Cooke couple were among the few Hamilton residents who owned an automobile. Nancy's dowry had provided that. Their auto was a rare sight in the city—just 196 cars were registered there at the time. When Ralph drove Nancy to the hospital that Sunday afternoon, the rain-slicked streets were virtually empty.

A woman's giving birth in a hospital was still unusual. The vast majority of infants born in Hamilton were delivered at home by a midwife. Besides the sterile advantage of a hospital, Ralph and Nancy Cooke were doubly blessed. City General had installed an operating room in 1910, a new concept for the times. Ralph and Nancy's good health and the modern facility helped to ensure a textbook birth. The wailing firstborn was a boy.

The two young Canadian immigrants named the baby Jack

Kenneth Cooke. Born on October 26, 1912 (not October 25, as many later records would state), the names of the infant and family members would appear differently on future documents as the memories of a humble Hamilton origin faded.[5] By the time Jack was five, the family had grown by three more children: Harold Edgar Cooke (born in February, 1914), Thelma Marion Cooke (November, 1915), and Donald Ralph Cooke (August, 1917).

"Johnny Cakes, Johnny Cakes."[6]

It was his father calling.

Jack Cooke, thirteen years old and full of himself, sensed he could be in trouble again. Ralph had found out he was skipping school. His father knew that Jack had been hanging out at Woodbine racetrack.[7] Ralph was probably going to lecture him about smoking too.

A small but tough Jack Cooke lay down on his back and slid down the steep ravine through the dust of the dry Toronto summer. He came to a stop near his back door, just a few steps from his father standing by the kitchen.

But Jack was home free. It was just a call to dinner.

Life was grand in their modest two-story bungalow, nearly fifty miles northeast of Jack's Hamilton birthplace.[8] It was built in 1921, after Ralph had bounced from Hamilton to Toronto in 1915, then to Montreal, on to Ottawa, and finally back to Toronto in 1918. The house at 194 Neville Park Boulevard, in a southeastern section of Toronto known as "The Beaches" was an ideal neighborhood for a lower middle class WASP family to call home. The city of Toronto was a typical twenties stew of ethnic diversity. Italians—the leading wave in numbers at least—had settled by the tens of thousands. The Irish had staked out their own territory in a neighborhood quickly dubbed "Cabbagetown." And while the east European Jews were forming their own ghetto to the west in Kensington, a burgeoning Chinatown had begun on Elizabeth Street and was spreading north.

Toronto was now a city, a big city, with well over half a million people—nearly 10 percent of the population of Canada. And it was so diverse that it printed the laws of the city in six languages.

It bubbled with the excitement of all new North American cities that were filled with immigrants armed with limited skills and unlimited dreams.

Above all, Toronto was the destination for the majority of families arriving in eastern Canada from the British Isles. More than six out of every ten residents of Toronto looked to the King of England as the ultimate head of state. "God Save The King" was still sung before or after sporting events or government functions with "Oh Canada" or "The Maple Leaf Forever" seemingly tacked on as an afterthought. Toronto was as British then as Montreal, to the east, was French.

The city had been founded about a century before the birth of Jack Kenneth Cooke by British merchants who wanted to trade flour to England. Originally, they gave the town the name of York. It started on what is a flood plain bordered by the Don and Humber rivers on the east and west, with Lake Ontario to the south. Each spring during the nineteenth century, the entire settlement of 2,800 would flood and the farmers who brought flour to the merchants on Yonge Street near the lake would curse the city, calling it bloody, muddy York. Yonge Street was lined with small farms north of York, stretching sixty miles out of town along a dirt road traveled by horses and ox carts. By 1830 the street was partially paved, and four years later the community was incorporated as the City of Toronto. Today, Yonge Street is lined with skyscrapers and can be compared to New York's Broadway. It is often called the main street of Canada, and if one wishes it can be driven on for more than a thousand miles, to James Bay, south of the Arctic Circle.

Toronto is a Huron Indian word that translates roughly as "Land of Opportunity" or "meeting place." Young Jack Cooke was ready for any opening, secure in the womb of the most British bastion of the city, where the number of Jews in a public school could be counted on one hand, and an Anglican or Presbyterian church spire could be found on nearly every corner. Many Americans might picture the city and country in which young Jack Cooke grew up as a slightly colder version of the U.S. Nothing could be further from the truth. Americans have grown up in this century being told they are living in the greatest country on earth, fostering a feeling of superiority. Canadians, growing up just north of this giant power, have been inundated with American culture. They usually get an opposite mindset. No wonder that one of the benefits of living in Toronto in the 1920s that was bragged about by its residents was "and we're close to New York!"

Jack Cooke received his American catechism early. He grew up listening to a radio station from Chicago. He would tune in late at night to hear his favorite type of music—jazz, a quintessential American art form. The "Georgia Peach," Ty Cobb, was his child-hood baseball idol. More than thirty years later, *Maclean's*, the leading Canadian magazine, would refer to Jack as "that most American of Canadians."

But while America at least tried to become a melting pot of cultures from around the world, Canada did not. Canadians have never really wanted to assimilate. Generally speaking, a person living in Los Angeles might think of himself as an American first, a Californian second, and an Angeleno third. A person living in Toronto or Vancouver might have a very different sequence, think-ing of himself as English first, an Ontarian or British Columbian second, and a Canadian third.

Unlike Americans, Canadians never fought a revolution for independence, never had a civil war, never had slavery or a pro-longed civil-rights struggle. Their own prejudices were more subtle. The British, who had won Canada, left their arrogance on the country. Canadians grew up in the early part of the century be-lieving that the only culture worth having was British, thus stunt-ing the growth of any real Canadian identity and totally alienating the French who make up 80 percent of the population of Quebec, an area much larger than Texas. The British in Toronto, strictly by virtue of their majority, were able to impose their values on nearly everyone.

It was a very "white" populace that walked the streets of Toronto in the 1920s. Racial and religious prejudice was evident. The terms "dago," "kike," and "mick" were in common use, and Canadians had their own derisive terms as well—DP and Dou-khobors.[9]

Some Torontonians believe that Jack's mother, Nancy Marion Jacobs Cooke, was a secular Jew who kept her family heritage hidden. If so, and there is no hard evidence either way, Nancy was acting with wisdom. The Beaches area of Toronto in the 1920s and 1930s was openly anti-Semitic. The *Toronto Telegram*, a "blatant anti-Jewish" evening daily of the times was the leading paper in The Beaches. Once in the 1920s, a local insurance company canceled most of the policies of its Jewish customers and only action by the Ontario legislature reinstated them. Leases for apartments were routinely denied Jews and a dance hall at Lambton Park in Toronto had a "Gentiles Only" sign installed.

In 1933, at the height of the rise of the Nazis in Germany, gangs of youths roamed the beaches of Toronto's east end terrorizing Jews and other ethnics under the name of the Balmy Beach Swastika Club. The club specialized in driving by the homes of Jewish residents, flinging garbage and shouting Nazi slogans. The club would also taunt the Jews by singing a song to the tune of "Home on the Range:"

> Oh give me a home where the Gentiles roam
> Where the Jews are not rampant all day
> Where seldom is heard a loud Yiddish word
> And the Gentiles are free all the day.

When Jewish youths tried to rip down swastika banners, fights broke out. The mayor of the city, backed by popular opinion, created an order prohibiting the wearing of the swastika on the beach, but the anti-Semitic *Telegram* maintained that the group had a right to demonstrate.

But in August, 1933, at the height of the Toronto anti-Semitism, an all-out battle erupted at a baseball game between Fascist groups and Jewish youths. The Nazi youths began yelling "Heil Hitler!" With more than 10,000 people present, the fight lasted for more than six hours and pieces of pipe and baseball bats were used as weapons. Scores of people were injured. Thus, it would be understandably prudent that a person with a Hebrew background living in a WASP neighborhood like The Beaches would choose to keep such a religious affiliation to himself.

Jack's father was a deeply religious member of the Anglican church. He also could play the piano decently, as could Jack's mother, who made her son practice daily. A half-century later, Jack would tell close friends that his father was good enough to have been a concert pianist. His judgment of his father's ability was probably exaggerated, but it is indicative of the closeness Jack and Ralph shared. Ralph wanted his son to become a lawyer. Jack's first registered ambition was to be an architect.

Not that Jack needed to worry. He already had his father's Saxon good looks and learned charm that would offer him a multitude of opportunities. School, however, was not on Jack's list.

Jack's higher education—what there was of it—was gained at Malvern Collegiate, a public high school just a little over a half-mile from the family's new house, which stood at the end of a cul de sac on the two long blocks of Neville Park Boulevard. When Jack attended (which was infrequently—neighborhood friends say he was absent for weeks at a time), he would climb up the steep ravine back of his house, cross Kingston Road, and be there in less than fifteen minutes.

And although young Jack Cooke could quickly grasp the concepts of math and had a keen interest in English literature and art, his mind was elsewhere. In the end, Jack completed three of the five years required at that time for graduation from a Toronto school. Two years were spent completing one grade and for a short time, Jack even switched to Riverdale Technical High, a vocational school. Money, and the making of it, was already his real major, with sports his minor.

At fifteen, Jack Cooke had an orchestra made up of school chums; they played at tea dances after school. The *Malvern Muse,* the high school's literary magazine contains a quarter-page ad for ''Jack Cooke and His Band'' offering ''Special rates for parties, dinners, banquets, and weddings.''

Some mornings he would get up and run to Woodbine racetrack. If a youngster got there by six in the morning, the men in the paddock would let him walk a thoroughbred and pay 25 cents an hour besides. For the lucky, it could be a horse from Brookdale Stables, the best of the lot. Then, rather than go to school, Jack would take his two quarters, hop the Queen Street trolley, and ride to the center of the city, a half-hour away. Ensconced at the music department of Eaton's, Toronto's largest department store, he would spend hours pouring over sheet music and listening to the recordings of the day.

Jack was particularly proud to be an east end "beach boy." If one walked to the other end of Neville Park Boulevard, south from the Cooke house, one would wander into the waters of Lake Ontario in less than a mile. The sands of Kew Beach, Scarborough Beach, and Balmy Beach attracted thousands from all over Ontario during the months of June, July, and August. Jack was in the center of it all, and thought of himself as being a Balmy Beach boy.

Balmy Beach boys played Canada's national sport, hockey, by day and practiced England's national sport, ballroom dancing, by night. Inspired by Vernon and Irene Castle in the 1920s, the boys of The Beaches dipped and twirled at dance halls all over Toronto. But for the boys of Toronto's east end, the ultimate place to "show your steps"—the fox trot, the waltz, the tango—was at that palace of dance, the Balmy Beach Canoe Club.

By the late 1920s, Jack Cooke was becoming Oley Kent, of "Oley Kent and His Bourgeois Canadians"—an orchestra that was twelve men strong. When he had first played at the Balmy Beach Canoe Club, at the foot of Beech Avenue near his house, his band had gone under the name of the "Balmy Beach Serenaders." But as the leader, he thought there should be a distinction—after all, he was the one who organized the band, made the deals, and scheduled the practices. Besides, he didn't want Malvern to know he was working in dance halls at night. So Jack Cooke/Oley Kent had taken the $60 fee from the club—$5 per man—and paid each musician $2.50. The day before he had bought a new suit and had gone downtown to purchase the latest Fletcher Henderson arrangement. He was ready.

Standing at the end of the mammoth Balmy Beach Club ballroom—nearly half the size of an American football field—on a raised podium gave Jack aka Oley an enormous sense of power. Nearly a thousand Torontonians had come to hear him and dance to his band. They had each paid 25 cents and nearly everyone was under the age of twenty-one. He was, at least for the evening, not just the leader of the band but the Pied Piper of his peers—the maestro of young Toronto.

That evening, a youthful Percy Faith was at the piano. And Jack—who was far from being the best musician; if anything he was one of the least talented—Jack was at the front alternating between tenor sax and clarinet. But above all, he was the envy of his peers in this growing metropolis on Lake Ontario.

It was striking how one could immediately distinguish the ethnics, the kids from North Toronto, from the beach crowd. The dancers from outside The Beaches all milled around in the center of the floor while the locals danced expertly around the perimeter. It was the youths from Scarborough and Kingston Road who were daring enough to dip. And when Oley Kent and his orchestra took a break, it was the boys of the beach who were the first to gently escort a young woman out through the wide doors that faced onto Lake Ontario and walk her onto the boardwalk or the dark beach sands to pet and share the warm, wet kisses of youth. Then the men would go off and refuel themselves with iced beer, and return ready for another hour of quick-stepping around the polished wooden floor of the Balmy Beach Canoe Club, dancing to the sounds of Oley Kent and his Bourgeois Canadians.

At night during the warm summers and the rare evenings when Ralph was home (he now sold Bibles and encyclopedias), the family would gather on the broad veranda that ran the length of the new thirty-five-foot-wide home, content in its secure middle-class Anglo status and talk, sing, or listen to Jack on his saxophone. They would catch the nightly sports broadcast on CKCL, where Al Leary would give the scores and baseball highlights of the day. The loud and boisterous family would sit there in its chairs, perhaps drinking O'Keefe's stone ginger beer or lemonade, the boys dangling their feet over the edge of the porch or sprawled over the front steps, spinning family fantasies about even better future years ahead. These dreams were still possible in the late 1920s. Jack or his mother Nancy usually led the conversations.

Jack was the musician of the family. Jazz was his choice of music and some nights he would spirit the family radio into his bedroom and stay up until dawn listening to the all-night show from Chicago which featured jazz bands performing live at the College Inn. Although the tenor saxophone was clearly his best instrument, he was also proficient on the clarinet and, like Ralph and Nancy, could play piano passably. Because the family home was at the dead upper end of the street, backing into the steep ravine, the sounds of Jack's playing, could be heard up and down the avenue. The Cooke family house was located at the center of what was a natural amphitheatre.

Jack's proficiency in music came from a couple of lessons and natural ability probably inherited from his father. Later profiles would say young Cooke was a student at the prestigious Toronto Conservatory of Music. But a file search for the years 1915–1930 by the Exam Board of what is now the Royal Conservatory of Music, found no record of a Jack Cooke ever being enrolled. Another myth that has been widely perpetuated by the press is that Jack was the "son of a wealthy picture frame manufacturer." Every available city directory for both Hamilton and Toronto between 1913 and 1939 that was checked lists Ralph Cooke's occupation as either agent, sales agent, or salesman. If Ralph Cooke made picture frames in a room in his house and then sold them, one could define him as a "picture frame manufacturer" but the reader would be misled. The Cooke family in the 1920s was neither wealthy nor upper middle class as many articles have routinely classified it. Jack's mother and father, though never poor, were clearly middle to lower middle class and struggling. The house on Neville Park Boulevard reflected that, although the family always had a car.

The Cookes' first home nevertheless had four white Ionic columns, eight feet tall, which went from the porch floor upward to support the roof. Jack sketched out the facade of the house for his father before it was built. It was the bungalow's most prominent feature. Jack would sometimes lean against these pillars as he practiced his music. A half-century later he would incorporate the columns, the most distinctive feature of his boyhood home, into the design of the Forum, the highly successful sports arena he would build in Inglewood, California, near Hollywood Park. At the right of the house, two modest stained glass windows had been installed to let light into the dining room. Above the one-story porch were two small centered lead-paned windows. There was even a small single-car garage, separated from the house and tucked into the hill.[10]

Although the details sound grand, the house itself was not. It wasn't even the best house on the street. On the contrary, it was one of the least expensive. Money was short for the Cooke family and the house was crowded.

Besides Ralph, Nancy, and Jack, there was Harold, Jack's second brother, and Jack's opposite in looks. His light locks and pudgy body contrasted widely with Jack's brilliantined brown hair and wiry frame. A boyhood friend who lived nearby said that Harold was "always hungry" and that Hal, as he was called, would always stop at his house after school for a snack because there was little food for snacking in the Cooke household. Jack's sister, Thelma, was the thirdborn. She too was blonde, and by all accounts a pretty teenager. Donald was the youngest, a carbon copy of Jack. Everyone else had a nickname—Harold was "Hal," "Nooks" or "Nooksy," Thelma was "Toots," and Donald was "Ginks." Only Jack was without one.

"All the kids were afraid of Jack, even then," remembers Vera Brady, speaking of Jack's ability to verbally intimidate. She grew up near the Cooke family and her husband Bill later worked for Jack, first as host of a radio show at Jack's Toronto radio station, CKEY, and later as an independent music producer.

"Every kid was given a nickname, but you wouldn't have given Jack one—he was too tough," another resident of Neville Park Boulevard told a writer. "Maybe Jack developed his own nickname, when he started calling himself Oley Kent."

"We still think of him as the high school hustler who hit it big," recalls Vera Brady. "He was always into something that made money—playing for tea dances after school, organizing his band."

Another woman, now in her seventies, who still lives in a suburb of Toronto, "went out with Jack" in her teens. Later she "partied with Jack" in the 1940s and still remembers the power of young Jack Cooke's devastating good looks.

"When Jack would crinkle up his eyes and stare right at you," she remembers, "he could melt your heart . . . or scare you half to death."

Indeed, the *Malvern Muse*, in a high school humor column titled "What We'd Like to See," lists one of its wishes as "Jack Cooke minus a grin and with straight hair."

By all accounts Jack made the most of his limited time in high school. Although absent almost to the point of expulsion, he hustled tea dances and played clarinet on cruise ships called the S.S. *Northumberland* and the steamboat *Dalhousie City* (where his band was called the Canadian Aces), which sailed the Great Lakes. The small, but seemingly unstoppable and popular Jack Cooke also excelled on the school's hockey, football, and rugby teams. Jack was one of the leaders of the school rugby squad, good enough to help lead the Red and Black of Malvern Collegiate to two city titles.[11]

In addition, Jack found time to be a quarterback on the football team. He was coached by the Canadian sports hero Ted "The Moaner" Reeve, who had led Balmy Beach to a Grey Cup championship, the last of the "neighborhood" teams to win a national title. Reeve would go on to a place in both the Canadian Football Hall of Fame and the Lacrosse Hall of Fame.

Reeve later said, "If I had known he was going to be so rich I would have let him start. He was a hard-eyed little guy with guts that wouldn't turn his head when a train went past. He could have been a good hockey player. But he could sell, boy, could he sell. He could sell stoves at a shipwreck."

"Of course in those days a quarterback rarely passed," remembers Joe McNulty, who is one year older than Jack Kent Cooke and who played various sports with Jack during their teen years. "Passing didn't come in until the mid-thirties."

McNulty says Jack's best sport was hockey. McNulty should know—he played professional hockey in northern Ontario for several years.

"Jack was a pretty good center and wing for Malvern in a city where nearly every boy could skate and play hockey well," he recalls.

Another teammate remembers it somewhat differently. "Cooke was a good center but he wouldn't pass the puck."

The young Cooke would play well enough to skate briefly for the Victorias, a semipro team. At this point, he was offered a hockey scholarship by the University of Michigan. But Jack had a problem with that: he was then two years short of the five required for a high school diploma, a dropout.

"Nancy, his mother, had a car," McNulty said, "and she would drive us to hockey practices. She had the same kind of nerve and gall Jack did. I think he took more after her than his father."

Jack later remembers the hockey scholarship this way: "It was tempting. Like most Canadian boys, I dreamed of being a big-league player. And the Michigan coach was Eddie Powers, who had coached Toronto into a Stanley Cup a few years before."

The young Jack Cooke, a realist and knowing what his limitations were in hockey, besides the lack of a high school education, decided that he was good, but not good enough to play in the same league as Eddie Shore and Howie Morenz. But being not good enough didn't stop the gall and nerve at school.

Miss Knight was having trouble with her Malvern English writing class. The boys at the back of the room were whispering and the class was being disrupted.

"If anyone thinks he can teach this class better than I," she said, "let him come up here and try it."

A sixteen-year-old Jack Cooke strode to the front of the room.

"Everyone open their books to page 84," he commanded the class. And Jack taught the class until the flustered Miss Knight sat him back down.

"Jack lived by his own rules, even then," McNulty remembered. "I'm a Roman Catholic so I had to be careful. The Cookes—as far as I know, they never went to church, so they didn't have to worry about religious rules.

"You know," McNulty concluded, "I've always gotten along

with Jack.[12] There was only one time I saw Jack really angry. And even though I'm bigger, I thought he might take a poke. . . . It was when I took Jeannie out for a canoe ride. We were late coming back and when we got to shore Jack was standing there, furious."

"Jack and I played and chased girls together," recalled Lloyd Nourse, another lifelong Cooke friend and a teammate of Jack's on Malvern's rugby squad, who still lives in the Fallingbrook section of Toronto. "Jean was a nice girl. I dated her before him."

Jeannie—Barbara Jean Carnegie—would be the best thing to ever happen to Jack Cooke and nearly fifty years later, she would cause him to make the biggest mistake of his life.

Notes

1. The real "armpit" of eastern Canada is probably Sudbury, Ontario. The town, dotted with nickel smelters, has so polluted the nearby land that it lies black and barren. In fact, the terrain is so like the dark side of the moon that NASA sent astronauts there to show them what to expect.
2. The city of Hamilton is also home to the Canadian Football Hall of Fame. Canada still claims to have invented modern day football when McGill University introduced a rough version of today's game to Harvard on May 15, 1874, in Cambridge, Mass. It is also fair to say that Canadians may be even more sports obsessed than Americans. The birth of hockey star Wayne Gretzky's first child, for example, was reported on the front page of the Hamilton *Spectator* in August 1990.
3. If one believes in professional seers or even Gypsy fortune tellers, one will want to nod wisely upon learning of an interesting event. On the weekend of Jack's birth, an American fooball team, the Carlisle Indians, led by the legendary Jim Thorpe, visited southern Ontario to play a pick-up game with a group of Canadian All-Stars under American rules. The Carlisle group shellacked the Canadians 51–0. Years later, shortly after Jack Kent Cooke purchased his initial 25 percent stake in the Redskins, the team began preseason training in Carlisle, Pennsylvania, "the home of Jim Thorpe," and have done so continuously for the past three decades. John Cooke, Jack's son, is a trustee at Carlisle's Dickinson College and Jack's grandson John received a bachelor's degree in English from there.
4. City Hospital today is known as Hamilton General Hospital. It is at the same address but has been expanded.

5. All of Jack's *Who's Who* and other biographical materials list October 25, 1912, as his date of birth. But the official birth records at City Hall put the birthdate on October 26. Jack Kent Cooke may be pleased to learn that he's a day younger than he thought.

6. "Johnny Cakes" is a Cooke tradition when addressing a family member by the name of John, much to the consternation of Jack's son John Kent Cooke. Jack still uses the term to address his middle-aged son in public, particularly when he's angry.

7. Woodbine racetrack is still there today but is called Greenwood. There is another Woodbine race track on the other side of Toronto, but it should not be confused with the paddocks of Jack Kent Cooke's youth.

8. The Cooke family's most likely route from Hamilton to Toronto in 1915 or 1916 would have been by steamship. Although today Hamilton is about a forty-five-minute drive on wide superhighways, there was no road at all at the time—just an Indian trail near Lake Ontario. The first road was not built until the 1920s.

9. DP stands for displaced person and was generally used for east European and Slavic peoples. Doukhobors were a Ukrainian religious sect; they are discussed in chapter 3, note 4.

10. Jack's boyhood home today is a boarding house. Part of the front veranda is gone, the result of a room addition. The garage is buried and partially hidden by an overgrowth of brush. It is still on the last street in the east end of Toronto.

11. The Malvern team nickname today is the "Black Knights," but when Jack was a student the school team was just referred to as "the Red and Black." Prophetically, twice in the student-written *Malvern Muse* the team on which Jack played along with Lloyd Nourse (also very successful in later life) is referred to as the Millionaires. Malvern lads were famous in World War II for wearing their school sweaters under their uniforms, and when captured, wearing them over their prison camp clothing.

12. After concluding his professional hockey career in northern Ontario, McNulty returned to Toronto and spent many years in the employ of the Balmy Beach Canoe Club. On a particularly important anniversary celebration given for McNulty at the club in 1989, Jack Kent Cooke sent McNulty a heartfelt and gracious letter to mark the occasion.

CHAPTER
3
JACK BE QUICK

"We were broke . . . without a dime, without a cent."

Barbara Jean Carnegie was, by all accounts, one of the prettiest girls at Jarvis Collegiate High School, Malvern's crosstown rival.[1] Her family was from Port Perry, Ontario, a small town of less than 5,000 about fifty miles to the east of Toronto, halfway between Lake Simcoe and Lake Ontario.

It was love at first sight. On Jack's part anyway.

They met, appropriately, at a dance in the early 1930s where "Oley Kent and His Bourgeois Canadians" were the featured attraction.

Oley Kent, aka Jack Cooke, spotted the pretty brunette standing near the bandstand at the Lakeview Pavilion in Oshawa, a large city hard on Lake Ontario.[2] Locking his piercing blue eyes on her soft brown ones, he put down his saxophone and began crooning love songs to the teenaged girl as if she were the only woman in a "forget-your-troubles" Depression crowd of hundreds. When he had her attention he moved toward her, dragging the heavy mike stand with him. His style was patterned after Rudy Vallee, and Barbara Jean Carnegie never knew what hit her. Later that night he sang another love song, whispering it in privacy into her ear.

"He came on so strong, I didn't much like him at first," Jeannie recalls. "But he was so strong, he beat back my objections."

Many of Jack's friends remember that Bill and Bernice Carnegie, Jean's parents, didn't much approve of a young bandleader sans high school diploma scratching out a living in the 1930s. By then, the Great Depression was creating pain for nearly every family in the country. The average annual salary for a civil servant in Toronto in 1931 was $927 and domestic servants worked for $50 a year—if they could find a job. But a good pair of new shoes could be had for less than a dollar and a bowl of vegetable soup was available for a nickel at the downtown food kitchens. Misery abounded. When the papers weren't reporting the Hindenburg disaster or the Lindbergh kidnapping or soup lines, they were full of graphic accounts of polio cases—grim statistics then—with adjoining pictures of children in iron lungs.

With this gloomy scene prevalent, Jack's band played on. Cheery songs like "Happy Days Are Here Again" and "Smile, Smile, Smile" were anthems for Jack's band as well as the campaign of Franklin Roosevelt. It must have seemed at times like Oley Kent and His Bourgeois Canadians were playing on the deck of the *Titanic*. Perhaps that's why—after several years of sporadic dating—Jack and Jean made the decision to both elope and later to escape.

The two were married without fanfare or much ceremony in a suburban Toronto chapel on May 5, 1934. Jack was twenty-one and Jean was seventeen. Jack's father was so upset that when he found out he insisted on a church wedding ten days later at nearby St. Aiden's Anglican Church on the corner of Queen and Silver Birch streets.

Jack's first move after marriage was to attempt to become a radio announcer. He applied for an announcing job at CFRB, Toronto, where owner Harry Sedgwick told him he'd be losing money on him at $10 a week. Jack's retort was to offer to pay Sedgwick $10 a week for learning privileges. Sedgwick refused, a move that he would remember later as a mistake.

"You knew Jack wanted to get into radio, when he started practicing radio announcing in the house," said Edna Tarver, who still lives next door to the Cooke house on Neville Park Boulevard. "You could hear him practicing up and down the street."

"I used to lie in bed at night trying to think of what I could do best," Jack remembered of his first try in radio in a 1952 interview. "I could play the saxophone, but not well enough. I could sell but I wasn't the best goddamned salesman in the world."

Jack, married, and needing to prove himself to his new bride, wanted to make money as soon as possible. That he had the nerve to believe this possible in 1934, when fear and a "give-up" mood had struck most North Americans, and when 25 percent of all Canadians were unemployed, is a testament to the spirit of optimism he had always shown.

Jack had hustled money at night as Oley Kent, at the race-track in the early morning walking horses, and door-to-door selling books during the day throughout the summer months. At his peak he managed a crew of eleven, grossing a profit of $150 a week, an unheard-of sum for a young man during the Depression.

So he decided to try a "honeymoon" that combined travel and selling. He borrowed an extra $50 from Ralph, packed a set of encyclopedias called the *New Educator* into the rumble seat of a 1930 Ford Roadster that had one curtain missing, and pointed the car west.[3] The trip was a disaster.

The first night wasn't so bad. Jack had sprung for the best room in a tourist home in Chatham, Ontario. Regular rooms were 50 cents but Jack and Jean's "honeymoon" night was spent in the "Regal" room for $1.75. "I wanted to start out big and it was really quite a good room, too," Jack remembers.

But as Jack and Jean drove further, they often couldn't find a hotel, and nights on the road were frequently spent sleeping in the car. And matters got even worse. There were 50- and 100-mile stretches of empty prairie in Manitoba. There were hours of driving through plains where the population was less than five per square mile. Perhaps it was fertile land for wheat but it was hardly ripe territory for an encyclopedia salesman. With many of the roads west either dirt or gravel, they must have felt like pioneers in a motorized covered wagon.

In what Jack remembers as "horizontal rain" shortly after leaving Canora, Saskatchewan, the old roadster sank deep into the mud, to the top of its tires. Again, the couple spent the night in the car.

The next day Jack and Jean walked into the town of Verigin, population 238, near the Manitoba border.[4] Broke and in need of money to get the car pulled out of the mud, Jack parked Jean in the town's only hotel, where she was made to sit in the kitchen. While pies and bread were baked around her—with Jean not being offered any—she waited for Jack to come back with enough cash to buy them their next meal.

"We were broke," Jack said, "without a dime, without a cent, just stoney broke.

"I went out into the rain and saw the grain elevator operator and the local minister and a doctor," remembers Jack, "whomever the hell I could stop. Finally, school was out and I saw the local principal. He didn't want to buy the books. I stayed with him from 4:30 to 7 o'clock. His wife had dinner on the table and she kept giving me dirty looks as if to say, 'Get out of here.'

"I was hungry, Jean was hungry. I think more to get rid of me, the principal finally gave me a $5 deposit. I got the car out of the mud, we bought a sandwich or two, and from then on, my luck began to turn.

"That was the all-time low," Jack concluded. "It was never as bad after that." Years later, Jack would say of his book-selling days, "A hell of a way to make a living. Just a lousy racket, really."

The two returned to Toronto and moved in with Jack's parents, his two brothers, and his sister Thelma. The little house on Neville Park Boulevard was packed with seven people but it was better than living out of an old Ford on the prairies of Canada. Nearly everyone went to work. Jack's sister labored as a stenographer and even Jean Cooke worked for a short time in a medical laboratory.

Before he had married, Jack had talked himself into a job as a runner on the Toronto stock exchange for the firm of L.J. West and Co. at $11 a week, with the aim of becoming a broker or trader. After a year, he had asked the owner, Jim West, to be a trader. A trader's salary was $25 but he was too young for the job. He was offered the opportunity to learn, but at $16 a week. He had quit instead. Now, Jack considered going back to the stock exchange but in the end, decided against it.

In 1936, the young Cooke swung a job selling soap and other products to stores for Colgate-Palmolive. He was given the northern Ontario territory. His product line included "toilet soap, toilet preparations, laundry soap, glycerine and antifreeze" according to a job description. It meant being away from home for weeks at a time, but the job, counting commissions, paid $70 a week, a handsome salary for the times.

It was in northern Ontario that Jack made a spontaneous decision that was to change the direction of his life forever.

Sitting in the lobby of the hotel in a small town called Kirkland Lake, far from Toronto, the young newlywed considered his future once more. While $70 a week was a princely sum for a twenty-four-year-old in 1936, particularly when so many would have been overjoyed to find any job for a small fraction of that amount, Jack was willing to take yet another chance.

He again reflected on the radio business. Being turned down once for a radio career or any work position must have only increased Jack's resolve. Rejection was something that fired him up.

Walking out the door of the hotel, he wandered over to the town's radio station, CJKL. He was impressed and grasped immediately the huge potential for profits. He asked for an interview with the owner. An appointment was arranged for him in the town of Timmins, a burgeoning mining community 100 miles to the west.

Timmins, the principal gold town of the region, had a population of less than 25,000 in the mid-thirties, but it was the largest city by area in all of Canada. Founded in 1911 by Noah Timmins and laid out grid by grid next to the Mattagami River, the settlement was built to house employees of the nearby Hollinger gold claims, the leading mines of the Porcupine mining district. The Hollinger mines had shafts that extended a mile underground, which would eventually produce more than a million ounces of gold a year—a quarter of all the gold produced by Canada. Timmins had a railway depot, a radio station, a newspaper, and a movie theater. It was the "big city" for miners, trappers, and loggers who made their living by bending their backs in labor in the vastness of northern Ontario.

It was in Timmins, in a small office on the second floor of the *Timmins Daily Press,* the first link in what would later become a chain of 170 newspapers, that Jack Cooke met Roy Thomson for the first time.

Notes

1. Malvern Collegiate was formed when Jarvis Collegiate grew too large in 1903. For a while it was called East Toronto High School until the permanent site at 55 Malvern Avenue was built in 1906. The first Malvern class numbered 128, with a staff of four teachers.
2. Oshawa in the 1930s was a town of 50,000. Today it has more than 130,000 people, with many of its citizens commuting to Toronto to work.
3. The *New Educator Encyclopedia* sold for $39.50 a set. But the profits came from the annual update volumes, which were $3.95 each year into infinity.
4. Verigin is named after Peter Verigin, the leader of the Doukhobors, a Christian religious sect that had emigrated from the Ukraine to western Canada, some 7,000 strong, at the turn of the century. Unusual, to put it mildly, the Doukhobors prohibit smoking, eating meat, and drinking. They also practice pacifism. But what set them apart was their belief that members of the religion were not bound by government or any other authority. When attempts by Canada to introduce basic schooling and to register births, deaths, and marriages were pressed upon them, thirty members, male and female, of an extremist wing of the sect—called the Sons of Freedom—paraded totally nude down the center of town in protest. The Doukhobors, who still have numbers totaling about 10,000 in Canada, resist government edicts to this day although some assimilation has taken place. Protests sporadically erupt from time to time, with nudism and arson the chief forms of disobedience.

CHAPTER

4

JACK JUMPS OVER . . .

". . . like a license to print money."

Roy Thomson, seventeen years Jack's senior, would become a mentor in the late 1930s and early 1940s. Thomson was a failed entrepreneur many times over before he struck it big in radio and newspapers in northern Ontario during the Depression. A former student at Toronto's Jarvis Collegiate High School, the alma mater of Barbara Jean Carnegie Cooke, Thomson was born in what is now downtown Toronto, four blocks south of Bloor Street, off Church Street, later gentrified into expensive town homes, in a one-block mews now called Monteith Street.

Thomson, the son of a barber, had many early business failures. After dropping out of Jarvis Collegiate, he was a bookkeeper for several years. Saving his money, he invested it all in a wheat farming operation in the province of Saskatchewan. Within two years Thomson lost the entire $15,000 stake he had scraped together—an enormous sum in those days. Thomson's second failure was as a distributor of auto parts. It was a matter of bad timing. The Depression was just beginning and gas stations everywhere were closing.

Thomson's next move was to travel to northern Ontario, where he sold radios off the back of a truck to miners who worked the gold, silver, iron, and other metal deposits in the region. The miners had little in the way of evening entertainment—Canada's government was not in favor of sanctioning prostitution—and selling them radios seemed like a great idea. The brands sold by Thomson were Rogers-Majestic and Stewart-Warner. At first he was enormously successful. But when the miners learned that the signals from the cities of southern Ontario came in only faintly or in fitful crackles, sales started to dry up. Thomson's genius was not to give up, but to use his profits to get a license to put a small station in each of the mining communities in which he was selling the miracle electric boxes. It was literally having it both ways. He had a profit from selling commercial time to Toronto advertising agencies who correctly believed that miners, isolated with money in their pockets, would buy anything. Thomson, who originated the phrase, "like a license to print money," was probably thinking of his early days in northern Ontario when he first made that quotable statement.[1]

Thomson's first foray into broadcasting was in North Bay, a small city on Lake Nipissing, some 200 miles above Toronto, and birthplace of the Dionne quintuplets. He opened the station, CFCH, with a borrowed $500 and a secondhand transmitter, above the local movie theatre. To get the old transmitter to North Bay, he heaved the machinery into the trunk of a car, hired an engineer from CKNC in Toronto to install and operate it for a fee of $25 a week, and then convinced his backer he needed another $160 for two transmitter tubes to make it work. The investor, already in for $500, had no choice but to get in deeper. The station today would be known as a "Mom and Pop" operation; Thomson was both the Mom and the Pop. He sold advertising time, introduced radio shows, and did interviews. In his spare time, he sold radios door-to-door.

Often Thomson couldn't pay his bills, and his checks bounced. An employee receiving a paycheck would sometimes be asked to hold it until Monday. Over the weekend, Thomson would attempt to collect money from advertisers in order to make the staff's checks good.

Like many entrepreneurs, Thomson went for broke—it was all or nothing. Thomson also operated on the principle of using OPM—other people's money—by borrowing to the hilt. It was a rule of business that Jack learned from Thomson, later using it to build his own communications empire.

Although Thomson was not ever close to being the natural promoter and salesman that Jack Cooke would become, he was not without flair. Roy instituted a "Christmas in July" promotion by playing Christmas music on his station in the middle of summer and staging a Santa Claus parade on the main street of town, with Santa passing out samples of the station's advertised products.

By the time Jack Cooke met him, in November 1936, Thomson had purchased two more radio stations in gold mining towns—CJKL in Kirkland Lake, nearly 370 miles from Toronto, and CKGB in Timmins, about 420 miles north. By the latter part of 1936, Roy Thomson had bought the *Timmins Daily Press* by putting down $200 in cash, which was nearly 4 percent of the total he needed. He committed himself to two and a half years of monthly installments. Thomson's philosophy at the time was to always repay the banks first, with other creditors second. That way, he reasoned, he would always have bank approval.

Both the *Timmins Daily Press* and the radio station, CKGB, were together, with the radio tower transmitter jutting skyward from a five-story building in downtown Timmins. In the 1930s it was the cornerstone of the fledgling Thomson communications chain.

The complete record of the initial conversation between Cooke and Thomson is probably lost forever, but a later report said that Jack's presentation was not unlike his pitch to the school principal in Verigin. The young Jack Cooke may not have been the best salesman of the twentieth century but he was probably one of the most persistent. When Thomson asked him if he had any radio experience, Jack answered that he was familiar with every aspect of the business, although his first time inside a radio station had just taken place in Kirkland Lake.

Within a half-hour Thomson said: "I like you. I'm going to hire you." Jack thanked him, left and went back to Toronto to resign from Colgate-Palmolive. Thomson hired Jack to manage a station that he was purchasing, CJCS in Stratford, Ontario, a small outpost nearly 100 miles northwest of Toronto. Jack Cooke's employment in Stratford was to begin on January 1, 1937. The salary was $23.85 per week.

Jack gave his version of the resignation from Colgate-Palmolive in a January 24, 1980, interview with the *Times-Globe* of St. John's, New Brunswick, a Canadian maritime province: "I was told I was a damn fool, that one day I could be president of Colgate-

Palmolive-Peet. They wanted to know how much he was paying me. I wanted to work for Mr. Roy Thomson."

Thomson probably found a lot in common with young Cooke. Both were frugal, although they expressed it in different ways. Thomson, the bean counter, avoided buying clothes in those days and one report of the early 1930s had him standing up at a governmental meeting in North Bay with a patch on the seat of his pants. Jack, the supersalesman, was always the snappy dresser—in later years he would twice make Canada's best-dressed list. Thomson was chunky, his 5'10" body often ballooning to over 200 pounds in spite of frequent diets. Jack would save by skimping on meals, or letting others pick up checks whenever possible. His most visible vice was cigarettes; he now regularly smoked three to four packs of Camels a day.

Both men believed in paying employees as little as possible, at the same time trying to keep morale high. The operating philosophy was to give a worthy associate who asked for a raise a new and more prestigious title or a perk, like the use of a car or a quick one-time bonus—anything but a permanent salary increase.

After the Christmas holidays of 1936, Jack met Roy Thomson early on New Year's morning at the corner of Bloor and Yonge streets in downtown Toronto for the two-hour drive to Stratford.[2] As they drove through the windy streets of Toronto early that day, the only sight was knots of shivering, unemployed men. Although they rode in Thomson's car, Jack drove much of the way. Thomson's eyesight was notoriously bad—he had to read everything by holding it up close to his eyes. His most unforgettable feature was always his glasses, huge round hunks of glass as thick as the bottoms of Mason jars. Thomson was a nonsmoker, a counterpoint to Jack's chainsmoking.

Jack was anxious to prove himself. Jeannie was pregnant and showing.[3] The little house on Neville Park Boulevard was getting cramped. But as they drove to Stratford, Jack received something of a jolt. On the way, Thomson told him, "You're manager but the former manager is still there. And, he gets to keep his title."

When Jack asked "Why?" Thomson told him about his rival's secret weapon. The current manager owned the transmitter.

Jack was hungry and could now alternate charm and snarls effortlessly. He had just taken a salary cut to work for Roy Thomson. He was willing to work from the moment his eyes opened to the time they closed. The existing manager, transmitter owner or not, didn't stand a chance.

The manager was gone in two months. And Jack had purchased the transmitter from him for $300.

CJCS was in the red when Jack took over. In the first months there were times when Jack couldn't even pay himself and had to keep Thomson's paychecks in his wallet for weeks. But by the middle of June, Jack had made the station profitable. In what was described as stunts combined with imaginative programming as well as Jack's superior salesmanship, he increased the sale of advertising time to near sell-out proportions.[4] Young Jack himself took to the air, at one time broadcasting live from the back of a milk truck where he did man-on-the-street interviews about the quality of the sponsor's dairy brands. After that, Thomson bumped his salary to $35 a week. The station became a success—so much of a success that it was quickly sold at a hefty profit. Thomson recalled his young find to the north, putting Jack in charge of the Timmins, North Bay, and the Kirkland Lake stations, giving him a small piece of each one and $100 a week.[5] Jack was a success right from the start. During his first month he doubled the ad billings in Timmins from $2,000 to $4,000.

Life in the mining towns of northern Ontario could be somewhat primitive in the 1930s. That was true in the radio business as well.

Roy Thomson's operation in Kirkland Lake had an announcer who often gave the weather report by sticking his head out the station's window and yelling to passersby about conditions. If the impromptu report came back as "real cold" he would tell the radio audience, "A fellow outside says, 'It's real cold.'"

One of his duties was also to read a commercial from Seymour's Men's Wear which ended with the slogan, "If Seymour's clothes don't fit, Seymour won't let you wear them." The announcer, tired of his job at CJKL, decided to quit. But as his final act, he delivered the clothing store's slogan as "If Seymour's clothes don't fit, Seymour doesn't give a shit, and neither do I." Then he left town before an angry Jack Kent Cooke could get to him.

Reaching Toronto, the ex-announcer joined the Canadian Army and was later captured by Nazis in Europe, becoming a prisoner of war. When Jack heard the news he was quoted as saying, "I hope the Germans shoot him, because if they don't, I will."

Al Dubin, a station engineer who worked eight years for Jack in Kirkland Lake and in Toronto remembers their first meeting in 1942 this way: "I had just started playing a Bing Crosby record. It's about 8:15 in the evening and the telephone starts ringing. I answer it and it's Jack. Except I'm not sure it's Jack because we've never met and besides Jack had a cold and was hard to understand.

" 'This is Jack Cooke,' " Al Dubin recalled the voice saying. " 'I'm calling from the Park Lane Hotel.⁶ I was listening to the station driving in. The modulation is too high. Turn it down.'

"I wasn't even sure it was him, but I went into the control room and turned it down. Jack was right. The modulation was too high."

Dubin, who remembers asking Jack for a raise and getting the title of Chief Station Operator instead, later had the responsibility of teaching the engineers of the fledgling Thomson radio empire the ropes.

"I taught the kids how to turn the station on and off, which buttons to push, that sort of thing. Jack bullshitted me out of so much money. I was only making $90 a month when Jack came on the scene and every time I asked him to get me a raise I wound up with another title. Times were tough, even though we were expanding. I remember Jack trying to collect advertising money on a Thursday to make payroll on Friday. He always made it."

Thomson, increasingly impressed with young Jack Cooke, offered Jack a half-interest in the next station he was buying. At first, Jack thought Thomson was giving him the interest for nothing.

"You raise $10,000 and you're in," he was told. Somehow, although the amount was a fortune, Jack found the money and the Thomson-Cooke radio chain was born. Later Jack and Roy even had a theme song of sorts, "Wishing Will Make It So." Jack would often play it on the piano for the two of them and sing it to groups at gatherings. And although the two were to invest in many communication enterprises together, Thomson's focus soon centered on newspapers while Jack kept to radio.

Those were heady days. Jack was still in his late twenties when he made his first big killing for Thomson and himself. Just over the Ontario border, in Quebec, sixty miles east of Kirkland Lake, there was a small mining town called Rouyn. The radio station in the town was for sale for $21,000. What Cooke and Thomson did there was to multiply their investment fiftyfold in less than a year.

Jack immediately saw that iron deposits around the town kept all other signals out, giving the Rouyn station a monopoly on radio for the area. Thomson and Cooke were able to buy the station for a $2,000 down payment—$1,000 each—and borrowing the remaining $19,000 from the Bank of Nova Scotia. Taking control, they named the station CKRN, the K probably after Thomson's son Kenneth and the R after the name of the town or possibly after Jack's new son Ralph. But Jack did more than discover Rouyn. It was his innovative programing that made the station the talk of northern Quebec.

A year later, the two sold the station for $105,000.

Jack's success up north gave him power. He was able to hire both his brothers Hal and Donald to work for him in the Thomson-Cooke radio chain. He even hired Don Horton, a friend who had lived on Neville Park Boulevard in Toronto. It was not a cushy job for any of them. Jack was much harder on them than other employees and Horton soon left. There were now two stations in southern Ontario, CHEX in Petersborough, and CKWS in Kingston, both opened by Jack in 1942. And stations were opened in the Quebec mining towns of Val d'Or and Amos.

Jack was thirty in 1942. A few years before, he had promised his father Ralph he'd be a millionaire by his thirtieth birthday.[7] He was one year late, reaching the magic number in 1943.

Thus, during the war years, while most of the world was in mortal combat, and when many young men Jack's age were fighting their way through North Africa or the islands of the South Pacific, Jack Cooke was becoming rich.[8] It wasn't enough.

A year later he was ready to go it alone and Toronto, as Alex Barris, the former entertainment columnist of the *Globe and Mail,* later put it, "was about to be hit by a comet."

Notes

1. Another memorable Thomson phrase is, "For enough money, I'd work in hell." Although the metaphor is wrong, he could have been speaking of the cold northern Ontario winters.
2. Jean often traveled with Jack throughout northern Ontario. Jack considered her an asset, particularly in closing business deals over dinner. She was generally home at the Cooke family house in Toronto during the holidays.
3. Ralph, Jack Cooke's oldest son, was born April 29, 1937. John, his other son, was born on September 27, 1941.
4. Jack was never ashamed of being a salesman. Twenty years later, a multimillionaire many times over, Jack Kent Cooke emigrated to the United States. The space in his passport for his occupation read simply, "salesman."
5. Jack often tried to wind up in Timmins on a Saturday night to play rummy and poker with Malvern buddy Joe McNulty and other Timmins friends after McNulty's hockey games.
6. The Park Lane Hotel, a seven-story building gone today, was once the pride of the gold mining town of Kirkland Lake. Business and government dinners for the community generally took place in its locally famed Normandy Room.
7. Jack and Jean didn't wait for Jack's certification as a millionaire to move out of the Neville Park house. The Cooke family of three moved to 65 Lawlor Avenue in 1939 and to 58 Fallingbrook Road in Scarborough the next year. Both addresses were near Jack's parents' home. Jack and Jean moved twice more before their first big possession—the Armour Heights house—purchased in 1944 after Jack bought CKEY. Ralph and Nancy moved the same year, to a more modest house at 45 Lawrence Avenue East, bringing the Neville Park Boulevard era to a close.
8. There is no evidence that Jack shirked his wartime responsibilities. Canada did not have a draft until late 1942 and that was instituted

by a special vote. Not surprisingly, in light of today's Canadian politics, 80 percent of English-speaking Canadians voted for a draft while 72 percent of the French-speaking population, voted against. Being a married man of nearly thirty, with two children, Jack would have been among the very last to be called. In spite of chainsmoking cigarettes, Jack's only health concern until he was forty was a painful kidney stone problem and a hearing deficiency that caused him to be deaf to certain tones.

CHAPTER
5
RADIO DAYS

"He is probably Canada's handsomest millionaire."

D day for the rest of the world may have taken place in June 1944, but Jack Kent Cooke's own D day began two months later in August of that year when he closed the deal to take over CKCL in Toronto, and changed the call letters to CKEY.[1]

"Make no mistake, Jack revolutionized radio in Canada forever," Bill Brady remembers. Brady had an evening show on the station in its early days called "Bill Brady's Boarding House," a live musical half-hour that had a cast of six singers and two musicians.

"He must have been planning it for years," recalls Al Dubin, who had followed Jack from the north, accepting an offer to be an engineer at the station for $200 a month. "He knew everything that needed to be done. He had it all ready like a commando operation."

Jack had wanted a Toronto station since he was a teenager. "I used to pass the station going home at nights on the bus," Jack told a writer years later. "I'd say to myself, Oh boy, wait 'til I own that place."[2]

Jack almost didn't get "that place." When he went to see the owner, Henry S. Gooderham, Jack had $100,000 in the bank and he naively thought that this amount would be enough to swing a deal for one of Toronto's six radio stations, particularly one of the lowest rated. He must have gulped when Gooderham asked for an even $1 million. Gooderham didn't care whether he sold it or not.[3]

Jack, going into his full-court sales press, somehow talked Gooderham down to $500,000. When Gooderham agreed, Jack whipped a contract out of his briefcase and filled in some blanks. But Gooderham added some caveats of his own. Young Cooke had one month to come back with the amount or lose his deposit. Gooderham wanted half of the $500,000 down and the other half in the form of a short mortgage. It was his belief that a thirty-two-year-old man fresh from northern Ontario, and with no family of substance, couldn't come up with the cash. He was nearly right.

Jack had sold his interests in the Rouyn, Amos, and Val d'Or stations to raise the $100,000 he had in the bank and perhaps thought that Roy Thomson might come in for a third or even half. Thomson, not wanting his star pupil to leave home, and probably thinking a failure would bring Jack back to the fold, declined. He may have been a little miffed, too, that besides Al Dubin, key staffers like Dan Carr, Don Insley, and Martin Silbert were headed south with his second-in-command.

Jack went to his attorney and friend, William K. "Bill" Zimmerman. It was Zimmerman's advice not to go hat-in-hand to the banks, but to form a syndicate of Toronto movers and shakers at $25,000 a share. There were to be only eight investors in the deal besides Jack, and Zimmerman himself came in for the first piece, writing Jack a check for $25,000. Zimmerman also got Jack the second investor, James H. Gundy of Wood, Gundy and Co., Canada's largest stock brokerage. Jack went around Toronto and picked up more high-stakes players—wealthy Ontario businessmen like Norman Urquhart, General F. Stuart Hogarth, and Charles L. Burton—who were willing to put up what in those days was a serious sum to invest in a thirty-two-year-old wunderkind. But with three more investors needed, Jack started running into dead-end streets. Everyone else began turning Jack, a salesman's salesman, down.

With less than a week to go before his option would expire—with Jack losing both his deposit and part of his boy-wonder reputation—the young Cooke was referred to a Canadian mining millionaire said to be one of the richest men in all of Canada.

Jack, palms sweating, went to him and talked for hours. The strain of acquiring the station was giving him sleepless nights and causing him to lose weight. But like the time in Verigin, or his first meeting with Thomson, the young businessman wasn't about to quit. Like a hungry dog with a bone, Jack Cooke wouldn't let go.

"I talked about everything," Jack remembers, "even the height of the [station's] building. I thought as long as I could keep him from saying 'no' I had a chance."

The mining magnate didn't say no but he didn't say yes either. He told Jack that he didn't want or need to invest in anything.

So Jack kept talking.

Finally it was agreed that his potential investor would at least sleep on it overnight and the prospective station owner would come back the next day.

When Jack returned, the millionaire had a surprise that would have put a lesser man on the floor. His potential investor not only agreed to give Jack Cooke the $25,000, but offered it as a gift. Jack wouldn't accept the free handout, but insisted the $25,000 be accepted on a business basis only.

"Being given that much money isn't good for a man," Jack said later.

With the influential mining man in, the other investors were found easily and Jack Kenneth Cooke, now beginning to call himself Jack Kent Cooke and to insist others do the same, was ready to change the direction of Canadian radio forever. The budding mogul now had the keystone property of what would become a media empire.

Jack began by breaking the unwritten rules of Canadian radio. It shook Toronto up and made the youthful entrepreneur the talk of Ontario.

Canada in the 1940s was a restrictive society by American standards. There were no Sunday movies, no Sunday sporting events or newspapers. Sledding by children on the Sabbath was illegal. Women were not allowed in certain bars on any day of the week. Thus Jack's first move, a change to twenty-four-hours-a-day radio, one of the first stations to go around the clock in Canada, was considered daring.

Next, Jack introduced the concept of singing station jingles, an enlivening move that somehow had escaped the rest of the nation. He speeded up the station, instituting a motto of "no dead air" (Jack was said to have entered a CKEY studio where a disc jockey was performing and tickling him in order to punch up the show). But Jack Kent Cooke's biggest change came in his move to install long block programming. In the early 1940s, most radio stations ran fifteen-minute time blocks. There would be fifteen minutes of news, followed by fifteen minutes of a singer, followed by a fifteen-minute comedy program.

Jack had run surveys that showed that Canadian women didn't like to turn the dial every fifteen minutes to find music. The surveys found that one hour or longer was the ideal program length. Jack Kent Cooke answered that need. But unfortunately one of CKEY's first new programs after Jack took over almost landed him in litigation.

A New York AM station, WNEW, had a show called "Make-Believe Ball Room," which had been invented by William B. Williams. The show featured the leading bands of the time on an imaginary stage, with a live host. CKEY put together an identical show with its own host, Keith Sandy, and put it on the air for an hour and a half in the morning and two hours in the afternoon. The owner of WNEW, Bernice Judis, wrote Jack several threatening letters, vowing to sue. Some of Jack's station performers, fearing they would be implicated in a civil suit began to slur the name of the show, so that it came out "Maple Leaf Ball Room." Jack ignored her and after a few months, the matter died.

Jack worked Sandy hard. When the announcer came to him a few years later to ask for Sundays off to be with his family, Jack's answer was: "What would you do on Sunday in Toronto if you had it off?" (He was apparently referring to the city's infamous blue laws.) "Why I would be lost myself for something to do here on Sundays if I didn't have my yacht."

Jack's biggest star at CKEY was undoubtedly Lorne Greene, who would go on to become a North American household favorite with his role in the TV series *Bonanza*. In the early 1940s, Lorne was known as the "Voice of Doom" in Canada because of the newscasts he narrated that detailed the deaths of thousands of Canadians in World War II. After the war, Lorne's resonant tones earned him the title "The Voice of Canada" and sometimes simply "The Voice of God."

Lorne anchored the "Sunoco News" four times a day and his combination of star aura and tough negotiating ability made him Jack's highest paid performer, by far, at $25,000 a year.

Once when arguing with Jack over money, Greene was asked to increase his time on the air. Lorne is reported to have said, "Jack, you sell time and so do I." He got his money.[4]

Boosting its power to 5,000 watts from 1,000, CKEY soon dominated Toronto radio. Within a year, the Elliot-Haynes rating service, the Nielsen or Arbitron of the day, gave Jack's station the major market position by far, a 35 percent share, making it Toronto's broadcast leader. And while another station, CHUM, attempted to duplicate the CKEY format, it never passed CKEY in the ratings. Jack was fighting for still higher ratings on another front as well. He lobbied hard to take away the NBC Blue Network affiliation from CJBC, a government-owned station, which would have given him even higher evening ratings. Instead, it made him a foe of CBC bureaucrats, even though he didn't get the NBC prize.

Jack, seizing on his listening numbers to boost advertising charges, also jammed in as many commercials as he could find. While the average Canadian station filled its time with an 8.4 percent commercial load, CKEY had 17 percent of every hour filled with ads. Nobody complained. Indeed, the all-night show called "House Party" with Johnny Williams as host was sponsored by a car dealer whose commercial spots were so frequent that it must have seemed to listeners like several hours of having a used car salesman in their homes. Not that it wasn't successful in moving automobiles. The car dealer who sponsored it did so for six years in a row. Among "cash cows," CKEY was a prize-winning Holstein, and it helped to make Jack Kent Cooke a millionaire many times over.

Although he first testified before the Canadian government in 1948 that he was ready to have a television station "on the air in six months" (Jack's quest for a private TV license would last more than a dozen years), it wasn't until the next year that he was able to put his huge cash flow to use in the broadcast field. But first the new multimillionaire eliminated his investor syndicate. Jack paid them $69,000 each, almost triple the $25,000 they had put in. CKEY now belonged 100 percent to Jack Kent Cooke, with the biggest profits still to come. The young mogul was ready to expand.

In 1949, when Canadian government officials, after turning him down for a private TV license (they weren't willing to grant anyone a private license yet), again prevented him from expanding in the broadcast field—this time from buying 40 percent of CKCO in Ottawa—Jack found a novel way to circumvent regulations. He simply signed a consulting deal with the station that called for him to get 40 percent of the gross profits before taxes and depreciation. This may have rankled the Canadian Board of Broadcast Governors and led to regulatory defeats down the road, but it was not illegal. Given a free hand by the station's president, a Cooke intimate by the name of Duncan MacTavish, Jack changed the call letters to CKOY, put in the CKEY formula, and watched the profits grow. During the decade of the 1950s CKOY's gross profits were $1,600,000, giving Jack "pocket change" for his consulting time that totaled $640,000.

Jack didn't hide his burgeoning wealth. When CKEY staffer Martin Silbert attempted to get him to buy some Irish Sweepstakes tickets he was selling, and told him he could win $140,000, Jack shot him a withering glance and answered, "Martin, I have $140,000."

Flushed with success, Jack started insisting that the Kent middle name go on everything. Later stories would say that there was another Jack Cooke in Toronto and that Jack added the middle name to differentiate himself. Actually there were two. First, there was the owner of James Cooke Motors, a well-known car dealer. There was also a Jack Cook, who was a leading Canadian auto race driver. Stories in the early 1950s, after Jack bought the Toronto Maple Leafs baseball team, would sometimes have both names on the same page, Jack Cook and Jack Cooke. Because of space limitations that headline writers often face, Jack's adopted middle name would be left out.

Some sources say that Jack chose "Kent" after the cigarette brand. But a Torontonian who knew him well says that it was taken from the Duke of Kent, a member of the British royal family who was a war hero, killed when his airplane crashed in 1942. Jack, who surely would want to have the last word, has sometimes told people that Kent is a tribute to a friend of his father. Kent is also derivative of Jack's real middle name, Kenneth, which is also the name of Roy Thomson's only natural son.

As Jack prospered, his frugality increased to the point that he sometimes became conniving.

Al Dubin had been asked to have dinner with Jack. He dreaded going. Oh God, he thought, somehow I'm going to get stuck with the check, I know it.

They went to the Lichee Garden at 118 Elizabeth Street.⁵ After dinner Jack said he had "forgotten his wallet." Get the cash from his secretary, Vera Fountain, he told Dubin. The bill was $7.80.

Al went to the secretary the next morning. Jack was out of town.

"Jack would kill me if I reimbursed you for dinner," she told him. "I can't do it."

Al needed the money. Eight dollars was a lot of money to a man making less than $300 a month. He knew that the station had several company cars and that Jack would always pay for a car wash.

So he walked to the corner where a 20-cent car wash was, and spent the morning picking up the receipts as the drivers dropped them in the trash before they sped away. When he had thirty-nine he brought them back to the station where Vera Fountain dutifully stapled them together and wrote out a slip. Then she took $7.80 from the petty cash box to pay him.

When Jack couldn't get the station filled with paying advertisers, he learned the value of barter.

Bill Brady, who was now composing and recording advertising jingles for one of Jack's first subsidiaries, Imperial Transcriptions, a studio that produced and recorded radio commercials on a national basis, remembers the Ted Davy escapade.

"It's funny, because I had just been to a business dinner with

Jack, the night before. I'd see Jack every month or so and Jack would always say at a point in the evening, 'Well, Bill I'm worth $3 million now,' and the next time he'd say something like, 'I'm up to $4-and-a-half million this month!' Perhaps he didn't believe how rich he was getting.

"So I was surprised he came to me one day when I was at the station and asked me about Ted Davy.

" 'Sure', I said, 'the car dealer down on Danforth Street.'

" 'Could you get him on the phone, Bill, and introduce me to him? I'd like to buy my mother a car.'

"Now," said Bill Brady, "This is right after Jack has told me he's up to five million, so I said to him, but Jack, Ted Davy is a *used car* dealer.

" 'That's right,' Jack said, 'I thought I could find something nice for about $800.'

"So I called Ted Davy and put Jack on the phone with him. The next day I'm at the station and here comes Jack and he's got Ted Davy by the arm. He reintroduces us and then he starts talking about doing a commercial for Ted.

" 'Bill, you know that old song, "Titwillow, Titwillow, Titwillow" '—and Jack sings it a little. 'I thought we could use the tune and say Ted Davy, Ted Davy, Ted Davy. What do you think?'

"Well," Brady recalls, "Jack not only wrote the damn jingle and got his mother a free car, but that jingle ran on CKEY for more than ten years. It was a goldmine!

"Jack knew how to do it," Brady concluded, "you have to hand it to him."

Brady also remembers the Tower Isle Magic caper:

"Jack and Jean went to Jamaica for a vacation and Jack comes back all enthused.[6]

" 'Bill, I've just been to Jamaica,' Jack booms, 'and we stayed at this marvelous resort called Tower Isle. I've invited the owner here—his name is Abe Essa—and he'll be staying at my house.'

"Jack was sitting across from me and you always knew he was about to make a point because he'd reach across and briefly touch your knee.

" 'I wonder if you'd do me a small favor.' "

Uh oh, Bill Brady thought, here it comes.

" 'Tower Isle has this fabulous jingle, called Tower Isle Magic, but it has a calypso beat. I'd like you to put it into a Canadian arrangement. Then when Abe Essa comes to my house I'm going to have two loudspeakers in the driveway and I'll play his jingle, Canadian style.'

" 'Well Jack, I'd be happy to but we'll have to hire some singers and musicians.'

" 'It's not necessary,' Jack said. He knew my schedule better than I did. 'You're doing the Nescafe commercial at Imperial Friday. Can't you just squeeze in ten minutes at the end of the session and run this off? It's for private use, be sure to tell them that.'

"So I recorded the Tower Isle Magic jingle for Jack and forgot about it.

"Two weeks go by and I get a phone call from one of the singers. Seems a friend of hers has called saying she's heard her singing on a radio commercial for a Tower Isle hotel in northern Alberta. Then I get a call about somebody hearing the Tower Isle jingle in Manitoba. Jack's running the Tower Isle spot all over Canada and he didn't even have to pay for it.

"So I go to Jack and confront him with it and tell him we've got to pay the talent. Jack hems and haws around and asks how much. I tell him $25 each for the musicians and $10 for each singer. Jack says he'll let me know—but he never paid anybody.

"The upshot is that two years later I'm down in Jamaica staying at a hotel and I go outside and hear my Tower Isle Magic arrangement being played on the beach. So I decide to go over to Tower Isle and look up old Abe Essa and tell him I'm the arranger. Abe Essa tells me it's the most expensive jingle he's ever had produced—Abe says, 'It cost me a month's lodging in my best suite!' "

Brady tells his Jack Kent Cooke stories not in an angry, vindictive manner. It's more of a bemused, almost admiring tone, as if to say, "That Jack!"

Jack's celebrity was now growing in Toronto. He was given movie star status. A reporter would ask him silly questions and Jack would give long, loquacious answers: Favorite food? "Softshell crabs. The finest food in the whole world." Favorite author?

"I like George Orwell because he has the highest intelligence in the world. He writes better than anyone in the last generation." Favorite playwright? "Christopher Fry, particularly *The Lady's Not For Burning*. To write English like that is not a science, but an art." Next ambition? "To produce a Broadway revue and to write a fine book."

"Jack would sometimes stay up nights reading the dictionary," a former CKEY staffer told a writer. "We'd always know because those were the mornings we'd come out of the sales meetings scratching our heads, wondering what he said."

When George McCullagh, the irascible publisher of the Toronto *Globe and Mail,* considered having a profile written about Jack in 1949, he asked about Jack's personality.

"He's ruthless, tough, and works every waking moment," one of his reporters told him.

"Good," McCullagh answered, "kinda reminds me of me."

Political candidates now sought his backing but Jack was anything but predictable. His 1948 Canadian *Who's Who* entry listed his political affiliation as Conservative, but he often backed Liberals for office. In the early 1950s Jack backed Allan Lamport for mayor of Toronto, probably on Lamport's promise to allow professional sports to be played on Sunday within the city limits. Jack was also active in get-out-the-vote drives for Toronto and in 1952 lost a $1,000 public bet with the owner of CHOB radio in Winnipeg when that city had a 52 percent turnout, much greater than the 34 percent of Toronto.[7]

Driving himself endlessly—he was often at the station literally twenty-four hours a day—so that his wife Jeannie would drive down to the station herself and drag him home, Jack expected the same hours of the staff as well. He would regularly schedule meetings at 12:30 and 5:30 so that employees would miss their lunch or dinner break. His only indulgence in the early years of CKEY was to host his own Sunday night book review show under a pseudonym.[8]

The new owner even wrote an operating philosophy of the duties of a successful radio station:

1. To be successful.
2. To provide information.
3. To entertain.
4. To serve the public interest.

This credo of Jack's was published by *Canadian Business* in 1947.

His devastating good looks were still an asset. One female writer, Thelma Le Cocq, would gush about him in a 1952 interview in the Canadian magazine *Saturday Night:* "Being the youngest, he is probably Canada's handsomest millionaire. He has a smile that not only lights up his whole face, but gives the impression that it could light up a whole night club. As though that weren't enough, he has fairish curly hair which is thinning only slightly, a finely shaped nose, noticeably good teeth, and an adequate chin. The only point of mystery is his eyes, which are said to be blue but which narrow to a fan of wrinkles at the corner so that the color as well as the expression is only guesswork. These lines, like the ones on his forehead, were put there early by facial activity and have nothing to do with the fact that he's nearly 40."

Jack began to attempt to live up to these rave reviews. He moved his suit buying from Toronto's Lloyd Brothers to Eddy Provan tailors, and dressed in a no-padded look, attempting to emulate Fred Astaire. As he grew even richer, he shopped for suits in New York City and eventually graduated to a tailor on Saville Row in London. He alternated between driving a Cadillac convertible and a Lincoln Continental, and went without a chauffeur except on special occasions when he had the company's delivery man, Eddie Parr, dress up to play the role. The staff at CKEY, which numbered eighteen when he took over (many of them resigned) was expanded to nearly 100. Jack's own office on the second floor was decorated in early Playboy style, including a leopardskin sofa and a built-in bar stocked with Jack's favorite Canadian whisky, Crown Royal. The normal work day was 7:00 A.M. to midnight, and then sometimes his boundless energy would cause him to nightclub into the early hours of the morning, a lifestyle that was beginning to be felt by Jeannie.

Along with the Cadillac, and the leopardskin sofa, Jack bought his first yacht. It was a Fairmile, which was a converted Canadian torpedo motor boat that had been used by the Navy during the Second World War. It was more than 100 feet long. With its flat bottom, it was uncomfortable at high speeds and gulped gas, but was perfect for Jack's business entertaining. The former bandleader would often have a Steinway wheeled aboard and delighted in playing and singing for his guests, while conducting business on a ship-to-shore radio. But Jack was criticized for his landlubber style of wallpapering the staterooms.

"Jack would love to buzz across Lake Ontario to Rochester on weekends," a Toronto employee told a writer. "In the winter he would have it driven down to Florida by a captain. One year he sent Jeannie and the two boys, complete with tutor. The trip really wiped Jean out."

Another new house was bought. This time it was a six-acre estate in the fashionable Richmond Hill section in the far north end of Toronto. Jack and Jean would often host parties at their home on Saturday evenings. While he rarely entertained groups of more than twenty, an invitation from Jack and Jean was sought after. The evening usually ended around the piano. The parties were quite liberal for Toronto. A newspaper of the day reported Jack as "being shocked" when he discovered some musicians smoking marijuana cigarettes in his garden.

"Jack was always selling, even then," a Cooke intimate told a writer in an "ice-to-the-Eskimos" story. "One Saturday night I was at the house and Jack took me aside and asked me to stay as the rest of the guests were leaving. I thought it was about a business deal. What Jack did was to walk me into his closet and try to sell me three used suits he had bought in England. He wanted $70 apiece. The funny thing is that Jack knows I owned my own menswear shop downtown. But I guess the joke was on me because damned if Jack didn't sell me his old suits."

But now, unflattering accounts were beginning to appear. The press already had began talking about Jack's "dark" side, along with his "wonder boy" title. A former employee was quoted as saying, "He'll promise you the sun and the moon. He'll give you everything but money." His office was called "the Kremlin" by some employees and "Cloud Nine" by others. A magazine wrote that "he'll fire somebody at a moment's notice just to show he's taken over." He was described as being "so stingy he'll refuse to okay an order for a dozen pencils." And his brother Hal, who helped to manage CKEY, was once screamed at in front of others when he parked Jack's Cadillac in the wrong place.

Pugnacious, ruthless as ever, Jack got in a fist fight with a Toronto newspaper man in a restaurant. And a magazine reported that "when Jack Cooke's name is mentioned in radio and publishing circles, the impression you get is that he's not liked."

Liked or not, the station under what most of the Toronto press was calling "the wonder boy" was both an artistic and financial success. *Variety*, the showbiz newspaper, gave Jack a plaque. A CKEY recorded-music show called "Sir Ernest Plays Favorites," hosted by the conductor of the Toronto symphony orchestra (Jack had talked Sir Ernest MacMillan into becoming a part-time disc jockey), was the only Canadian radio show to win an award by an American radio-TV organization. The station was clearly the most successful broadcasting enterprise in Canada.

With a huge success on his hands in CKEY—the station became one of the top ten dollar-grossing stations in North America by the early 1950s—Jack's libido began to stray. Toronto models and singers were his first conquests. He would book the King Edward hotel for a few hours in midafternoon so he could "clear his head of migraine headaches." Bigger names would come later. And never satisfied with just a single success, Jack was already looking for new businesses to acquire.

His biggest would be *Liberty* magazine.

Notes

1. Jack's CKEY took to the airwaves on Monday, August 28, 1944 at 5:00 A.M. with a program called "Rural Route 580." The station's frequency was 580 AM (FM was rarely used anywhere at that time). Toronto had six stations in 1944 and four U.S. stations were popular enough to be listed in the Toronto papers.
2. The reader is referred back to chapter 2. CKCL was the radio station of Jack's boyhood and he may have wanted to own it since he was a child; also see chapter 3.
3. Gooderham didn't have to. The Gooderhams had substantial interests in the liquor industry—they originated the Hiram Walker Canadian

Whisky labels. The Gooderhams are also a yachting family, a social and competitive strata Jack would later enter.

4. Lorne Greene was met with indifference when he went to Hollywood to try his luck. He existed by doing radio and television commercials until he got his first break, by going to New York to do a Broadway play, *The Prescott Proposals* with Katherine Cornell. The play, a cold war confection about the U.N. and Communist intrigue, earned him good notices and led to his famous *Bonanza* role.

5. Lichee Garden, as most old-time Torontonians know, moved to its new address at the corner of Bay and Dundas, in 1983.

6. In 1990, Jack would assert that he had taken only one vacation since he was eight years of age.

7. As the reader might suspect, Conservative in Canada is roughly comparable to Republican in the United States and a Liberal is akin to a Democrat.

8. Jack treasured the letters he received for the program and is said to keep them in his small private museum next to the stables on his Far Acres estate.

CHAPTER
6
LITERARY WAYS

"Jack had won, and . . . helped to change Canadian law."

Packing entrepreneurial weapons—charts and binders full of figures—Jack Kent Cooke and Roy Thomson swaggered into the boardroom of *Liberty* magazine on a cold Toronto day in October 1947 and received a shock. Expecting to see only a handful of executives of the failing enterprise, they instead were greeted by a force of twenty-five—accountants, lawyers, editors, and ad salesmen. Jack didn't mind being outnumbered. That meant he would have to fight harder. And he loved the challenge.

Thomson and Jack were back together again. The year before they had purchased the small Skyway Drive-In movie theatre chain. Then they bought two national radio sales agencies together, National Broadcast Sales in Montreal and Radio Broadcast Sales in Toronto. They had still found time to grab businesses separately as well. Jack had just started Guild Radio Services, a syndicator of radio shows in Toronto. He had also purchased Lawrence Advertising, a small ad agency. All of these businesses helped add to the profits of CKEY. Business jargon today would call it "vertical integration."

Meanwhile, Thomson was still acquiring small newspapers and radio stations in Canada whenever they came up for sale.

Most of the men in the room were Americans. *Liberty* had begun in the 1920s, as the idea of Joseph Patterson, then the publisher of the New York *Daily News*. It was an American publication. The magazine didn't even have a name when it first appeared—that was selected by its readers in a contest that resulted in national publicity. The periodical's most distinctive features included timed articles ("Reading time for this article: six minutes and forty-five seconds") and no features that were continued in the back section of the magazine. The weekly specialized in racy titles. Perhaps its best known story was "My Sex Life," an article written by Mahatma Gandhi explaining his vow of celibacy. Both fiction and articles were given equal weight and a mass readership developed, second only to the *Saturday Evening Post*. But advertising did not.

With a huge circulation, but not enough ads, Patterson decided to get back into what he knew best, newspapers. He traded his creation to America's best known health enthusiast of the day, Bernarr McFadden, in exchange for a Detroit tabloid newspaper.

McFadden couldn't make a go of it either. Although circulation continued to grow, advertisers failed to get on board. The magazine was like a growing child with a voracious appetite and whether it consumed health food or junk food, what it was doing was eating up at the profits spun off by McFadden's other publications.

McFadden dumped *Liberty* on the printing firm whose presses cranked out the copies each month. During this part of *Liberty*'s life, a separate Canadian edition was begun. Although the magazine carried some Canadian advertising, a Canadian editorial, and some Canadian articles, it was still very American in tone. Often, the editors would try to Canadianize the content of a piece of fiction by changing, for example, the word Cleveland to Vancouver or the Missouri River to the Fraser River. But the editor would often miss a nuance or two so that perhaps the name of "Vancouver's" football team might be left as the Browns instead of being changed to the Lions.

When Jack, Roy, and Roy's accountant burst into the boardroom stuffed with Yank lawyers and accountants, *Liberty* magazine had become Canada's largest weekly publication in terms of circulation but every edition that hit the streets was losing thousands of dollars.[1]

Even though Jack and Roy were outnumbered twenty-five to three, it was Jack Kent Cooke who took over and dominated the room. Roy would later tell friends, "I didn't say a word. Jack talked the entire time. When it was over, Jack had bought the magazine for about half of what I thought we'd get it for."

The "half" that they paid for *Liberty* magazine in late 1947 was $400,000. Jack and Roy took 45 percent each, with the other 10 percent being divided between friends and employees of the two.

Although Cooke and Thomson were equal financial partners, creatively it was Jack's show from the start. The editor, when Jack walked in, was Jim Harris. A British newspaper man by the name of Beverley Owen, who had run *Liberty* for years, had just quit. A Canadian, Joe Rutledge, handled the business side. The magazine's editorial office was in Toronto; there were advertising sales offices in both Toronto and Montreal.

Jack began by firing the entire editorial staff, installing a hand-picked group of editors he had personally discovered. It was led by Wallace Reyburn, a thirty-five-year-old New Zealander, who had been editor of the *Montreal Standard*'s Saturday magazine.

Jack chose Reyburn because he was the type of editor who wanted to "walk to the boundaries," and "step on the toes of famous people," a concept that was almost unthinkable in the ultrapolite Canadian society of the late 1940s. At the *Montreal Standard*, Reyburn had constantly fought with management for articles that pushed the envelope. "We never used to hear from any readers," Reyburn said in a 1949 interview, "and sometimes I used to sit at my desk and wonder if we really had any readers and if so, how many were really interested in what we wrote."

With Jack pushing for controversy, and Reyburn willing to push boundaries, it was no wonder that Jack Kent Cooke promptly got sued for libel in a case that could have sent him to prison.

Jack had already made a few superficial changes. He immediately raised the price of the magazine from a nickel to a dime and changed the magazine's name to *New Liberty*. It was an article titled "Babies for Export," written by a Harold Dingman with information supplied by an informant, Dr. Charlotte Whitton, who had written a report on the situation for the Imperial Order of the Daughters of the Empire, that brought criminal charges against Jack Kent Cooke.

The piece had run in the December 27, 1947, edition and charged that a black market existed for Alberta babies, because of looseness in western Canadian provinces' adoption laws. The Alberta provincial government, learning that the magazine was about to publish the story, had requested that Jack and Reyburn withhold the offending piece. The reason given was that a special commission was doing its own investigation and hadn't had time to publish its own findings.

Alberta's attorney general wanted to charge Jack, Dingman, and Whitton with criminal libel. To do so however, meant sending the Royal Canadian Mounted Police all the way to Toronto, a distance of 1,800 miles. The Alberta government was sufficiently angry enough to do so, and two officers from the RCMP were dispatched to Toronto to take Jack and Dingman into custody under section 888 of the Canadian criminal code. Jack's lawyer, Joe Sedgwick, got wind of the Mounties' impending arrival. When they got to Toronto, Dingman was in New York, covering the United Nations. Jack was in Buffalo at a sales meeting. The Mounties returned to Edmonton, Alberta, empty-handed. For once, they did not get their man.

The Alberta attorney general then changed the main charge to "conspiring to publish defamatory libel" plus twelve other lesser charges. By making the change in the charges the province of Alberta was able to compel Jack Kent Cooke, Dingman, and Whitton to appear in Edmonton for trial, which began on April 3, 1948.

Privately, Jack enjoyed the uproar immensely. The Mounties had ransacked the files in *New Liberty*'s offices. Jack and his new magazine were getting millions of dollars worth of free publicity.

"I could have never have bought that kind of advertising," Jack would later tell a friend, "and it came just at the right time."

In fact, when it was all over, *New Liberty* had added 100,000 to its circulation because of the notoriety. Only one Canadian newspaper failed to report that *New Liberty* was the periodical in question: the *Toronto Star* always substituted "a national magazine" in place of the magazine's name. Jack did not forget that. He later ran a critical article in *New Liberty* on the *Star*'s president, H. C. Hindsmith. He also instructed his editorial staff to feed any news tips to the *Star*'s rivals, the *Globe and Mail* and the *Telegram*.

As the "Babies for Export" trial progressed in the Alberta Court, the lesser charges were quietly dropped, one by one.

Jack, in a preliminary statement to the Alberta Court on January 22nd, 1948, gave an eloquent defense for freedom of the press in Canada:

> There are two distinct issues in this case. One of them is the question of the innocence or guilt of Mr. Dingman and me on a charge of conspiracy to commit a libel. The other is the question of the freedom of the press in Canada.
>
> The first of these issues will be decided in court in Alberta. We shall answer to the charge when the time comes. It would obviously be improper for me to comment on that phase of the case at this time.
>
> The second issue, that of the freedom of the press, should be decided by the passage of a new law which will prevent for all time a recurrence of the backdoor method by which the Alberta authorities have sought to penalize me for publishing this article.
>
> Straightforward libel actions are not unusual in Canada, or for that matter in any other country where citizens are free. If a man or a group of men feel they have been wronged by a publication, they have legal rights to vindicate themselves and can do so with libel proceedings.
>
> But this charge against *New Liberty* is not a straightforward libel action. It is a charge of conspiracy to commit a libel. The emphasis in the charge must be on the word CONSPIRACY, because only through this legal subterfuge, could the Alberta Government cause Mr. Dingman and me the loss of time, inconvenience and great expense we are now facing. Incidentally, I understand that this is the first time in the history of British law that this charge has been made.
>
> In laying these conspiracy charges, the Alberta authorities have deliberately evaded the true purpose of the section written in 1888 for the protection of the freedom of the press. The law passed at that time was written by Sir John Thompson, who explained:
>
> "The object is to make two changes in procedure relating to criminal libel. First, that the place of trial in criminal libel prosecutions against the publisher of a newspaper shall be within the province in which the newspaper is published—the publishing office of the newspaper."
>
> There is no reason why we should depart from the general rule

that an offence should be tried where it is committed and I do not understand why a newspaper should not be tried where it is published.

Sir Richard Cartwright added these comments:

"The bill, I suppose, is intended to prevent what appears to be an injustice, the taking of a man from one province to another province to try him. The bill is an excellent one and I am glad to see it introduced."

Jack concluded:

I believe that this action of the Alberta authorities is a dangerous precedent. Using the same method which the Alberta authorities have employed, any disgruntled or power-seeking person in Canada can harass, persecute, and intimidate any publisher, editor or writer in the country who dares to criticize him or any government or group with which he is associated.

The situation created by Alberta's action is completely intolerable in a country where a free press has been cherished for generations. If this law remains in our criminal code as it now stands, every publisher and writer in the country who dares to publish any critical article does so under the threat of being arrested and hauled off to any part of Canada to stand trial.

The trial ran for five days and in the end Justice J. Boyd McBride acquitted Jack and his associates of all charges. Although the prosecutor in the case, C.S. Blanchard, rumbled about bringing new charges, the case was over. Jack had won, and in doing so helped to change Canadian law. On June 30, 1948, the Canadian government amended the statutes to ensure that future libel charges would have to be tried in the defendant's own province. In addition the RCMP's action in searching *New Liberty's* files to gather evidence was roundly condemned. Harold Dingman was also lauded and Charlotte Whitton was later elected mayor of Ottawa.

"Cooke emerged victorious," *Canadian Business* magazine commented, "and if not covered with glory, at least littered with press clippings."

Jack, exultant over the results, began to make bold moves on behalf of *New Liberty* to solidify its position as Canada's leading magazine. His first action was to acquire the 160,000 subscribers of *New World,* the Canadian imitation of *Life.*

The magazine was now over 500,000 in circulation, but each copy cost Jack and Roy six cents to print. The ten cents the magazine cost the reader gave them a four-cent profit before editorial and mailing costs. At that time, advertising was minimal. On the bottom line, Thomson and Cooke were losing money with every issue. To stem the red ink, Jack raised the advertising rates from $900 to $1,600 for a black-and-white page.[2] And unlike CKEY, where he had increased the personnel from eighteen to nearly 100 in a year, Jack cut the *New Liberty* editorial staff to the bone, reducing it to just four people, and employing free-lancers for nearly everything. Still the magazine lost Jack and Roy an additional $300,000 before it went into the black.

"I remember the first time I met Jack Cooke," recalls Alex Barris, the former *Globe and Mail* columnist. "I had heard about him of course, and how rich he was. I was in Wally Reyburn's office talking about writing a free-lance piece when Jack walks in and without introducing himself looked right at the editor and asked him for a wire coathanger.

" 'Sure, Jack,' the editor said, 'but what for?'

" 'See my Cadillac down there?'

"At this point we all looked out the window," Barris told a writer, "and sure enough there was a blue Cadillac convertible.

" 'I'm locked out—the keys are inside. That's what I need the coat hanger for.'

" 'But Jack,' the editor says, 'you're parked right in front of the locksmith, he'll have you out in a minute.'

" 'My God,' Jack Kent Cooke roared, 'that's five dollars.'

"And he took the wire coathanger and went outside. I laughed about it to myself all the way home."

Besides free-lancers such as Barris, *New Liberty* hired "name" Canadian writers of the time like Leslie Roberts, Bruce Hutchinson, and Samuel Gardiner. True crime pieces were written by J.V. McAree of the *Globe and Mail.* But the most popular article was a feature called Vox Pop, a regular column that featured the opinions of the readers themselves. "How to" articles were featured often, as well as human behavior/amateur psychology pieces. Until 1950, no author was ever paid more than $300 for any article or short story.

Still, the magazine had a hard time catching its competitors in advertising pages. The *National Home Monthly* was more focused, even though it had far less circulation. And *Maclean's* magazine had the smallest circulation of the three, but the most advertising due to its prestige.

Nothing escaped Jack's attention. *New Liberty* was sold on street corners out of metal boxes, like newspapers, in addition to newsstands and mail subscription. Jack spent days agonizing over whether to paint the boxes red or orange. He also made sure that the editorial staff knew that Bodoni was his favorite typeface.

To combat *Maclean's*, Jack began adding a little prestige of his own. He hired Canadian's best known poet, E.J. Pratt, to check every word in the magazine for clarity of language. He made Toronto professor Marshall McLuhan, who would later gain fame as a pop philosopher and would receive a measure of immortality by coining the phrase "the medium is the massage," and the term "global village," a regular contributor.

Like CKEY, Jack and Wallace Reyburn drew up a manifesto that contained guidelines for *New Liberty:*

1. Entertainment first, information second. No uplift, no great significance to the articles.
2. No Canada-first attitude. *New Liberty* doesn't aim to be primarily Canadian, as other Canadian magazines do. Articles depend upon interesting subjects whether or not they are Canadians. [It was Reyburn's belief that the Canadian desire to talk about itself was part of an inferiority complex.]
3. Provocative articles, straight from the shoulder. Let the chips fall where they may.
4. In personality articles, give them the works. No puffs. But avoid ripping people up the back unnecessarily.
5. Definite articles on various subjects. Tell all there is to know about such subjects as television, the new motor cars, oil, etc., with charts and diagrams. [Reyburn called this being a miniature *Fortune.*]
6. Television is a must for Canada—so play it hard. [This was *New Liberty's* only straying from a hands-off editorial policy.

Jack's interests were in radio. But Jack wanted television in Canada, therefore *New Liberty* wanted television].³

7. A more broad-minded attitude toward liquor. [It was *New Liberty*'s belief that Canadians were childish about the liquor business and should be more grownup. Blaming temperance advocates, *New Liberty* ran frequent articles on social drinking.]

8. A more sensible attitude toward Sunday. [Although Monday newspapers were allowed to be sold on Sunday night, Canada didn't, and still doesn't have many Sunday newspapers. In 1948 Torontonians were not allowed to buy such items as cigarettes and ice cream on Sunday. Neither professional baseball games nor motion pictures were played on Sundays.]

9. No prejudice against publicity good or bad. *New Liberty* will mention company names in its articles, with praise or criticize products and will mention price. This will make some advertisers mad but so be it.

With this approach, bold for its time, *New Liberty* did indeed offend some advertisers. A profile on the head of a large company mentioned his false teeth and lost advertising because of it. An article on athlete's foot cures attacked one of the magazine's advertisers with predictable results. And a 1955 article about comedian Jackie Gleason titled "Away I Go" brought another libel suit and fresh notoriety.

While it could be said that *New Liberty* became an artistic success for a mass medium magazine, it was never a truly huge financial success. Although Jack and Roy managed to make their $400,000 investment back and *New Liberty* continued to make regular, though unexceptional, profits in the early fifties, Jack never gave up on publishing.

Indeed, Jack Kent Cooke, looked into buying the Toronto *Evening Telegram* in 1949 and 1952, but astutely reasoned that the numbers were too much against him. The *Telegram* folded a decade later.

Jack was also one of several who submitted a sealed bid after George McCullagh, owner of the *Globe and Mail,* died in 1952.⁴ But his reputation as a hardliner on salaries frightened the newsroom reporters.

"When we heard that Cooke was in the bidding we were

terrified," Alex Barris of the *Globe and Mail* remembers. "We were nonunion then, but we reinstated the Guild, just in case he got it, so he couldn't cut salaries."

But Jack lost out on the *Globe and Mail* and it wound up in the hands of R. Howard Webster, a Montreal businessman.

Jack was now a very rich man. One Toronto newspaper reported his income at a million dollars a year, although that figure was probably greatly exaggerated.

With *New Liberty* profitable, and solidifying its position as Canada's leading mass magazine, Jack was ready for quality. As do many men with limited education who find great success in life, Jack undoubtedly felt a need to surround himself with a prestige endeavor. For all the pomposity that he affected, particularly in his enthusiasm for language and words, Jack Kent Cooke genuinely understood and had a love for English literature. He really did spend evenings reading Aristotle and George Orwell. His popular fiction was not lowbrow either. Hemingway, E.M. Forster, and John O'Hara were about as "popular" as his reading became. He spent much time reading Fowler's *Modern English Usage* to learn the precise use of a word or phrase. And while he had heroes in hockey, baseball, and popular music, the person he may have admired most was Robertson Davies, Canada's most lauded author of fiction and essays, though he would have been careful to whom he confided that pleasure.

And while Jack gained a reputation by 1950 as "one mean son of a bitch" about whom one of the nicest things being said was that "he has a mercurial personality," he was, at least at that time, fair in many ways. He was awarded plaques many times by Toronto Jewish groups for the hiring of minorities. Beth Shalom Synagogue presented Jack with one such plaque in the 1950s and Toronto Rabbi David Monson remembers Jack as being a "help to Jewish causes."

In fact, Jack in 1951 credited his success partly to having the "gift of the *mazel*"—the Yiddish word for luck.

When Cooke received the Jewish Brotherhood award the same year, he was cited for hiring "Italians, Jews, Swiss, Japanese, Filipinos, and Negroes" at CKEY.

Jack's typically tough response: "I'm not crusading for minorities. I'm looking for someone who can do a better job. I have never hired anyone because I felt that their race was discriminated against economically, but on the other hand, I have never turned down a person because they were not white, Gentile, or Protestant.''

Any sentimentality or softness that existed within the boy wonder of Toronto was kept inside. Perhaps he felt that such displays would be viewed as a weakness by competitors.

Thus, with financial success and a measure of respectability gained, it was perhaps natural progression in the publishing field for Jack Kent Cooke next to purchase one of Canada's most respected periodicals, *Saturday Night,* in October 1952.

Saturday Night was, at the time, a magazine said to be a cross between the *New Yorker* and the *Saturday Review of Literature,* the two middlebrow American icons of coffee table good taste. With an audited circulation of 61,011, the magazine was the crown jewel of Consolidated Press.[5] A publishing empire, Consolidated Press included a five-story building at 73 Richmond Street in downtown Toronto, a printing press on Duchess Street, two national magazines, the *Canadian Home Journal* and *Farmer's* magazine, and a slew of profitable trade magazines with names like *Canadian Baker,* the *Canadian Cigar and Tobacco Journal, Motor Magazine, Trader, Canadian Jeweller, Food in Canada, Manufacturing and Industrial Engineering,* and *Canadian Service Data Book.* There were annuals like the *Canadian Jewellers Year Book.* And Consolidated represented the *Canadian Dental Association* magazine and *Chemistry in Canada* for advertising space. The trade publications were sold off one by one over the next five years at various profitable prices, leaving Jack with what he really wanted, *Saturday Night.*

So enthusiastic was Jack about his new enterprise that he moved his headquarters from CKEY to 73 Richmond Street[6] and waxed rhapsodic about his plans.

''*Saturday Night* is going to be a news magazine for Canadians,'' he said at the time. ''I can see a real future for such a publication in Canada. Readers will be looking at world news through Canadian eyes rather than through American eyes, which up until now is the best we've had. But that is a condition that's going to be changed just as fast as we can change it.''

Jack was treading on hallowed ground. *Saturday Night* had been published in Canada since 1887. The original editor, Edmund Sheppard, had begun the magazine as a weekly commentary on the news under the name of *Toronto Saturday Night* and had had steel art engravings shipped from England. Some were too wide for a magazine page but, undeterred, Sheppard turned them on their sides and ran them anyway. The readers loved the unconventionality of it and *Saturday Night*, as it had become known after going national, became a success. Jack's other two acquisitions had been around for nearly half a century. The *Canadian Home Journal* had begun in 1904, and *Farmer* started a few months later.

This time there was no Roy Thomson as partner. The two had separated permanently as a business tandem. Although Jack and Roy would remain lifelong friends and would partake in each other's triumphs, a business divorce had taken place. The separation occurred when Jack failed to invite Roy in on the lucrative CKOY consulting deal in Ottawa. Thomson was privately put out over the matter and never did a business deal with Jack again.[7]

Jack never revealed the purchase price he paid for Consolidated Press. The company had grossed $4.5 million the year before he took control and was marginally profitable. Jack bought all of the stock that belonged to Mabel R. Sutton—about 60 percent—who had run the board of directors but had not taken an active hand in management. After taking over, Jack uncharacteristically would tell reporters that he now had a net worth of $5 million and was the largest magazine publisher in Canada.

Jack also told the press how he intended to raise the profits of the magazines. "If you give the public what it wants," he said, "you are going to gain more influence with your publication. Once you gain acceptance for your medium, the profits will look after themselves."

Reaction to Jack's plans for the magazine and Jack's reputation as a tough taskmaster kept the *Saturday Night* staff up nights refreshing their resumés. Within a week after Jack took over, the editor, R.A. Farquharson, the Ottawa editor, Michael Barkway, the editor emeritus, B.K. Sandwell, and the advertising director, Norman McHardy, all resigned. Sandwell, it was said, removed his bag lunch from his desk drawer the moment he learned of Jack's acquisition and headed home, never to return.

Jack treated this as an opportunity. He put together an editorial board of his idols—author Robertson Davies, John Irving, a professor of philosophy at the University of Toronto, and the poet E.J. Pratt, who was already working for *New Liberty*. The new staff included Gwyn Kinsey, a newspaper editor whom Jack knew from his Thomson years in Timmins, and Hugh Garner, the Toronto novelist. Garner was a heavy drinker whose office overlooked a government liquor store, much to his delight. Jack assigned him to write a column titled "Backward Glance."

Garner remembered his tenure under Jack Kent Cooke in the Canadian book, *The Monthly Epic*, by Fraser Sutherland.

> I quickly developed a formula for writing these pieces about former issues of the magazine and once when I got sick of writing them, Jack Kent Cooke . . . threatened to beat my brains out if I so much as mentioned giving them up. Friday afternoon was our editorial deadline on the magazine and after procrastinating the first four days of the week, I would realize that I still had my weekly piece to write. I missed the deadline once. Usually I would sit down shakily at the typewriter, hoping for some inspiration, or better still, hoping the old building would collapse and give me a legitimate excuse for not writing anything at all.
>
> At first I researched some of the pieces, but stopped this nonsense when a three-part piece on cemeteries and funeral customs resulted in all the undertakers taking their ads out of the magazine. They were replaced by beer and liquor ads eventually, which were not only more aesthetic and eye-pleasing but far more profitable.

Jack's boast, "Give us six months and we'll be on the road to a brilliant journal of Canadian comment and opinion," seemed to be suspect with writers like Garner aboard, but actually the novelist turned out a prodigious amount of good writing through his haze of alcohol. Later he would write a novel in which the principal character was patterned after Jack Kent Cooke.

But whether *Saturday Night* became a "brilliant journal" under Jack's control is debatable. His ownership years were certainly stormy. He added a "Letter from London" column as well as one from Montreal. Robertson Davies became the book review editor. And two years after he bought the magazine Jack changed it from a weekly to an every-other-week schedule, which resulted in both record numbers of advertising pages and seven more resignations.

With CKEY and *New Liberty*, Jack Kent Cooke had gained financial riches. *Saturday Night* fueled his fantasies as a man of letters. The third part of the triangle, that of sportsman had taken place a few months before when he purchased the Toronto Maple Leafs baseball club.

One can only speculate what would have happened if Jack Kent Cooke had focused his life only on publications or the electronic media. Certainly he would have been in the same league as a Rupert Murdoch or a Robert Maxwell. But Jack would probably squash such a thought. He would probably say it wouldn't have been half the fun.

If Jack's days were filled with juggling his many different businesses—he now had six different offices spread around Toronto and like the silver ball inside a pinball machine would bounce to all of them in his Cadillac convertible on any given day—his evenings were filled with romance. He was writing romantic ballads and wooing the most popular female singer of the era, Kay Starr.

While Jack Kent Cooke is a genuine lifelong lover of English literature and the language itself, he is also an unashamed populist when it comes to music.

Once, at a 1952 baseball game he was attending with his wife Jean, a devotee of dance, he attempted to compare ballet with baseball.

"There is more grace and form in a double play from second base to first, than in any ballet," he firmly told her.

His love of big band jazz and pop was still steadfast and true, rooted in his own saxophone and clarinet days as Oley Kent. With success after success coming his way in commercial radio, it is unsurprising that Jack's next artistic enterprise was that of composing popular music.

Bill Brady, who is credited on the sheet music as lyricist of "Funny About a Dream," one of two published songs written by

Jack Kent Cooke, remembers Jack's songwriting days this way: "Jack's recording studio that did advertising jingles, Imperial Transcriptions, was headed by Dan Carr. One night I was at Jack's house, and he started humming this tune to me. Then he pounded it out on the piano.

" 'Bill,' he told me, 'you've got to do something with this.'

"So I jotted the chords on a drink napkin and put them in my pocket. A few days later Jack asked me how it was coming, so I went over to Imperial Transcriptions and made an arrangement. Jack came to the studio and my singers and I performed it for him. Jack loved the lyrics and my arrangement and had it recorded."

When shown the sheet music by a writer forty years later, Brady said, "Oh yes, that's my arrangement. I always put C-13th notes in my music, see, there they are."

"Funny About a Dream" was the "A" side to Jack's first and only attempt to jump into the recording business. While the more poignant of the two songs—"Love Is Gone" was on the flip side— over the years "Funny About a Dream" is the arrangement that has earned the most royalties, according to Brady. The lyrics, typical of the day, have direct sentimentality.

> Funny about a dream, it's seldom they come true.
> I dreamt last night I kissed you dear,
> although we were through.
>
> Funny about a dream, you say romance is past
> But I can see no reason why
> It shouldn't last.
>
> When you go dancing by, I seem to get the notion
> That when I catch your eye,
> There comes a spark of emotion.
>
> Funny about a dream, I pray that mine comes true.
> And if you find that I'm on your mind
> You're dreaming my dream true.[8]

"The most I ever got was just under $700," Bill Brady said. "Today sometimes I get a small check, but it's under $10."

Jack once told a writer he got as much as a few thousand dollars a year, but that would have been for both songs. Jack Kent

81

Cooke has actually composed more than a hundred tunes, but many of them don't have titles and are numbered Jack 1, Jack 2, etc. In later years Jack Kent Cooke would have them recorded privately by orchestras and give the music as gifts.

"Someone used the song in a movie, once," recalls Brady. "It was a film about the Calgary Stampede, something called *Golden-rod*.[9] Then somebody used the music as the theme for a late night show. I heard it once and could hardly recognize it."

Jack's other song, "Love Is Gone," was both composed and lyricised by him in 1950, though Brady remembers doing the arrangement at Imperial. It is a sad and tender ballad, perhaps revealing of Jack's mood at the time.

> I've been a fool to compromise dear,
> It was all so sadly in vain.
> I've had the time to realize, dear,
> I won't do it over again.
>
> Of lover's quarrels, we've had our share,
> I've done my part, but you weren't fair,
> There's no use continuing,
> The flame has died.
>
> Oh why go on! The thrill is gone,
> This is the end of all our dreams,
> I won't change as I've done before,
> For love is gone.[10]

"Everyone liked to record 'Love Is Gone'," Brady recounts. Indeed, Charlie Kunz, the well-known British pianist included it in an album on the London label and Jean Vallain did a French version for Mercury where the song was known as "L'amour Se Meurt." In all, eleven different artists recorded the tune, including Ray Anthony and Helen O'Connell although neither "Gone" nor "Dream" was hit parade caliber.

"I think Ray Eberly recorded 'Funny About a Dream'," Brady says, "and Kay Starr may have done both."

Kay Starr was a great, passionate romance in Jack Kent Cooke's life. His involvement with her was the first time he strayed publicly from his marriage to Barbara Jean Carnegie Cooke.

Kay Starr's singing career was still ascending when she met Jack Kent Cooke on the evening of August 31, 1950. Born Katharine Starks on July 21, 1922, in Dougherty, Oklahoma, a hamlet of less than 200 people in the south-central part of the state, Kay had gotten her husky singing voice in a most unusual way.

A country hillbilly singer, she had begun winning talent contests in Dallas and Memphis when she was nine years old. By the age of eleven she had her own radio show on WRR in Dallas, and at fifteen she was featured on the "Grand Old Opry" in Nashville. Kay began branching out to pop music and toured with Joe Venuti's and Bob Crosby's big bands, recording with Glenn Miller before she was eighteen.

Just as her booming career was about to explode, Kay Starr became seriously ill. Part of the illness was a throat infection and Kay could barely speak, let alone sing, for more than a year. When she recovered, she found that her voice had become lower and huskier. The unique sound of her voice made her the biggest female recording star of the 1950s. Her biggest hit, "Wheel of Fortune," was number one on *Billboard*'s hit parade charts for nine weeks in a row.

Kay Starr was beautiful in a sultry manner, partly because of her Cherokee Indian heritage.[11] When she met Jack Kent Cooke, she had had four consecutive top ten tunes and was riding high with her first duet single, "I'll Never Be Free," with Tennessee Ernie Ford. Songs like "Wheel of Fortune," "Rock and Roll Waltz," and "Side by Side" were yet to come.

Kay had just been featured in two movies, one of which, *Make Believe Ballroom*, was based on the New York radio show. Since that was also one of CKEY's most popular shows, it is likely that Jack went to see the movie when it played Toronto in 1948. Kay opened in Toronto at the cavernous Casino Theatre, an 1100-seat former burlesque house at 87 Queen Street West. By the 1950s, it was used for musical acts on the way up or down. The old bump-and-grind palace had once been Toronto's center of sin in the 1930s and 1940s, serving up strippers four times a day. But now it was just an adjunct to the last days of the summer of 1950 and the

Canadian National Exhibition, which was going full tilt a mile away, with Danny Kaye as the featured attraction.[12]

"I remember it well," said Al Dubin, who by now had quit CKEY and was serving as a publicist for a number of nightclubs around town.

"Jack sent her flowers. Danny Kaye sent her flowers. And so did this businessman from Windsor and Detroit, who had mob ties."

"Kay went out with Jack," Dubin recalls, "but what he didn't know was that she also went out with Danny Kaye. Some nights, she'd beg off from Jack and go over to Danny Kaye's hotel suite and have dinner in his hotel room. I know, I had to cover."

"Jack was infatuated with Kay Starr," one former CKEY staffer remembers. "When she went back out of town he'd go into his office and play her records for hours."

"The long-distance bills were horrendous," Bill Brady said, "even the accountants were raising their eyebrows. It was very open, too. Once we saw Kay and Jack at the racetrack together. I was embarrassed because we were friends with Jeannie as well and would have to show up at their house as if nothing was happening."

"Jeannie knew. Oh, she knew," Al Dubin recalls. "Once I drove Jack home at five in the morning. Jack was going to change clothes and shower. I waited while Jack and Jean had a two-hour fight. Jack was really generous with Kay and maybe Jean was aware of it. He gave her a fur coat and a car."

"Once we were riding in the back of a limousine," Jean's close friend, Margo Reid, told a writer. "I had just delivered a stillborn child by Caesarian and Jean was worried about Kay Starr. 'We're the two unhappiest women in Toronto,' Jean said to me."

"She came to me once in a nightclub." Al Dubin said. "She said she was going to leave Jack, she couldn't take it any more. But she never did until later.

"Kay and Jack and Dan Carr were in an automobile accident once, going up to Ottawa," Al Dubin continued. "Jack hit a haywagon, but nobody in the car was hurt. The haywagon driver, when he saw he had been hit by a Cadillac convertible, . . . Jack had to pay him off."

Kay Starr took her romance with Jack seriously. In a 1988 statement to *Maclean's* magazine, she said, "He was so full of life and joy. I loved him."

Jack and Kay Starr's relationship lasted between two and three years. Today Jack tells intimates that Kay Starr was one of the three great loves of his life, Barbara Jean Carnegie being the second. The third name changes from time to time.

"All of Toronto knew about the romance," remembers Alex Barris, "and we all knew when it had fizzled. I was out at the ballpark one night prior to a Maple Leafs baseball game. They always played recorded songs before the game started. Somebody in the booth hadn't got the message, I guess, because here comes "Wheel of Fortune" by Kay Starr over the loudspeakers. It got about four bars in and you heard the needle being dragged across the record and then there was silence. That's when we knew it was over."

Notes

1. The accountant was most likely Sidney Chapman, Thomson's right hand on the business side of his organization.
2. Jack's salesmanship rather than the quality of the magazine was the key factor that attracted new advertisers like Bulova watch and Chrysler to *New Liberty* by 1949.
3. Jack applied for a private television license for the city of Toronto as early as 1948, saying he "could be on the air in six months."
4. The Toronto *Globe and Mail,* for the benefit of some American readers, is perhaps Canada's most prestigious newspaper. It can be compared to the *New York Times* as a newspaper of record. Ironically, it is now owned by Thomson Newspapers which is controlled by Kenneth Thomson, Roy Thomson's son, whose net worth is double that of Jack Kent Cooke.
5. By 1990, *Saturday Night's* circulation was 135,000 but it was still losing money. It worked out a deal with Southam Newspapers to insert the magazine into papers in five major cities, thus moving the circulation up to 700,000. In early 1991, this experiment was still being tested.
6. The building still stands today and is home to Hy's restaurant, an upscale seafood place. Jack's large office is now a private banquet room. The only artifact remaining of the Consolidated Press empire

is an ornate *Saturday Night* brass emblem, built into the railing. It is noticeable as one enters the restaurant.

7. It wasn't Jack's decision to cut Roy Thomson out of the consulting deal. It was the station's bankers who controlled the mortgage owed by what was called the CKCO group, who soured Jack and Roy's business relationship.

8. "Funny About a Dream,"' copyright 1950, Blue River Music, Studio City, California. Reprinted by permission. In Canada, reprinted by permission of Jobina-Quality Music, Toronto, Ontario.

9. The Calgary Stampede in Calgary, Alberta, is Canada's largest rodeo.

10. "Love Is Gone," copyright 1950, Blue River Music, Studio City, California. Reprinted by permission. In Canada, reprinted by permission of Jobina-Quality Music, Toronto, Ontario.

11. Washington Redskins fans will be pleased to know that many of Jack Kent Cooke's romances have been with women who have Indian blood. Besides Kay Starr's Cherokee roots, Suzanne Martin Cooke is part Penobscot, a Maine tribe, and his current wife, Marlene, is said to have at least some Inca blood.

12. The Canadian National Exhibition is Canada's national fair and is held every year in Toronto during the last week of August. Several hundred thousand people attend daily and Canadians come from all across the country as well as Americans from nearby states.

CHAPTER
7
A MAJOR IN THE MINORS
Maple Leaf Stadium became the place to be.

Of the hundreds of men and women who are chronicled in *Forbes* or *Fortune* as being among the richest individuals in the world, most are unknown to the general public. The exceptions are moguls like Donald Trump or Robert "Ted" Turner who lead lives of notoriety and controversy. Many would prefer it that way, but many more hanker for some public attention, preferably of course on their own terms. Most get attention through philanthropic works, where their names are placed on the side of a hospital or when a library at their university is named after them. Or they build profitable entities such as an office building and name it after themselves, thus giving them not only a cash flow source, but a small measure of immortality. Public service as an elected official is another avenue but few take this route. Not only does it mean that one's blemishes and warts are exposed for all to see, but it entails being stuck in a low-paying job for several years, stifled by an entrenched bureaucracy which limits power.

Another way one avoids anonymity is a broad participation in what Wall Street likes to describe as the "leisure industries." A publisher or broadcaster is far more likely to be quoted in the press or to be recognized at his country club than, say, an owner of a wholesale plumbing firm. Indeed, just controlling such a business provides a podium from which the owner can speak to the public about any concern on a regular basis.

Jack Kent Cooke had already felt the power that came from owning Toronto's most popular radio station and Canada's leading magazine. It was a natural progression then, that when one of

Toronto's sports franchises came up for sale, in 1951, Jack would be a spirited bidder.

Toronto, whose population was now well over a million, was a major league city without a major league baseball team in the early 1950s. Baseball had not yet begun its big expansion, but some could see it coming. Jack was one of them, and he reasoned that a successful owner of Toronto's minor league baseball team would be one of the first in line when a major league franchise became available.

Jack gained control of the Toronto Maple Leafs International League baseball franchise at 5:00 P.M. on July 5, 1951, by purchasing the stock of president Donald Ross, the owner of a local brokerage house, and that of two members of the board, Max Haas and John McCausland. Besides becoming president himself, Jack installed his brother Harold and his friend and lawyer, Bill Zimmerman, on the board and gave his wife's brother, Peter Carnegie, a job in the front office.

Although the price that Jack paid was not announced, a knowledgeable source told a writer it was just under $200,000. He didn't get a lot for his money. What Jack bought was a team that was both a competitive and a financial loser. He inherited a club that had a losing record, was firmly in fifth place in an eight-team league, and was already virtually out of the pennant race, eighteen games behind the front-running Montreal Royals. The attendance was often under 2,000 per game, and the yearly total less than 250,000. That was virtually inevitable. The Maple Leafs had not been competitive for years and were a perennial fixture in the lower half of the standings. Only the hard-core fans attended.

In spite of the Maple Leafs' poor performance, Jack wasn't the only bidder. Burleigh Grimes, who had managed the team to a pennant in 1943, wanted the team badly. Bill Veeck and Branch Rickey, who were Jack's friends and mentors, were interested. And the Leafs were bid on by the Pittsburgh Pirates, the New York Yankees and the Brooklyn Dodgers, who each wanted Toronto as part of their farm club system. But Jack Kent Cooke was the lone Canadian in the running and nationalism won.

What Jack got for his $200,000 besides the franchise in the International League was a lease to Maple Leaf Stadium, owned by the Toronto Harbor Commission, the contracts of twenty-five players, and a working agreement with the doormats of the American League, the St. Louis Browns, which was due to expire in two months.

The International League was the top of the minor league system. Founded in 1884, it contained three Canadian teams— Toronto, Montreal, and Ottawa—plus teams in American cities as large as Baltimore and Buffalo and as small as Springfield, Massachusetts.

Like CKEY, Jack didn't wait for a shakedown period to take charge. He changed nights at the ballpark to a happening and attendance skyrocketed. Just one week after buying the team, an ad placed by Jack on July 12, 1951, in the Toronto *Globe and Mail* announced: 5 STAR BASEBALL! IT'S FAMILY NIGHT—LADIES 25 CENTS! CHILDREN UNDER 14 ACCOMPANIED BY PARENTS ADMITTED FREE! But that was just the beginning of the ad. There was A COMIC BOOK GIFT FOR EVERY YOUNGSTER UNDER 14! and, 10 SPECIAL PRIZES FOR YOUNGSTERS! But Jack offered something for everyone. In the same ad there was MARILYN COT-LOW METROPOLITAN OPERA STAR TO SING "MY HERO" FROM "CHOCOLATE SOLDIER"! Next in line, HUBERT DIL-WORTH, STAR OF "BLOOMER GIRL" SINGS "I GOT A SONG" and "THE EAGLE AND I!" If that was too highbrow, the night at the ballpark also advertised COMEDIENNE CAROLYN ADAIR, PIANIST MARIO BERNARD, AND THE SINGING CHORUS! Finally at the bottom of the ad were the teams: MONTREAL VS. TORONTO. To top all this vaudeville, Jack had fireworks exploding every time his team scored a run. Toronto had never experienced anything quite like it and it wasn't the roar of the skyrockets that left them shell-shocked. Maple Leaf Stadium became the place to be on a summer's night.

Jack Kent Cooke reveled in his afternoons and nights at the ballpark. His box on the third base side of the field was nearly always filled. Jack had a black phone installed and kept in touch with his various businesses between innings. As might be expected, guests included a sprinkling of local movers and shakers as well as out-of-town celebrities, much like the present day variety of high-profile faces that populate his box at Washington Redskins games. Branch Rickey, who informally helped Jack find talent, was twice a guest in 1953. Jack insisted on Jean joining him for many evening games and would often have her travel on road trips with him to Buffalo and Rochester.

For the next several years Jack's promotional efforts on behalf of his ball club were relentless. There were endless appreciation nights for cabdrivers, streetcar operators, students, and municipal workers. Prize fights were staged in a ring near the pitcher's mound before and after the game. Jack hired a flagpole sitter to sit in center field until the team won a game. Unfortunately, the team went into a prolonged losing streak and the flagpole sitter nearly set an unintentional record. There was a "black cat" night where everyone who brought a black cat on Friday the 13th got in free. Hundreds took Jack up on his offer and no dark cat was safe in Toronto that evening. Diapering contests were held at home plate. An audacious "3-for-1" promotion, in which free admission was given to a pregnant woman, accompanied by her paying husband or "friend" took place. Magicians, crooners, and comedians performed in the infield. The opening day ceremony of throwing out the first ball was given to Canada's leading names, ranging from Olympic skating gold medalist Barbara Ann Scott to Prime Minister John Diefenbaker. A Toronto newspaper editorialized that "it would hardly be surprising if the players forgot why they were there, or wondered if they were part of the main act or the sideshow." The same paper also praised Jack for making Toronto "baseball mad."

Within a week after buying the club, Jack was personally taking a role in player selection. "Three Negroes are on the list," the *Toronto Star* reported. "He is extremely interested in Honey Lott of the Indianapolis Clowns. The 25-year-old second or third baseman is hitting over .300."

Jack personally asked Bill Veeck to find players for the team. He very much wanted the team to draw people and win games immediately so he took charge himself. Inevitably, the general manager, Joe Ziegler, resigned at the end of the 1951 season and the manager, Joe Becker, was let go.

Later Jack installed Frank Pollock as his general manager. Pollock, who had begun a long career with the Maple Leafs in

1939 by selling programs and working the concession stands, held the job until the end of Jack's ownership.

"Frank knew everything about the team," Mary Pollock, Frank's widow, told a writer. "I like to think that Frank taught Jack Kent Cooke a lot about the business side of baseball. Frank was the only Jewish general manager in the minors and Hank Greenberg of the Cleveland Indians was the only one in the majors. Hank got my husband a lot of good players.

"Jack was demanding, too," Mrs. Pollock continued. "He would call Frank at all hours. Once he telephoned at two in the morning just to ask Frank why an outfielder dropped a fly ball."

Jack was a fast study. At the minor league draft in Columbus, Ohio, a few months later, he was already in full control. "His name is Leon Foulkes," Jack said of his first pick, a pitcher. I'm quite sure it's F-o-u-l-k-e-s but by this list it's F-o-u-l-k. Anyway, he's a righthand pitcher, who won fifteen and lost eleven for Des Moines last year."

Jack's first full year as owner of the club, in 1952, may have been the high point. Although critics say that Jack overpaid for players and "never saw a $10,000 ballplayer he wouldn't pay $15,000 for," the Maple Leafs finished in the first division and made the playoffs for the first time in seven years. Counting post-season attendance, the team attracted more than 500,000 paying customers, double the number of the year before. Jack was named minor league executive of the year by *Sporting News* and was elected to the board of the International League. The year after that he was elected vice president, a ceremonial but prestigious post.

By now the Canadian wonder boy, duplicating the success he had gained through a combination of hard work, ruthlessness, and P.T. Barnum showmanship, had his sights on the big leagues. When the expansion move rumors of 1952 fingering the St. Louis Browns, Philadelphia Athletics, and Boston Braves began to filter through the major league baseball community, Jack was already lobbying for Toronto as a destination. But there was a snag. Maple Leaf Stadium seated 18,600 for baseball and at least 30,000 capacity was necessary for a major league team to consider moving to Toronto, even though it now had 1.3 million people inside the city limits.

The Toronto Harbor Commission had owned the ballpark since 1933 when the Maple Leafs ball club of the time was nearly bankrupt. The commission had inherited the stadium when the club couldn't come up with $41,000 in back taxes, and although they tried to sell it in the thirties there were no bids. By the fifties, the ballpark was old and not even close to major league caliber.

Still, it is possible that if the Harbor Commission had heeded Jack's request and put bleachers in center field, the St. Louis Browns would have moved to Toronto instead of Baltimore and Toronto would have had baseball as early as 1953. Jack offered to buy the stadium but the commission declined that offer as well, citing the need to study the impact of additional traffic congestion at the waterfront location of the ballpark.[1]

Jack, at least publicly, wasn't discouraged. He now had a profitable ball club. His name was splashed on the sports pages at least once a week. And he had extra programming for CKEY, in the form of nightly baseball play-by-play broadcasts by his veteran sportscaster, Joe Crysdale. He even became viewed as somewhat of a philanthropist, by continuing a tradition to donate the proceeds from one game a year to the Variety Village children's home, which often raised more than $50,000.

With an empire composed equally of sports, broadcasting, and publishing, Jack's six-acre estate in the Richmond Hill area of North Toronto became too remote. He no longer had time for his hobbies of horseback riding and gardening. Jack also felt that the Bayview Avenue property was too far out so he chose a more sophisticated mansion closer in at 3 Frybrook Road. The house had been built in 1910 for Robert Christie of the Christie Biscuit Company, Canada's leading cookie maker. The small mansion, in the posh lower Forest Hill section of Toronto, was coincidentally (or perhaps not) on the same street and just blocks away from George Gooderham, of the same Gooderham family that Jack had talked into selling CKEY. It was also just around the corner from a titled member of the Eaton department store family. Jack was now in the midst of some of the cream of Toronto society. A Toronto Realtor remembers that Jack paid "just under $150,000" for the three-story French-style chateau that came with a partially stocked wine cellar.

"Jack gave a housewarming party outside in the garden that was the talk of the town," remembers Mary Pollock. "He hired jockeys from the racetrack to dress in their racing silks and park the guests' cars."

Ralph and John, Jack's two sons, were sent to Forest Hill Collegiate, an upscale public high school.

Ever restless, Jack Kent Cooke, moved frenetically through the mid-1950s. As might be expected in one moving so fast, mistakes were made. One of Jack's ballpark promotions drew an illegal lottery charge and wound up with a $250 fine in July 1953. The Social Credit party, one of Canada's more radical political groups condemned Jack for an article in *New Liberty* which compared members of the party to Nazi storm troopers. And Jack was censured by the Canadian government for "radio piracy" on CKEY.

It was the radio piracy charge that may have made Jack Kent Cooke permanent enemies with the Canadian government broadcasting hierarchy and thus forever ruin whatever chances remained for owning a second radio station or gaining Toronto's first private television station license.

Jack was charged with unlawful reconstruction of hockey broadcasts. Although CKEY had baseball in Toronto sewn up by virtue of Jack's ownership, competitor CKFH had the exclusive rights to the "other" Maple Leafs, the NHL hockey team. But a reconstructed description of the game, using wire service copy on a short delay was legal. So CKEY, using its two most popular sports announcers, Joe Crysdale and Hal Kelly, began broadcasts recreating the action in the CKEY studios. The two used a short time delay and sound effects that, as broadcast, seemed to give an even more colorful account than Canadian broadcasting legend Foster Hewitt did on CKFH.

This was all well and good until CKFH began to suspect that CKEY wasn't using wire copy or phone-ins from the game site but were taping Hewitt's own broadcasts, and broadcasting them re-created by Crysdale and Kelly moments later. Hewitt's station laid a trap for the CKEY pair. They had Hewitt make up nonexistent penalties given to players who weren't even on the ice and describe nonexistent goals. When the same description was repeated in a more lavish manner by Crysdale and Kelly seconds later, CKFH went to the Canadian Broadcasting Corporation Board of Governors and charged Jack's station with "radio piracy."

Hauled before the Board of Governors, Jack denied the charges. But after the comparative tapes were played to a guffawing CBC group, the boy wonder backpedaled.

"I would say that Mr. Hewitt has apparently scored a point with the tape recordings," Jack said. "However I would also say that the program director of CKEY, the production manager, the station manager, Hal Kelley, Joe Crysdale, and myself are prepared to swear under oath that we didn't take the material from Mr. Hewitt's broadcasts, and what's more, we didn't listen to his broadcasts at any time."

Although Jack Kent Cooke and his employees were never asked to testify under oath, the Canadian Broadcasting Corporation, protestations aside, ruled that the reconstructions were illegal and CKEY was to desist.

Nevertheless, the baseball Maple Leafs were both an athletic and a financial success throughout the 1950s. The average Maple Leaf attendance while Jack owned the team was 385,000. The team was usually in the playoffs and won four International League pennants (1954, '56, '57, '60). After a pennant win, Jack would fly his key executives to New York for a party at the '21' Club, inviting major league people as well, lobbying for a Toronto club. Now, with the team's success, Jack became a born-again baseball evangelist.

"I wanted to be a professional baseball player and an orchestra leader," he told the *Toronto Star*. "I played baseball as a kid at Main and Gerard with fellows like Tuba Brennan, Bobby Porter, and Leo Deadeye," he said naming three famous Torontonians. Later at a club dinner, Jack would tell his audience:

"Every kid should have someone to look up to. When I was a kid I had two idols. One was Ty Cobb, who I think was the greatest baseball player of all time. The other was William Jennings Bryan. The closest I ever came to Cobb was that I hit like William Jennings Bryan. Even when they caught my fly balls I wanted to argue. It's alright to lose gracefully, but it's better to win gracefully."

Perhaps Jack's most famous player during his ownership of

the Maple Leafs was catcher Elston Howard. Howard played for the Maple Leafs in the 1954 season, hitting a home run the very first time at bat. Howard was voted the Maple Leafs' Most Valuable Player that year, batting .330, with twenty-two home runs and 109 runs batted in. The next year he was gone, becoming the first black player on the New York Yankees and a mainstay of the Bronx club for more than a decade. Howard uttered a memorable quote nine years later when he became the American League MVP. "I've just won the Nobel Prize of baseball," he said.

Jack also gave Dick Williams his start as a manager. Williams subsequently would pilot the Boston Red Sox to their first American league pennant in decades and later enjoy similar success as the skipper of the Oakland Athletics.

In the summer of 1955, after the Browns, Braves, and Athletics had found homes in other cities, Jack despaired of ever getting a major league franchise for Toronto. So he submitted a secret sealed bit of $5,180,000 for the Detroit Tigers, which were up for sale by Walter "Spike" Briggs. Jack's bid was $70,000 lower than the highest bidder, Bill Veeck. But Spike Briggs didn't want anything to do with Bill Veeck, and he didn't want to sell the team to a Canadian, even though Jack promised to keep the team in Detroit and make the Maple Leafs one of the farm clubs. Instead he sold it to a group of Michigan broadcasting millionaires headed by George Storer and John Fetzer, who had bid lower than both Veeck and Jack.

"Don't be mad at me Jack," Briggs told Jack when he called to tell him of the decision, "You have two pitchers we're interested in."

Next Jack put in a bid for the Chicago White Sox. His name was published when the Crosley family put the Cincinnati Reds on the block. In fact the name Jack Kent Cooke was now mentioned when any major league team was rumored for sale.

More or less giving up on getting the Harbor Commission to expand and refurbish the Toronto ball park, Jack tried a new tack. He would build or participate in getting his own stadium built. He was quoted as willing to join in a plan to construct a ball park with the city fathers of Etobicoke township at a location near Woodbine racetrack northwest of downtown Toronto. He also volunteered to build a $6 million stadium at Riverdale Park in the Don Valley but the Toronto city fathers wouldn't give him the land. In the end, nothing came of either trial balloon.

Teams in the International League seemed to come and go. Toledo came in for a year and then went back to the American Association; Richmond, Virginia, replaced Baltimore; and pre-Castro Havana, with a club called the Sugar Kings, entered the league with a big 28,000 seat park and fans who waved white handkerchiefs instead of booing.[2]

Jack had never been much of a joiner. But in the 1950s, perhaps wishing to soften his tough image and to be more accepted by his new upper crust neighbors in Forest Hill, Jack began joining scores of private and public clubs and charitable groups. He had joined Lambton Golf Club, the Board of Trade, and the National Yacht Club in the 1940s. Now he added more exclusive clubs like the Granite and Waspy Thornhill Golf and was active in charities like Variety and the St. John Ambulance Brigade. His most enthusiastic membership though, was in the Royal Canadian Yacht Club, where he spent weekend after summer weekend racing a new passion, a fifty-four-foot, German-built yawl he named *Pompadour*.[3]

Jack had arrived. The Royal Canadian Yacht Club was the oldest and perhaps most prestigious club of its kind in North America. Founded in 1852, its first clubhouse was an old boat anchored at the foot of Simcoe Street. But by the time Jack joined, it was an aspiring blueblood's fantasy—graceful old white buildings on one of the Toronto islands (Olympic) in Lake Ontario. There was lawn bowling and tennis played as it should be—on grass. There was a swimming pool and a fine bar and restaurant. But what Jack liked best was how one arrived. Only by boat. And you couldn't step ashore unless you were wearing a jacket and tie. Of course short trousers could be worn, even Bermudas. But a blazer and four-in-hand were required to disembark. After you were on land, you could wear anything. Jack was always natty, even in sailor's stripes and dungarees.

On Saturday, August 11, 1957, Jack and a crew of ten were

part of the fleet leaving Rochester, New York, on a 270-mile race that would skirt part of the perimeter of Lake Ontario. The race would last nearly three days.

It wasn't the racing yachts from the Rochester and National clubs that concerned Jack. It was the fleet of the RCYC, his own club, particularly Ray Engholm's *Ivanhoe II*. Engholm was the commodore of the RCYC and Jack and Ray's rivalry was friendly, but competitive.

"Brisk winds, about 15 knots from the west," Jack told his crew, "perfect for a spinnaker run all the way to the Niagara River."

Jack's *Pompadour* and Engholm's *Ivanhoe II* quickly outdistanced the fleet, with only the RCYC's *White Squall* in contention. On the second leg, toward Main Duck Island, the winds calmed and Jack could see Engholm. But the breeze began to shift.

"Put out the other spinnaker," Jack yelled.

But now the wind gusted to 25, then 35 knots an hour and Jack's spinnaker snarled on the turn.

"Let out the smaller one . . . oh hell, I'll do it," Jack yelled.

Engholm put out his spinnaker as well but it wrapped around the forestay and the halyard, became tangled and stayed there. His auxiliary canvas was ripped to shreds.

Now the 35-knot gusts filled both boats' sails and they came side by side back toward Rochester, *Pompadour* crossing the finish line 63 seconds ahead.

"Sonofabitch," Jack said, because he knew he'd lost to Ray Engholm. The corrected start times would give Engholm the victory. Jack hated to lose.

Jack won many races with *Pompadour*. He won the Freeman Cup in a 90-mile run to Port Dalhousie, the Olcott trophy, the Yacht Racing Union Trophy, and the Mackinac yacht race. He talked about forming a Canadian group to head south and bring back the America's Cup. But yacht racing, although "one of the great thrills of my life" wasn't a lifelong passion. Jack liked to win and compete but it was more fun to win and compete when profit was involved.

Before giving up on major league baseball for Toronto, Jack made a few more stabs at getting a team.

He applied for a National League expansion franchise on Sep-

97

tember 10, 1957, and was turned down. He said that Toronto would have gotten the California American League franchise if it had a new stadium. It was a streak of bad luck, the worst he had felt since his arrest in Florida in a traffic dispute on April 5, 1954.

The patrol car flagged down the Canadian in the Cadillac in Sanford, Florida. The prosperous-looking driver said he was on his way to an International League Baseball meeting.

"You're charged with improperly passing a police vehicle," the patrolman told him. "You'll have to follow me to the justice of the peace."

The Canadian businessman was livid. And he let the justice in Orlando know it.

"Do you plead guilty?' the J.P. asked.

"Certainly not," Jack answered. Then he spoke to the judge using a legal phrase in Latin.

"Do you understand what you said?" the elderly jurist asked.

It was the wrong thing to say to Jack Kent Cooke.

"I don't think you understood," Jack retorted. "I used a Latin phrase which you, as a justice, should understand." Then Jack really let him have it, giving him several minutes of his best invectives.

The justice sat stunned for only a moment. "That's contempt of court," he said. "Take him to jail."

Flanked by two policemen, Canada's handsomest millionaire was led across the street to the jailhouse. "Get me a lawyer," he told the police.

He used his one phone call to contact International League president Shag Shaughnessy. Shaughnessy called the mayor of Orlando and Jack was out of the cellblock within an hour.

But he had to apologize to the justice of the peace and put up $35 bail.

The contempt charge was dismissed, but the Canadian businessman was still livid.

*   *   *

Jack's last big hurrah in attempting to get major league baseball for Toronto came in 1959. The Dodgers and the Giants had left for California and New York City was without a National League franchise. Mayor Robert F. Wagner tried to get a new National League franchise and Warren Giles, the National League president said, "Who needs New York?"

Those were the wrong words to say to a New Yorker.

Wagner formed a committee headed by a youthful fifty-two-year-old attorney by the name of Bill Shea who also headed a Manhattan law firm that had his name on the door.[4] Shea tried to entice the Cincinnati Reds but was turned down, partly because with an unsuitable Polo Grounds and Ebbets Field about to be made into a housing project, there was no viable stadium.

Shea, Wagner, and a committee decided that if they built a new stadium then surely a new team would follow. They found a site in Flushing Meadow and named the multiuse sports park after Bill Shea.

Sniffing profits and prestige, virtually every powerful man in North America wanted part of a league that would have a team with a new stadium in the largest city in the United States. It was decided to start a new major baseball league, the Continental League and Branch Rickey was brought out of retirement to run it.

Jack was in from the start. The league lineup of cities was formidable. Besides New York and Toronto, there was Buffalo, Houston, Denver, Minneapolis–St. Paul, Atlanta, and Dallas.

The powers of baseball moved quickly to squelch the threat while Shea Stadium was being built. The American League expanded in 1960 and the National League added a team in 1961. The Continental League collapsed city by city as each defected to the majors. Minneapolis–St. Paul and Los Angeles were new franchises in the American League. Houston jumped into the National League and New York was willing to play in the Polo Grounds for two years until Shea Stadium was completed. The dream of a third major league ended abruptly. Toronto and Jack were out in the cold again.

Jack Kent Cooke seemed to give up on the Maple Leafs after

that, although he would be the first to deny it. He had made at least a dozen attempts to either bring major league baseball to Toronto or to purchase a major league team. Once, when baseball commissioner Ford Frick said that Toronto had "weather problems" that prevented it from having a major league team, Jack prepared a detailed presentation entitled "Why Toronto Belongs in Major League Baseball." It said that Toronto's mean annual temperature was the same as that of Cleveland, Detroit, Milwaukee, and Chicago. And it added that precipitation in Toronto was less than in Detroit and Milwaukee and just fractionally higher than in Cleveland and Chicago. Frick brushed Jack aside and said that the majors were looking toward the northwest and west for new teams.[5]

On July 20, 1961, the Maple Leafs ball club marked Jack's tenth year as the owner with a special celebration. The ads as usual, hyped the extras: FREE SHOPSY HOT DOGS AND FREE PEPSI COLA, and continued, TONITE IS LADIES AND FAMILY NIGHT. LADIES FOR 50 CENTS—CHILDREN UNDER 12 ADMITTED FREE ACCOMPANIED BY AN ADULT! And COME OUT—HAVE A PARTY![6]

But it was over. The Maple Leafs were back in sixth place, firmly in the second division. The turnout was pathetic—just 2,015 people were counted in the park, less than 200,000 would attend that year. And on the field it was worse. The Leafs lost to the Buffalo Bisons 8–0, getting just three hits to their American rivals' fourteen.

But it didn't matter to Jack because he wasn't there. He had already moved from Toronto to California and would return to his country of birth the next time as an American citizen.

Notes

1. Jack also tried to buy the Toronto Argonauts of the Canadian Football league in 1952. His reasoning was that by purchasing the Argos he would force the Harbor Commission to expand and refurbish Maple Leaf Stadium if he promised to play the Argos' home games there.
2. Weeks before Batista fell and Fidel Castro took over, Jack was on a

yacht in Havana Harbor. He could see the fighting in the hills via flashes of gunfire.

3. *Pompadour* was not named after Jack's hairstyle but in honor of the Marquise de Pompadour, the mistress of Louis XV in 1764.

4. The Shea and Gould firm became Jack's main legal arm. The Shea and Gould relationship began in 1956. Bill Shea has been on the board of many of Jack's sports enterprises and Milton Gould handled Jack's divorce from Suzanne Martin Cooke in 1989–1990.

5. Jack was a better seer than Frick. In 1990 Toronto set an all-time major league record for attendance in its new stadium, drawing nearly 4 million.

6. Shopsy, as many Torontonians know, was the late Sam Shopsowitz, a local meat packer who cornered the corned beef and hot dog market in the city. Sam sold the company some years later, but some oldtimers still call a hot dog a Shopsy in Toronto.

CHAPTER

CITIZEN COOKE

". . . a new future for himself and family in the United States of America."

By the end of the 1950s, Jack Kent Cooke was a lawyer's dream. As the age of Dwight Eisenhower and John Diefenbaker gave way to a youthful, playful 1960s, of which the leaders were John F. Kennedy and Pierre Trudeau, Toronto's best-known millionaire was embroiled in civil suits on every front.

Jack had purchased three industrial firms in October 1956. Two were plastic factories, in London and Acton, Ontario, the third an aluminum foundry in the west end of Toronto. Jack paid just under $4 million for the group.

The first firm, Robinson Industrial Crafts, made plastic injection moldings for automobile dashboards and also manufactured toys. The second firm, Microplastics, manufactured 60 percent of all the plastic pipe in Canada, as well as plastic sheeting and refrigerator parts. Precision Dyes and Castings of Toronto specialized in aluminum fabrications.

Jack's statement at the time he bought the companies was the same as the advice given nearly a decade later to Dustin Hoffman in the film *The Graduate*. "Plastics have an enviable future. The surface hasn't even been scratched yet. It's an intensely interesting industry and we feel great progress can be made."

But within a year, a suit was filed by Jack Kent Cooke against Robinson Industrial Crafts for fraud, claiming that the inventory was $105,000 less than stated and that much of it was obsolete.

Jack asked for $400,000, but he settled with Ray Robinson, the former president of the firm, out of court.

In another action, a former sales manager of CKEY sued Jack and his brother Harold for $7,660 for back sales commissions. But more importantly, he testified under oath that CKEY had doctored the station's logbooks in 1959 to conceal the fact that more commercials were broadcast than were permitted by law. The former employee, James Armstrong, said that the excess commercials were written in using pencil, then erased. He testified that the practice was "caught up with" and stopped in 1960. Armstrong was not cross-examined on that point. The case was dismissed in Jack's favor with the magistrate saying Armstrong breached his contract by going to work for another radio station.

Jack also sued a potential buyer for his yacht, *Pompadour*, for reneging on an agreement to buy the racing yawl for $35,000.

Even CKOY, the Ottawa station Jack had consulted with for more than a decade, didn't escape litigation. CKOY canceled the contract in which Jack had received 40 percent of the profits for consulting, claiming that a move to the U.S. rendered him useless. Jack disagreed and said that the agreement was in perpetuity unless CKOY's profits fell beneath a certain percentage. The judge agreed with him and awarded Jack Kent Cooke $100,000.

Lawsuits like these, all of which were splashed across newspaper pages, and a dozen years of press stories had left Jack Kent Cooke with a controversial image in Canada. This was part of the reason the Toronto city fathers continued to deny him an expanded baseball park. But it was not the reason Jack made the decision to leave Toronto and his native Canada after nearly fifty years of unparalleled success there.

After a dozen years of lobbying and trying to get Toronto's first private TV license, Jack was in the running when the Broadcasting Board of Governors decided to hear final applications. Undoubtedly, he felt that as owner of Toronto's leading radio station and as an extremely successful broadcaster, he should be given the television prize. But Jack Kent Cooke had rankled the BBG once too often. He hadn't even subscribed to the code of ethics of the Association of Canadian Broadcasters. A few years before the

BBG had suggested that Jack team up with another broadcaster to get the license. Jack's answer: "That's like asking Eaton's and Simpson's [Canada's two largest department stores] to go into business together."

There were nine applicants for "the rich plum," as Jack described it to the press, a candid description that would work against him as the hearings wore on. The applicants drew straws to determine the order in which their presentations were to be made. Each was given half a day to make a pitch. Jack's presentation came near the end of the hearings.

The Board of Governors wanted to hear from an operator who had deep pockets, would promise programming content that was more than 50 percent Canadian, and would keep advertising to a minimum. When Jack's turn came he outpromised everyone who had come before him. While his competitors had promised 55 percent Canadian content, Jack pledged 64.4 percent. He vowed to devote his entire financial resources to the station by not making it a separate corporation, but by merging it with his holding company, Consolidated Frybrook. And he based his revenue projections on broadcasting just one commercial every fifteen minutes.

When he was questioned by the Rev. Emlyn Davis, a Baptist minister, about what would happen if the station were operated without him (rumors were already reaching Toronto about Jack's possible move to California) Jack answered as if his mortality were at stake.

"I come from a hardy, almost indestructible line," he said. "I have no intention of dying within the next twelve months." If he did, though, he told the board, his brother Hal, assisted by "the great little band of men who have been with me so long," would take over.

Jack's conversion to Canadian content, after years of American pop music on CKEY, and his promise to limit commercials to four per hour after the heavy commercial load on his radio station actually drew laughter from the gallery.

Pierre Berton, one of Canada's most respected writers, wrote a column in the *Toronto Star*, that ridiculed Jack's testimony. It was titled "Mr. Jack Kent Cooke's Amazing, Mystical Conversion."

It seems to me that the chief diversion offered the general public during the recent TV hearings was the conversion of Mr. Jack Kent Cooke, the well-known philanthropist, to the new religion of Canadian Culture.

. . . name dropping was honed to a fine edge. Every applicant worth his salt managed to sprinkle the names of a score of leading Canadians through his opening remarks. One man got Cardinal McGuigan and Rabbi Feinberg into a single sentence. Another, who had a book publisher on his board, managed to toss off the names of most of our leading novelists.

By the time Mr. Cooke got up, there were no big names left. *Who's Who* had been exhausted. The *Social Register* had been squeezed dry. Undeterred, Mr. Cooke entered the witness box alone—a man who had received the message and seen the light. He was dressed in his best suit, a dark conservative number with matching vest and four-in-hand, as befits a Patron of the Arts and a Champion of Culture. There he stood—a so truly blue Canadian that he may easily replace the beaver, the maple leaf and the New York Rangers as a symbol of the nation.[1]

Now you may remember, a while back, that there was some whimpering and hair-rending by the private interests over the BBG's insistence that all programming be 55 percent Canadian in content. I'm happy to report that the carping has ended. Indeed, the applicants at the Oak Room were falling all over themselves to top this figure. It remained for Mr. Cooke to lead the field with 64.4 percent "the second the station opens."

If Mr. Cooke came to the hearing under certain disadvantages he turned not a hair. He is the sole owner of CKEY, a radio station which has devoted 58 percent of its time to popular records, more than 20 percent to commercials and less than one-half of one percent to public service, children's programs, drama, interviews and documentaries. Yet here was Mr. Cooke, promising to deliver great gobs of these things on the screen. . . .

Until his recent conversion, Mr. Cooke was a member of the You-Gotta-Give-The-Public-What-It-Wants school. The closest he got to culture was when he described The Fabulous Sixty Tunes on his station as "the folk music of the American continent." He once ran afoul of the Fowler commission for broadcasting too many commercials. But now here he was talking about a TV station as "the servant of the community" and referring, discerningly, to only one commercial announcement every 15 minutes.

105

I don't know if Mr. Cooke has undergone some kind of mystic experience or not but surely this is the greatest about-face since the days of Apostle Paul.

"For many years I have observed with deep sympathy the efforts of educational groups in the field of television," said Mr. Cooke earnestly. Well, he was preparing to devote two hours a day, six days a week to pure education. "And I promise you gentlemen, that is a minimum."

With that Mr. Cooke began to reel off the names of organizations who would help him in his work. The Toronto Symphony Orchestra, the Art Gallery, the Royal Ontario Museum, the Opera Guild, the National Ballet, etc. A titter rippled across the audience. They had heard those names in previous verbal briefs.

Later, Mr. Cooke was asked if he actually approached these various cultural groups. He said he hadn't. He planned to wait until they were a little less busy.

One got next, a fascinating insight into Mr. Cooke's new concept of programming. I do not recall that he mentioned the Top Sixty Tunes, but we did hear about live music, concerts, and live union performers (whom Mr. Cooke has never employed). There was talk of a weekly 90-minute drama "from the great classics of literature— English, French, Greek. . . ." There was a panel discussion on democracy; there was a reference to a conversation program between a man and wife team, discussing such tonics as: how to fix a leaky drain; the problems of juvenile delinquency; their personal concept of Arnold Toynbee, and so on.

Well, Mr. Cooke's performance only served to point up the overall air of unreality which covered over the proceedings before the BBG. Everything seemed just a little too good to be true. Personally, I longed for someone to produce a blood and thunder drama of the Living West. Sandwiched in between the endless Chopin recitals, the wholesome children's programs, the religious choirs, the earnest panel discussions, and the National Ballet, it would have come as a breath of fresh air.

This, however, no one could afford to do, the climate being what it was. Oddly, the one note of reality was introduced by Mr. Cooke himself when he described the private TV license as "a rich plum."

And that really was what all the talk about culture and all that breast-beating about Canadianism and all the name dropping was all about.

For once, all of Jack's forceful speeches didn't get the deal. A group led by John Bassett of the dying *Toronto Telegram,* won the day. The station was given the call letters CFTO.

Except for losing on a big deal, the one thing Jack Kent Cooke hated most was to be ridiculed. Scathing articles like Pierre Berton's and losing out on getting Toronto's first private TV license hastened Jack's departure from Canada even more than the failure to achieve major league baseball status. In addition, the Toronto Maple Leafs were floundering in 1959 and CKEY had just two years to go before its broadcasting license came up for renewal. Jack's battles with the Canadian Broadcasting Board of Governors assured that the hearings would be anything but a cakewalk.

A more wide-open America beckoned. There were lower taxes, warmer weather, and best of all, fewer government regulations on multiple ownership of broadcast properties. Jack, unappreciated in Toronto, was itching to show Americans how to succeed, Jack Kent Cooke style.

So Jack quietly gave the go-ahead to Shea and Gould—the New York law firm he had begun using in 1956—a month after losing the TV station license, to proceed with a historic application for restorative citizenship in the U.S. The bill made Jack Kent Cooke an instant citizen, without having to wait for the customary five years of American residency. In fact, the bill dated Jack's citizenship back ten years. Bill Shea approached Representative Francis Walter, a twenty-seven-year veteran of the U.S. Congress from Easton, Pennsylvania. Walter, known as "Tad" to his friends, was reputed to be a "wheeler dealer" according to John Monahan, then chief assistant to the Speaker of the House, John McCormick. Walter was both chairman of the powerful House Un-American Activities and Judiciary committees and a Democrat.

A memorandum from Walter to the Congress stated that Jack had gone to the United States to study broadcasting techniques and was impressed with the freedom of opportunity usually accorded U.S. citizens. "To become a U.S. citizen became an ambition of Mr. Cooke," the memo added.

Walter's House bill said that Jack had attempted to buy eight U.S. radio or television stations, the Philadelphia Athletics, the Detroit Tigers, and several newspapers. It said he had business interests in the U.S. that included a company in Cleveland, a record company in New York, a corporation called Broadcast Equipment in California, and an advertising representative organization, also in New York City.

"In Canada, Mr. Cooke is well liked and is a favorably known public figure. He has wealth, status, and social position there," Walter's memo said, "yet he would forego these material advantages if given the opportunity to build a new future for himself and family in the United States of America."

The bill, HR 8156, "for the relief of Jack Kent Cooke" was passed without debate by the House of Representatives on May 3, 1960.

Still, Jack's application did not sail straight through, even though Walter's memorandum read: "Mr. Cooke has long admired this country, its customs, people, and way of life. Mr. Cooke was impressed with the freedom of opportunity usually accorded U.S. citizens. In Canada, his energetic and aggressive espousal of the United States and its people is a matter of public record—along with some minor criticisms." The memo said that Jack had at least $1 million in U.S. investments. But Jack's private law still had to clear the Senate.

The sports columnist for the Toronto *Globe and Mail*, Scott Young, foreseeing Jack's exit, wrote a sad report in his May 4, 1960, column about a reception on the opening day of the Maple Leafs baseball season:

"Leading in [to] 26 years to this day where he stood a rich and restless man, at the door of the vice-regal suite of the King Edward Sheraton," Young's column concluded, "Greeting the men he had invited to come to greet him. . . . Saying steadfastly, 'No comment' to all questions as to why he had decided to become a U.S. citizen."

But as the bill to make Jack an instant citizen hit the Senate, it became bogged down. By June 1960, a spokesman for the Senate judiciary committee had this statement: "Usually a bill of this kind tells us why it is urgently needed, but this one doesn't. We need stronger arguments to back up what this bill demands."

A member of the Senate committee grumped: "This man never even took the trouble of getting a visa. We still haven't been told why the bill should pass."

Although the bill still had to clear the Senate and still had to be signed by Dwight Eisenhower, who was serving the last year of his presidency, it didn't take long for all of Toronto to begin a debate about the pluses and minuses of Jack Kent Cooke. Jack's son Ralph, now in his early twenties, pleaded ignorance when asked by a Toronto newspaper about what he thought about his father's move to the U.S. Ralph said that he had just learned about it himself by reading the newspapers.

A newspaper wondered about Jack being allowed to keep his CKEY license. Canadian law at the time said that a radio station had to have a Canadian president and two-thirds of the board had to be Canadian. Walter's bill would have changed that. It called for Jack to become an American citizen retroactively to September 28, 1950.[2]

Jack tried to soften these queries by saying that he would spend six months of each year in the Westchester County suburb of Hartsdale, New York (where Jack owned a house), and six months in Toronto. But Torontonians were disbelieving.

The most severe criticism came when a Toronto sportscaster, Wally Crouter of CFRB radio, said on his 7:55 A.M. broadcast on September 14, 1960, that Jack Kent Cooke would be a "deserter if it was wartime" by the way he "condemned" his own country. Within a half-hour, Crouter said he received fifty supporting phone calls.

According to Crouter, "Many of them said: 'It's about time somebody said something like that.' "

Jack, contacted at his Waldorf Towers suite in, appropriately, New York, brushed off Crouter's diatribe. "I can save you a lot of time and money by telling you I have no comment," he told everyone who reached him.

More short and to the point was a Toronto columnist who wrote, "Jack Kent Cooke has stepped on enough toes in this town to make a foot doctor wealthy."

But the *Globe and Mail* defended Jack. In an editorial headlined "Why Pick On Jack Cooke?" the paper said that Jack was just following the footsteps of the "famous and wealthy like . . . Lord Beaverbrook, Cyrus Eaton, Mary Pickford, Ned Sparks and Marie Dressler.[3]

"Mr. Crouter owns up to resentment against Mr. Cooke's 'ungrateful' admiration for the U.S., its customs, its people, its way of life and its opportunities for making money.

"One line of business in which Mr. Cooke engages in the U.S. is radio stations, which employ disc jockeys. His sour-grapes farewell to Mr. Cooke would seem to cut off the prospect of Mr. Crouter finding a job, at least on some U.S. stations."

Jack's application for instant, retroactive citizenship continued to move slowly through the Senate. On August 31, 1960, the *Congressional Record* shows that at least one U.S. Senator, Lyndon Johnson of Texas, who also had interests in radio and television broadcasting, made a feeble attempt to delay the legislation:

THE LEGISLATIVE CLERK. A bill (H.R. 8156) for the relief of Jack Kent Cooke.

THE PRESIDING OFFICER. The question is on agreeing to the motion of the Senator from Texas.

The motion was agreed to; and the bill was considered, ordered to a third reading, read the third time, and passed.

MR. JOHNSON of Texas. Mr. President, I move to reconsider the vote by which the bill was passed.

MR. DIRKSEN. Mr. President, I move to lay that motion on the table.[4]

The motion to lay on the table was agreed to.

The bill was finally approved by both houses on September 14, 1960, and signed immediately into law by President Eisenhower. It is listed as Private Law 86-486.[5]

Now the *Globe and Mail* had second thoughts. "Perhaps with his cosmopolitan background and his large business interests in the United States, there should be no great mystery about his intention of becoming a citizen of that country," the newspaper wrote in a September 17, 1960, editorial.

"He has been a valuable citizen of Canada—far more valuable in most ways than most of us—and we are sorry to see him go.

110

But what worries us is the power of Congress and the President to make residence as retroactive as an increase in wages. Surely there is danger in this. What's to stop a misguided session of Congress from passing a bill decreeing that some chap who touched down at Idlewild the day before yesterday actually came over on the Mayflower 340 years ago—thus creating a new breed of pioneer descendants and even, a few proper Bostonians to boot?"

The charade of "six months in Canada and six months in the U.S." was over. Jack's Frybrook Road mansion was sold by March 1962 for $170,000. *Saturday Night* and *New Liberty* had been sold in August 1961 to a Toronto entrepreneur, Percy Bishop, who specialized in bringing small oil firms' stocks to the public. Bishop was speculating that the Canadian government was about to restrict the distribution of American magazines in Canada. He was wrong. By 1964 Bishop had nearly drowned the magazine in red ink and it was sold again for the price of its back printing bills.

CKEY was sold, ironically, to a group led by the firm he had tried to buy ten years earlier, the Toronto *Globe and Mail.* Jack decided not to sell the plastics groups right away. The companies were solidly profitable and there was no problem with a foreign owner. Although the baseball team was available, Jack didn't find a real buyer until 1964. A group of Toronto businessmen—a virtual Who's Who of the city—stepped in when it was thought that the team might be allowed to fold unless an owner were found. They paid about $50,000 for the club that Jack had bought for $200,000. Jack said he had lost "a small fortune."

"There was a difference of $297,000 between what I had in the ball club and what I received for it. I am still interested in the game," he said, "and had I remained in Toronto I would never have sold."

But an old-time Cooke friend told a writer, "Jack never lost money on anything. He got a lot out of the club during the time he owned it. The loss probably helped on taxes."

If Jack did lose money on the Maple Leafs sale it was the only asset in Canada in which he ever lost cash. All the others were sold at a profit.

The new owners of the ball club were led by two Toronto thoroughbred breeders, Robert Hunter and Sam Starr. Among the

111

investors was the hot dog king Sam Shopsowitz; a banker, Frank O'Neill; and the former owner of the club who had sold to Jack in 1951, Donald Ross. They apparently needed Ross, the stock broker. With the club continuing to draw poorly, the new owners took the team public at $1 a share. By the late 1960s the club was drawing less than 100,000 a year and faded into the oblivion of bankruptcy.

When Jack Kent Cooke's Leafs were sold, the assets included the contracts of only six players and the field manager, Sparky Anderson, who would later become famous as manager of "the big red machine," the Cincinnati Reds, and also bring a 1970s renaissance to the Detroit Tigers. The rest of the assets included balls, bats, uniforms, field lights, and the contract of one "Smoky" Smith, the trainer. The group retained Frank Pollock as general manager, who had now been with the team twenty-five years.

Not that Jack was without a sports toy to play with. A few years before he had been in a cab in New York going to The '21' Club for dinner with a group of friends that included his friend and attorney, Bill Shea. He was told that a chunk of an NFL football team was for sale—Would he be interested?

"Hell, yes."

The call was made from his table at the restaurant and shortly afterward Jack Kent Cooke and Bill Shea put up $350,000, which gave them 25 percent of the Washington Redskins.

Notes

1. At the time, the New York Rangers were made up of all Canadian players but had not made the playoffs in the NHL for three years.
2. Making Jack a citizen retroactively to 1950 gave him an immediate okay to buy a broadcasting outlet. One must be an American citizen to own a radio or television station.
3. Mary Pickford, "America's Sweetheart," who was Canadian, is typical of many Canadians who emigrate to the U.S. and develop an All-American image. For instance, many of the key people on the original *Saturday Night Live*, the epitome of American humor in the 1970s and 1980s were Canadians. Lorne Michaels, the producer, Paul Shaf-

fer, the musical director, Gilda Radner, and Dan Ackroyd as well as two of the original show's writers were all from Ontario.

4. Lyndon Johnson was the Senate majority leader at the time and Everett Dirksen of Illinois was the minority leader.

5. Jack would later tell *Maclean's* magazine: "It was done entirely by friends in the United States who wanted me, desperately apparently, to come down here."

LOS ANGELES

CHAPTER

9
CONTESTS AND INDIANS

**"He wanted KRLA to be the ratings leader
like CKEY had been."**

Jack purchased a 25 percent stake in the Washington Redskins
in partnership with his close friend and attorney William Shea on
April 17, 1961. The shares became available when Harry Wismer,
the New York sports broadcaster who had once been the voice of
the Washington Redskins, became upset with George Preston Marshall, who controlled the team.

Wismer, who had paid $65,000 for his shares, observed that
Marshall was running the team as his personal fiefdom, charging
such items as out-of-town liaisons with women, and a house, to
the Redskins. Marshall was even using Redskin office people as
his personal servants—having them drive him to parties and do
his gardening. Wismer felt he would never get any benefits out of
the team so he sold his stock back to Milton King, a vice president
of the team and used the money to buy a controlling interest in
the New York Titans (which later become the Jets) of the new
American Football League.

In order for Jack and Bill Shea to buy the piece of the team,
they needed Marshall's blessing. Shea called Marshall from the
table at '21' and made a pitch for Jack Kent Cooke.[1] Marshall gave
his okay because he heard that "he was the only owner of a minor
league baseball club who always paid his bills." Jack's net worth
at the time was reported to be between $10 and $12 million.

Jack and Bill shared the stake 60–40, with Jack getting the
larger amount. Jack also assumed a seat on the club's board of
directors. Shea said at the time that he considered Washington his

second home since he had gone to Georgetown University and its law school and had sent his son there. He also called George Preston Marshall "a longtime friend." Shea had also once owned a football club called the Long Island Indians, a Redskins farm club.

After Jack and Bill bought the 25 percent stake for $350,000, with an option to buy a controlling amount from Marshall at any time he wanted to sell or from his estate upon his death, Shea had an argument with Marshall. It was over the hiring of black players. The Redskins had none and would eventually become the last NFL team to integrate.[2] Disgusted with Marshall, Shea sold his part of the team back to Jack, saying he "didn't want to be a part of it."

George Preston Marshall was a blatant racist and didn't care who knew it. At a 1953 Washington Redskins luncheon for fans at the Washingtonian Golf and Country Club in Gaithersburg, Maryland, he told a gathering, "I'm not going to have any niggers on my team." Jim Gustafson, an employee of Washington's WTTG-5 television at the time, was at the lunch, and remembers no reaction to the Redskins president's remark "except maybe a dirty look directed towards Marshall by a black waiter."

In 1964, Jack attempted to purchase another 13 percent that was owned by C. Leo DeOrsey, a Washington attorney who was by then acting president of the football club. DeOrsey had taken the place of Marshall, who had stepped down because of ailing health.[3] Marshall would remain ill until his death in 1969. Leo DeOrsey had several good reasons for selling his shares. He was in bad health too: he had suffered four heart attacks by 1964 (he was sixty-one). The profit would not have been bad either. Jack's check for $910,000 was 450 percent more than DeOrsey had paid just two and a half years earlier.

Jack wired DeOrsey on April 11 confirming their agreement that DeOrsey would sell 130 shares in the Redskins for $7,000 per share, totalling $910,000. Jack agreed to mail the $910,000 to DeOrsey by April 15.

But the DeOrsey deal didn't go through. George Marshall's guardian, a protective John J. Carmody, blocked the sale, saying the contract was bad for the now ailing Marshall.

Jack nearly gained majority control of the Redskins that same year by another avenue. A sick George Preston Marshall offered Jack control of the team by selling him his shares so he could enjoy life "on the money you'd pay me." A price was agreed on and Marshall sent one of his aides to Los Angeles to work out a contract. But the aide tossed Jack a curve ball.

Jack was told that in order to get the deal, he would have to give Marshall's man 10 percent of the stock or else he would tell Marshall that he was being taken. Jack told him to stuff it and Marshall's man went back and told Marshall not to do the deal. The agreement died.

"It was blackmail, actually," remembers Jack. "I always felt that the blackmailed is just as bad as the blackmailer."

But he still had 25 percent of the club. It was an auspicious beginning.

Although Jack Kent Cooke had made a great debut on the East Coast of the United States, his first foray into broadcasting on the West Coast was anything but that. His purchase of a Pasadena, California, radio station was a debacle that resulted in a major embarrassment for him.

Jack's youngest brother Donald had moved to the U.S. in the early 1940s, becoming a citizen in 1947 in order to run Jack's business interests in New York City—Strand Records, which produced recordings like "Let's Polka with the Polka Serenaders," and Jack's advertising sales agency. Because Jack wasn't a citizen in 1959, he used Donald's name and Donald's American citizenship when he purchased a small AM radio station in Pasadena, KXLA, 1110 on the dial. The money came from Jack Kent Cooke. His own private bill hadn't yet been even introduced.

But no government agency could keep him out of the country. Jack was firmly ensconced in Los Angeles by 1959, preparing to use his twenty-five years of radio know-how in making the radio station the talk of southern California. He first bought a house in Beverly Hills, presenting it to Jean as a slightly belated twenty-fifth anniversary present. Later he would buy a pink Mediterranean stucco house at 310 Saint Cloud Road in Bel Air, a Los Angeles neighborhood that rivals Beverly Hills for snob appeal. The estate, on 2.7 manicured acres backing into woods on the side of a mountain, was described by a friend of Jack's as "not all that big—it has fewer rooms than some hotels." What it also had was a three-hole putting course, a swimming pool, fountains, and a badminton court. There were electric-eye gates to keep out the curious, and celebrity neighbors like Greer Garson and Tony Curtis.[4] He purchased a new celadon Bentley and put his initials, JKC, on the driver's door. He brought his faithful CKEY retainer Eddie Parr and family to Los Angeles to chauffeur and do odd jobs. He then established a three-room office at 9888 Wilshire Boulevard in Beverly Hills. Jack put no name on the door and didn't even bother to list the phone number. And because one had to be a citizen to own a radio or television outlet, the station was unlisted too as far as Jack's name was concerned. Nonetheless, his mark was everywhere. The station was Donald's in name only. Jack gave his brother the $900,000 to purchase KXLA and began to work his magic.

Jack's plan for the station was almost like combining the best of what had worked for CKEY and the Maple Leafs baseball team. First Jack changed the call letters to KRLA, increased the power to 50,000 watts, and then unleashed a new format—the Top Forty hit parade.[5]

The 50,000 watt signal was aimed at the number two U.S. radio market. Jack changed KRLA from a hillbilly country format to a pop sound in order to be competitive in the Los Angeles ratings. But Jack wanted more than that. He wanted KRLA to be the ratings leader, as CKEY had been in Toronto. So he invented a series of contests that involved finding his new star disc jockey, Perry Allen. The prize was $10,000. The second contest, with an advertised award of $50,000, involved finding a golden key that was to unleash the new 50,000 watt signal.

Meanwhile the Federal Communications Commission was looking at all this activity closely. The agency questioned documentation which showed that all but $10,000 of the purchase price had been put up by Jack Kent Cooke. It asked why Broadcast Equipment Corporation, a Jack Kent Cooke-owned firm, had the option to buy Donald out at any time until November 1965 providing its "owner qualified to be a licensee." Donald Cooke, sensing the FCC's scrutiny, upped his share in the station and struck the option clause. However, the FCC later concluded that "while it was bought in the name of Don, a man of limited means, Jack was ultimately to become licensee of any station to become acquired." Indeed, the station was up and running four months before Donald visited the facility.

With KRLA now under examination by the FCC in 1960 and scheduled to begin its new format and its new supercharged 50,000 watts of power on Labor Day, Jack became dissatisfied with the station's master plan. He burst into the studios ten days before the "grand opening" and decided he didn't like the disc jockeys. Lighting up a cigarette first (he had switched to Marlboros when he moved to the U.S.), he spent the day listening to demonstration tapes. Jack decided that Perry Allen of WKBW in Buffalo was the one for the prime-drive time slot, even though the station manager had already turned him down as having a "too frantic" delivery. Jack called the deejay and offered him a job on the spot. Then he started his "Find Perry Allen and Win $10,000" contest to highlight the new employee.

What Jack failed to calculate is that the disc jockey fraternity is rather small. Most radio people know other personalities in competing metropolitan markets or are at least aware of them through trade publications. Although KRLA began broadcasting clues that suggested Perry Allen was near various Los Angeles landmarks, the real Perry Allen was still finishing up the two-week notice he had given to WKBW in Buffalo. Two rival disc jockeys on L.A.'s KFWB didn't buy the Los Angeles location clues and flew to Buffalo the next day, claiming the $10,000 prize. The FCC later reported, "After extended negotiations . . . the $10,000 was paid to Purcell [one of the finders] on behalf of KFWB."

Jack's reaction, upon learning he had lost the money to a rival station about two weeks before he had planned to award the amount, was: "Good God! Do you know how much $10,000 is?"

Meanwhile, Jack was running other contests as well. Every fifteen minutes, various amounts of cash were given to anyone who answered the phone and said, "Don't say hello, say KRLA."

The big, $50,000 contest was the one that got Jack into the most trouble. Starting at midnight, September 1, 1960, the station began broadcasting clues to the "Find the Golden Key" contest. For the next fifty-four hours the station broadcast nothing but clues for the various contests, hoping to whip Southern Californians into a frenzy. After a few clues were given, the $50,000 prize dropped a couple of thousand dollars, and then again after a few more clues, and so on. Jack had already decided that $5,000 would be the amount awarded and that an obvious clue would be given on day seven that would focus on a place within Marineland where the key was hidden.

The problem was that the writer doing the clues wasn't even told where the key was hidden until three days into the contest. Nor was the key even deposited at Marineland until midway through the week, well after everything was underway. These omissions did not escape the eyes of the press. Questions were raised by the bible of the industry, *Broadcasting* magazine, and it was only a matter of weeks until the FCC pounced, asking for an explanation and a look at the station's logs.

The FCC held hearings. In question were the misleading contests and falsified logs. They also charged that owner Donald Cooke had given control to Jack, who was not then a citizen. The result was to order KRLA off the air, effective April 16, 1962, on the grounds of fraudulent practices and allowing KRLA to fall under control of an alien—one Jack Kent Cooke. It even said that the station entered into its logs religious broadcasts which "in fact, were not broadcast." The FCC also found that Donald Cooke had actually left the station in 1959, turning over working operations to Jack and was unaware of any deception or alteration of records.

After the FCC ruling, Donald said he was "shocked" by the decision and would appeal. He said that Jack had loaned him $500,000 but that Jack was being repaid in monthly payments. The appeals dragged on until April 1964, when every avenue was exhausted including the U.S. Court of Appeals in Washington.

Jack made one last-ditch attempt to salvage something out of the disaster. He and Donald proposed to donate KRLA as a gift to the nonprofit Broadcast Foundation of America, which in turn pledged to donate 80 percent of the station's profits to a local PBS (educational television) station. The catch-22 was that the foundation assume a $360,000 debt owed by Donald Cooke to Jack and also assume a five-year lease on the station site, payable at $90,000 a year to Jack Kent Cooke. The FCC voted four to two to reject this gambit on the grounds that Donald, as an owner without a license, had nothing to assign to anyone.

The station's power and dial position were valuable but Donald and Jack got nothing. Lining up for the potential million dollar bonanza of the new FCC license were a long list of celebrities—Bob Hope, Art Linkletter, Nat King Cole, McDonald Carey, bandleader Horace Heidt—plus the Bible Institute of America. In all, twenty different groups applied. KRLA stayed in limbo for fifteen years with PBS indeed getting a cut of the earnings until it was finally awarded to the Hope-Linkletter group. Donald and Jack lost a license to a station that was now worth between $5 million and $15 million, depending on which expert one talks to in Los Angeles.

Jack traveled north to Pebble Beach to lick his wounds. Moving into a $100,000 contemporary house bordering the links, he played golf nearly every day for five months, reducing his handicap to five. It is now part of the conventional wisdom included in many magazine and newspaper articles that Jack moved to Pebble Beach to "retire," although a minority reported that he was "stricken ill." Jack Kent Cooke himself has fostered that portion of countless profiles by telling reporters variously, "It was the biggest mistake I ever made. I don't think the Lord put me on earth to play golf," or "I decided I had worked hard and hadn't had a vacation in my life. I played golf everyday, got my handicap down. It was as useless a diversion as I ever engaged in. I'd wake up every morning . . . and think 'Oh God, we're going to play golf again today—we should be doing something constructive.' " But Jack Kent Cooke, never a quitter at anything in life, was just contemplating his next move.

Like the time in 1936 at Kirkland Lake, Ontario, when he had realized the huge amounts of money that could be made in radio, Jack made plans for the future. He took long, solitary walks each day to think. He remembered being amazed when looking at a remote piece of real estate in the California mountains that he was one of the few people in town who could get television that day. The reception in his hotel room came in perfectly and he was told that the lodge was wired for cable.

"You mean people are willing to pay $5 a month for this?" Jack was reported to have asked.

Jack Kent Cooke is a student of the campaigns of Napoleon. Most likely, Napoleon's observation, "The combative urge is within us all," was ringing in his ears when Jack headed south to his office on Wilshire Boulevard and purchased his first group of cable television antenna systems for $4,600,000.

It would be cable television, an industry in which Jack would be one of the pioneers, that would give him some of his biggest triumphs and help push his net worth from mere millions to a fortune in excess of a billion dollars.

Notes

1. The table at '21' is marked today by a Redskins helmet, which is suspended from the ceiling above it. The table is located along the wall, just to the left as one enters the main floor dining room.
2. When the Redskins finally got around to picking their first black player, they chose a real winner. Running back/wide receiver Bobby Mitchell played seven seasons for Washington, beginning in 1962, after four years with the Cleveland Browns. His total of four Pro Bowls, lifetime 5.3 yard rushing average, and 521 pass receptions got him inducted into the NFL Hall of Fame in 1983. In 1990, he was the Redskins' assistant general manager, enjoying his thirty-third consecutive year of employment in the NFL. Some football historians might dispute this, as the Redskins had drafted Syracuse running back Ernie Davis, but traded its rights to Davis, the number one choice, for Mitchell. Davis became a major tragedy of the time when he died of leukemia after graduation without ever playing in an NFL uniform. The Redskins didn't really want Mitchell either. It was an unspoken condition for letting them play at the new D.C. stadium, later RFK stadium, which was built with federal funds.
3. Although it was never described as such, Marshall had what is known today as Alzheimer's disease.
4. Neighbors weren't necessarily friends. Greer Garson stopped speaking

to Jack after he told a national magazine that her house needed painting.

5. The increase to 50,000 watts was begun by a man whose name was Loyal King, the previous owner of the radio station, who drafted the FCC application. One of his claims to fame was that he "discovered" singer Tennessee Ernie Ford.

CHAPTER

10

CABLE FIGHTS

"He arrived at ringside with an entourage worthy of a fighter."

There are no sure things in American enterprise. But one can come close. And the closest one can get to certainty in business is to find a fast-growing industry, in its infancy, that offers a needed service, is unregulated in price, and has a monopoly in the community it serves. That described the still fledgling cable television industry that Jack Kent Cooke jumped into with an initial $4.6 million investment in the fall of 1964.

For those who had vision and the ability to do a little math, it was not difficult to project almost certain profits from a protected cable franchise. Jack would correlate the advantages of such a system with his early days as a radio pioneer in northern Ontario. Roy Thomson had often repeated at the time, "It's like a license to print money." Now that same opportunity was available in cable television.

The cable formula was simple. It matched current market penetration and system growth projections against current and expected future subscriber charges. Cable was novel and not yet replete with a hundred basic channels, public access, or premium services. It was simply a way to bring a half-dozen television channels into a small community where viewers until then either had to erect individual ninety-foot antennas or get a snowy signal.

Cable television, then called CATV—for community antenna television—was still unknown in most of the country when Jack bought his first systems in 1966. It had begun in 1948 when residents in a tiny Pennsylvania community installed an antenna

126

system to bring in TV signals over the mountains, thus creating television reception where there was none. Areas of Oregon and Washington were next, a few months later.

Jack Kent Cooke's initial systems were in Graham and Palestine, Texas; Barstow, California; and Keene, New Hampshire. Jack paid just under $300 per subscriber for 16,000 paying households. Collecting $5 from each subscriber monthly gave him a beginning cash flow of $80,000 a month.

"CATV is a natural for him," the *Globe and Mail* of Toronto, which still covered him avidly, reported, on October 30, 1964, "because it is a hybrid of broadcasting, of which he is an expert, and also a profitable investment field."

Jack moved fast. By 1965 he had added Camarillo, Laguna Beach and South Laguna Beach, Thousand Oaks, and Troutsdale Estates, in California; Lewiston, Idaho; Independence and Parson, Kansas; Ocean City and Berlin, Maryland; Brainerd, Rochester, and Winona, Minnesota; Gallup, New Mexico; Moab, Utah; Clarkton, Washington; La Crosse, Wisconsin; and Casper, Wyoming. All of these were small communities in rural areas—perfect places to buy existing CATV franchises.

The new cable television mogul gave his son John a job with the young company, which he named American Cablevision and headquartered at the 9888 Wilshire Boulevard offices in Los Angeles. John had attended two Canadian colleges—Upper Canada and Waterloo, both in Ontario—but had not graduated. When Jack sent John to the La Crosse, Wisconsin, system in early 1966 he made him start as a cable installer but later promoted him to system manager. John, 3,000 miles from home, used the opportunity to marry his girlfriend from Phoenix, Arizona, Rebecca Ann Gilliam, known as Becky, in a ceremony in La Crosse on March 12, 1966.[1]

The new far-flung, fast-growing cable empire required frequent travel by Jack, a situation that often aggravated his claustrophobia. Attorney Jay Ricks of the Washington law firm of Hogan and Hartson remembers one flight with Jack and Jean Cooke from Washington to Cape May, New Jersey, on September 11, 1964. "We picked them up at the Sheraton Carlton in Washington and drove to Page Airways terminal. . . . My brother was flying. The plane was a four-passenger Navion, I believe, a single-engine air-craft. As the plane taxied out on the runway Jack was upset . . . perspiring heavily . . . pale, on the verge of fainting. He had us return to the terminal where the canopy was opened for more air. I suggested Jack move to the front seat where there was a more . . . open feeling. He did and we proceeded on to Cape May."

Jack brought William J. "Bill" Bresnan and James Lacher into his cable enterprises in 1966. This gave him the ability to expand and put together two subsidiaries—a company that engineered other CATV systems, and a company that sold cable equipment. Although Bresnan would eventually leave, Jim Lacher stayed and today is Jack's chief lieutenant. Lacher later got a real estate license and listed Jack's $11 million house on Chalon Drive in Bel Air, California, when Jack put it up for sale in 1990.

After Jack got heavily into sports ownership in the mid-sixties he sold the majority of his cable empire to H&B Communications for stock in H&B that was worth $30.8 million at the time. American Cablevision had 85,000 subscribers. Jack still continued buy-ing and owning a few cable systems under his own name, particularly systems in southern Arizona—Tempe and Tucson—and 51 percent of the cable system of Clark County, Nevada, which he owned with Las Vegas newspaper publisher Hank Greenspun. Jim Lacher moved into sports with Jack, and Bill Bresnan became Jack's listening post at H&B. H&B then was bought by Tele-PrompTer, the largest cable television company in America, and the only one with a presence in the highly prized New York City market. Jack owned nearly 11.9% of TelePrompTer, a publicly listed company, and when H&B was merged, Jack's stake was worth $40 million.

TelePrompTer was run by an entrepreneur named Irving Berlin Kahn, a communications dynamo who, like Jack, had been a radio broadcaster during the 1930s.[2] Kahn had named the corporation TelePrompTer, after the electronic cue card he invented in the 1940s and which is still widely used in television and motion pictures. Kahn had entered the cable business after a stint with Twentieth Century Fox. Knowing a good thing when he saw it, he quickly parlayed TelePrompTer into a company that would have over a million subscribers in more than 100 communities by 1970. But illegal bribes would soon nearly drive TelePrompTer into oblivion, and almost cause Jack to lose most of the $50 million fortune he had created during his first five years as a cable pioneer.

Although Jack Kent Cooke owned or had owned a majority interest in six different sports teams by 1971, it was his knowledge of the potential of cable television, particularly the new "pay-per-view" technology, that caused him to make a quick decision on December 28, 1970, to write a check for $4.5 million to Chase Manhattan bank for a letter of credit (Madison Square Garden put up the other $500,000) that guaranteed Joe Frazier, undefeated at 26–0, and Muhammad Ali, unbeaten at 31–0, $2.5 million each for their first encounter on March 8, 1971. Billed modestly as the "Fight of the Century," it was "one of the few fights at Madison Square Garden that actually exceeded expectations," former Garden promoter Harry Markson told a writer.

Jack put up the money, planning first to stage the fight at his recently completed "Fabulous" Forum in Los Angeles (conflicting dates and Frazier's reluctance to fight in California made it impossible). He was joined by rock concert promoter Jerry Perenchio.[3] Jack and Jerry knew that if the fight was to make money, the revenue would have to come from pay TV. The potential live gate at the Garden, assuming a total sellout of the 19,500 seats priced from $20 to $150, was $1.5 million. The Garden got the live gate in exchange for its $500,000. All other revenue was to go to the Cooke-Perenchio team. After expenses, Jack and Jerry would need about $20 million just to break even and they had only two months to put everything together.

Ironically, Wilt Chamberlain, one of the players with the NBA basketball team Jack bought in 1965, the Los Angeles Lakers, had come to him a year before and told him about a $500,000 offer he had to fight Muhammad Ali. Jack, in what later could be termed, "do as I say, not as I do" advice, said to Wilt:

"Avoid and desist from it. The fight crowd's a sleazy bunch. Don't ever get mixed up with them."

After Jack got involved in putting together the Ali–Frazier

fight, he saw Chamberlain again. "You know," Wilt later told a writer, "the man didn't even blush."

It was Jack and Jerry's chutzpah combined with the Jack Kent Cooke bankbook that pulled it off. Perenchio put together a worldwide network of thirty-five countries that, besides the United States, included Canada, the United Kingdom, Argentina, Bermuda, Brazil, Chile, Colombia, Costa Rica, the Dominican Republic, Ecuador, El Salvador, Guatemala, Honduras, Hong Kong, Indonesia, Japan, Mexico, Nicaragua, Nigeria, Okinawa, Panama, Peru, the Philippines, Puerto Rico, South Korea, Thailand, Uruguay, Venezuela, West Germany, Italy, Switzerland, the Netherlands, Austria, Romania, and Yugoslavia. Jack and Jerry, with just a little excess bombast, estimated that the audience outside the U.S. would be more than 300 million.

Franchises for closed-circuit TV in America and Canada were parceled out to celebrities—particularly those in sports. Former California Angels pitcher Dean Chance got the West Virginia territory. George Chuvalo, Canada's best heavyweight of the decade, teamed with Boston Bruin defenseman Bobby Orr and got Quebec, Ontario, and parts of Manitoba, in Canada. Angelo Dundee's brother, Chris, grabbed Miami Beach, and Jack's one-time rival for the affections of Kay Starr, Danny Kaye, got most of the West Coast by putting up a $1 million guarantee.

The average price for a closed-circuit ticket was about $12, although prices varied widely. Seats at the Hilton in Washington, D.C, were $30. The 6,200 seats in New York's Radio City Music Hall were sold out weeks before the event at $20 and $25. A total of thirty-three movie theaters in New York's five boroughs carried the fight. The largest national venue was at Three Rivers Stadium in Pittsburgh. The 50,000-seat stadium—unheated and outdoors— did not sell out. In Chicago's Coliseum, which did sell out, a riot would erupt when the equipment brought in to project the fight broke down.

After everything was put together Jerry Perenchio tried to sell commercials on the closed circuit at $400,000 a minute. But the price was a little too ambitious and time ran out on the Hollywood promoter.

Jack, with his years of experience in cable and microwave, helped work out a system in which the Madison Square Garden signal was microwaved to the American Telephone Building on Canal Street in Manhattan. Then it was sent to the domestic theaters via AT&T long line cable. It was also sent to the Empire State Building, where it was beamed up to the three satellites that fed it to the thirty-five participating countries. There was also a standby system set up in case anything went wrong.

Radio City installed a new 30 × 40-foot screen for the fight, one of the largest. The smallest was a 9 × 12-foot screen for media nabobs at a private party held in the Time-Life building.

Jack and Jerry protected their investment fiercely. They wouldn't even give Armed Forces Radio a free ride but at the last moment relented slightly, allowing it to broadcast the fight to the troops in Vietnam. When Mutual Radio tried to broadcast the fight on a delayed summary basis, Jack took them to court and won.

While Perenchio and Jack were putting together the financial part of the event, the two contestants were doing their part in selling the fight, both consciously and otherwise. Frazier's manager, Yank Durham, grabbed headlines by saying his twenty-seven-year-old fighter would retire after the match. Frazier added to the hype, saying he would give up boxing for a singing career. Next, Joe Frazier's camp reported a death threat that advised Joe to "lose, or else." The threat got him front page headlines, wall-to-wall protection by eight of New York's finest detectives, and new, secret lodging, "somewhere in Manhattan."

Muhammad Ali, a natural promoter, did more than his part. His movie *aka Cassius Clay*, distributed by United Artists, opened around the country the week before the fight. Arriving in New York, and learning of the potential $25 million gross, Ali yelped "we wuz robbed" and threatened not to show up unless he got more money. Ali also promised a secret envelope that would predict the round (sixth) in which he would knock Frazier out.

Just before the fight, Jack gave an interview to the *New York Times* in which he complained about all the crazy business offers now coming his way. "You wouldn't believe what they want me to do," he said. "One deal, they want me to build totem poles as a tourist attraction in Louisiana. You see, I told you you wouldn't believe me." Jack developed a form letter to answer every oddball business partnership offer.

Jack told the *Times* that New York was his third favorite city. His first was Los Angeles, and his second was Glennville, California, where his new 13,300 acre ranch, Raljon, was based.[4]

Jack admitted in the interview that he would "only make $1.5 million from the fight" (later estimates made Jack's cut between $500,000 and $3 million) and that he probably could have done just as well with short-term notes. "But then," Jack said, "I wouldn't have had as much fun."[5]

Other members of the Cooke family were involved in the fight. The program was credited as a Ralph Cooke–Sidney Tillman Production with the contents "not to be copied in whole or part without the written permission of Ralph Cooke Enterprises, Inc." The cover of Ralph's program was tastefully headlined "Somebody's Going To Get An Ass Whipping" with "Joe Frazier, Undefeated Champion and Muhammad Ali, No. 1 Contender" in smaller type.

Jack may have had the most fun of all on the night of the fight. He arrived at ringside with an entourage worthy of a fighter. Lorne Greene and old chum Roy Thomson flanked Jack, and in his group were Bill Shea, Elia Kazan, and Pete Davis "of the Davis Tennis Cup Davises." The fight was clearly a celebrity event. At ringside were Hugh Hefner and his flame of the moment, Barbi Benton (wearing a see-through blouse that made her in the words of one newspaper, "a walking centerfold"), Michael Caine, George Plimpton, Jason Robards, Ben Gazarra, Count Basie, Diana Ross (wearing velvet hot pants), Peter and Cheray Duchin, Andy Williams with Ethel Kennedy, Teddy Kennedy, Sargent Shriver, and Eunice Kennedy Shriver. Media titans included William Paley of CBS, Robert Sarnoff of NBC, and John Hay Whitney, whose *New York Herald Tribune* had once been Jack Kent Cooke's favorite American newspaper. Three astronauts attended, led by Alan Shepherd. The New York Knicks basketball team and the hockey Rangers all got in free because they played in the Garden. Stars were everywhere. Peter Falk, Curt Jurgens, and Herb Alpert arrived together. Burt Lancaster was the ring announcer and Frank Sinatra photographed the fight for *Life* magazine. Norman Mailer wrote about the deeper meaning of it all for *Esquire*, Budd Schulberg handled the literary duties for *Playboy*, and William Saroyan was on hand for *True*.

Perenchio, who at various times had also been an agent for both Richard Burton and Marlon Brando, saw the whole thing as a happening: "It's Woodstock all over again," he told *Newsweek*, referring to the musical event of the previous decade.

Things got a little punchy just before the fight. The New York *Daily News*, probably running out of prefight copy, devoted two pages to predictions on the winner by "100 prominent Americans." Among these august citizens were the following for Muhammad Ali: Ed Sullivan, Jacqueline Susann, Bill Russell, Joe Garagiola, Tiny Tim, and Zsa Zsa Gabor. Weighing in on Joe Frazier's side were Gil Hodges, Mae West, Toots Shor, Bob Hope, and Henny Youngman. On a more credible level, the three fighters who had fought both Ali and Frazier—Jerry Quarry, Oscar Bonavena, and Jimmy Ellis—all came out for Ali, citing "his superior speed." At fight time, Frazier was an 8–5 favorite.

Both men had worked themselves up to a lather of hatred by the time they stepped into the ring. The first words Ali said to Joe Frazier as the referee brought them together for their final instructions were, "I'm going to kill you, nigger." Ali, who had said for weeks that the people were coming to see him, not Frazier, had been his usual mouthy self before the fight, so the blaspheme shouldn't have shocked anyone. Although his title has been stripped from him in 1967 because of his anti-Vietnam War stance, which had made him a martyr for many blacks and whites, the controversy that always surrounded him had begun years before when he became one of the first prominent African-Americans to convert to the Black Muslim faith, a religion that clearly threatened many whites. But it was his refusal to enter the draft, on the grounds that he was a Black Muslim minister, that fueled the controversy which follows him to this day.

"Joe Frazier must win by a knockout," Ali told a press conference (with Jack Kent Cooke by his side) before the fight, "he can't outpoint me. It's impossible. Even if he catches me with a good punch, I'll know what to do."

133

When Frazier heard Ali's "I'm going to kill you nigger" remark he responded, "I'm going to do the same to you." Frazier was more to the standards that the American public expected of a fighter. He had a maroon Cadillac with two white telephones inside, in a time when any car phone was a rarity. He had a fancy motorcycle and he had learned to be a fighter at night while working days inside a South Carolina slaughterhouse. And while Ali spent his spare time with the controversial Black Muslims, Frazier performed in his off hours as a singer with his rock band called The Knockouts.

The reinstated Ali became the underdog on the Las Vegas betting line because of his long layoff. He had warmed up with two fights—a third-round knockout over Jerry Quarry and a fifteenth-round TKO over Oscar Bonavena on December 7, 1970, where he had put the Argentinian down three times and the referee was required to enforce the three-knockdown rule. But the experts were not impressed with Ali's two comeback wins, except in London; there the British bookmakers had him an 11−8 favorite.

With more than 600 accredited press personnel in the garden, the two charged to the center of the ring as the bell rang for round one of the fifteen-round match. Joe Frazier missed his first blow, an attempted left hook, while Ali landed his first, also a left hook. The round was close, with one judge and referee Arthur Mercante voting for Ali.

Frazier's straight-ahead approach, like a train with extra pistons, won him the majority of the first five rounds on all three cards, with one judge giving him four rounds and the other two decision makers awarding him three. Ali took particular delight in taunting Frazier, calling him "chump" instead of "champ" and leaning against the ropes, slipping punches.

Ali nearly took charge in the middle rounds, putting together four- and five-punch combinations that went unanswered. In the eighth round, the crowd, who was clearly for the challenger, began chanting, "Ali, Ali," and Muhammad raised his right hand, playing to the mob. And in the ninth, a two-punch left-right combination had Frazier wobbly. But in the final third of the match, Frazier took control. The eleventh round began with Frazier backing Ali into a corner and banging his gloves into Ali's face and body as if

134

he was working out on a punching bag. Most of the punches were slipped or picked off, but a left hook toward the end of the round had Frazier's challenger reeling, his legs like warm pudding. Joe Frazier won the round big on every card. And in the fifteenth, the fight was decided when Frazier landed a crushing left hand early in the round that landed flush on Ali's chin, breaking his jaw (a later report said it was "just a severe hematoma of the right jaw") and putting him down. Ali bounced up at the count of three, but had to take a standing eight-count. It was the knockdown that probably gave Joe Frazier the unanimous decision. In the end Mercante scored it 8–6–1 and the two judges had it 9–6 and 11–4.

After the fight, which was raved about for several days in the press because of the quality and the drama of the night, Jack Kent Cooke crowed that he had rematch rights "in perpetuity" and that the next fight would be held in Los Angeles at the Forum, which he had built five years before. Jack, in anticipation of an encore engagement, bought out Perenchio and prepared to go it alone. There were reports that Perenchio had spent too much money. Most of these allegations were spread by Bob Arum, the promoter and Ali's attorney, who was trying to line up a second fight between the two. On May 3, 1972, Arum told Dave Anderson of the *New York Times*, "Perenchio blew a million in needless expenses and his TV locations were disorganized." Arum claimed he was in close negotiations with lawyer Bob Schulman, who was representing Jack Kent Cooke for the rematch. Jack originally wanted an August 1972 date but backed off because of the Munich Olympics. September and October were out because of the World Series. The fighters were guaranteed $5 million each for the encore engagement.

One of the more unusual sidelights in the proposed reunion came from Jack's birthplace of Hamilton, Ontario. A local sports promoter, George Goodrow, backed by Hamilton Mayor Vic Copps, promised a live gate of 50,000 by staging the fight in Ivor Wynne Stadium, home of the Tiger Cats football team, with closed-circuit TV next door at the baseball park projected at 20,000. The whole Hamilton package was estimated to gross $7 to $10 million for the live gate alone.

Jack's unsentimental answer: "No way."

When was the last time he had visited Hamilton?

"Eight or nine months ago, I think, the last time I was in Toronto."

"Are you coming back to Hamilton for the 125th anniversary this summer?"

"What birthday?"

As the months dragged on, Jack began using the terms "if there is a rematch" and was no longer adamant over the Forum as the site for the bout. Yank Durham, Frazier's manager was saying that "there are two or three things in the contract I can use to break it," and that Jack "only has a two-year option," a conflict with the "in perpetuity" statement. The real reason was that, as Joe Frazier told Jack's lawyer, Bob Schulman, in late 1972, he didn't want to fight in California because of the scoring rules, the weight of the gloves, and the size of the ring. These were all factors that were against him, he felt.

Three other events made a presentation of a second bout between the two boxing legends by Jack Kent Cooke void. The first was Frazier's surprise defeat by an undefeated (and svelte) George Foreman on January 22, 1973, delaying a championship rematch. The second was Jack Kent Cooke's heart attack, on March 8, 1973.

The third reason was caused by the cornerstone of Jack's cable empire, TelePrompTer. At the time of the fight between Ali and Frazier in March 1971, the stock, of which Jack now controlled nearly 16 percent, was trading at $59 a share. Two years later, shortly after Jack's heart attack, the stock was down to less than $2. Jack's investment in cable, which had a paper worth of more than $60 million the night of the fight, was now worth less than $2 million despite Jack's continuing stock purchases. It was enough to give a lesser man an ulcer as well as a heart attack.

Irving Berlin Kahn was responsible for the rise of Tele-PrompTer and also its downfall. Jack Kent Cooke was to become its savior, resurrecting it.

Kahn first jumped into cable in 1959 after the Twentieth Century Fox job. He bought a 750-subscriber system in Silver City, New Mexico, for $130,000 cash. His reason for buying the tiny

CATV operation was to run experiments in pay television. Irving Kahn had a long background with pay-per-view prize fights in a few cities, using microwave, particularly in San Francisco and Philadelphia. In his public papers at Pennsylvania State University's National Cable Television Center and Museum, titled "An Oral History," Kahn analzyed why he chose Silver City, New Mexico as his first system.

Silver City, a small town of just over 6,000, was 250 miles southwest of Albuquerque, near the Mexican border. It was an isolated community far away from any metropolis, large or small. The airport's single runway was unpaved. It was a great place to test pay-TV theories under a cloud of anonymity.

Kahn reasoned that if his pay-TV tests worked, his organization would have plenty of time to work out any bugs. And if they failed, nobody would find out. He wouldn't be embarrassed.

But shortly after he bought the system, he got a call in the dead of the night from his financial consultant. The consultant woke him up to tell him that he had gone over the books and that the system had a fantastic cash flow of more than $30,000 per year. Kahn had had no idea as to what the financial numbers were and he became very interested in the future of CATV. In the next sixty days he bought two more CATV operations: Farmington, New Mexico, and Rawlings, Wyoming—highly profitable systems in small unregulated areas.

Kahn next bought Elmira, New York, from Warner Brothers for 30 percent less than the going rate. Elmira was about to get its first VHF television station and the conventional wisdom at the time was that if a small town got a television station there would be defections from cable subscribers. Kahn played on those fears and was able to "steal" the system.

At first, both TV stations and subscribers paid to get on a cable television system. Television stations paid about $180 a month and subscribers paid $3 a month. The system would usually peak at about 50 percent of homes and then would remain static. Kahn started reducing TV station fees in order to get more stations on the system. Finally he reduced the fee to zero and then started paying the stations. The more stations that were available, the higher the subscriber count became and Kahn could then sell ancillary advertising at a higher price and also raise the subscriber fees. Kahn also began premium giveaways for sign-ups. One of the more successful was free installation and a cherry pie for anyone signing up on George Washington's birthday.

By early 1971, TelePrompTer systems and its franchises took up fifty-one lines of listings in the trade publication *TV Factbook*. But then Irving Kahn made a stupid mistake. He bribed Mayor Kenneth Tompkins of Johnstown, Pennsylvania, and two city councilmen, paying them a total of $15,000 when the Tele-PrompTer system was threatened in Johnstown under a rebidding process.[6] Then he lied about it to a grand jury and was socked with seventy counts of perjury. Kahn next sold all his Tele-PrompTer stock, driving down the price. The taint of scandal didn't help the company either. The stock went into free-fall, sometimes dropping several points a day. Kahn got the maximum penalty and was sentenced to five years, doing twenty months at Allenwood, a minimum security prison in Pennsylvania.[7] He spent part of his time studying cable by mail and actually getting a degree as a cable television technician.

Kahn resigned as president of TelePrompTer on the last day of March 1971, just weeks after Jack's triumph with the Ali–Frazier fight. Although Jack Kent Cooke had become almost a passive investor in TelePrompTer, he was the largest stockholder and had the most to lose. He had assigned the voting rights for more than 500,000 shares, the majority of his holdings, to Kahn, and even though he was on the board of directors, he had little power. He would have preferred to stay in California where he had a full plate. Besides the busy day-to-day operation of his new California sports empire—the Los Angeles Lakers, the Kings, the Forum—and his working Raljon cattle ranch of 13,300 acres, his marriage to Jean was beginning to crumble. There had already been suicide attempts by Jean, the result of Jack's years of frenetic business activities.

With Jack at first powerless, Irving Kahn was able to install his cofounder and close friend Hubert Schlafly as chief executive. Under his employment contract, Kahn remained as a consultant, getting his full salary of $225,000 a year, an apartment in Palm Beach, Florida, a company limousine, and a yacht that although purchased by Irving Kahn, was maintained by TelePrompTer. Jack, thinking this a bit excessive for a convicted felon on appeal, prepared a dissident slate of directors for the company's annual meeting in November 1971.

A bit of skirmishing delayed the election of a new board of directors until January 1972. On January 11, Jack Kent Cooke took effective control of TelePrompTer by electing eight members of the fourteen-person board of directors. Jack shoehorned Raymond P. Schafer, the former governor of Pennsylvania, into the chairman's position by February 1972, and put his trusted employee Bill Bresnan in as president. Although Schafer was brought in to give the company respectability, the investment community had lost faith, and the stock of TelePrompTer continued to plunge.[8] It didn't help that in 1973 TelePrompTer's trading was halted by the Securities and Exchange Commission.

With Jack now recovering from his March 1973 heart attack and both TelePrompTer and his marriage falling apart, a lesser man would have stayed in bed. But Jack flew to New York in October 1973 and installed himself as chairman and CEO, taking charge of every aspect of the country's largest cable operation, which now owned 139 systems in thirty-eight states, the background music system called Muzak, animated television programming, closed-circuit sports and entertainment programming, and electronic surveillance systems.[9]

When asked how he planned to run TelePrompTer, the Lakers, the Kings, and the ranch while recovering from a heart attack, Jack answered, "When you want something done, ask a busy man." He added he was in great shape and planned to be in the office everyday.

"I've never felt better," Jack Kent Cooke said, adding that the TelePrompTer board of directors had said the same thing. According to Jack, his doctors had just told him that he was among the 15 percent of heart patients whose electrocardiograms showed no evidence of previous heart attacks.

Jack brought in attorney Barry Simon of Shea and Gould, his New York law firm, and made him vice president and general counsel. He also made Richard Sykes, a CPA from Arthur Young, his head of accounting.

Shuttling between New York and Los Angeles, running two diverse operations on two different coasts, took a toll on Jack Kent Cooke. He was rumored to have had another heart attack in 1975, but denied it. At TelePrompTer, Jack implemented a defensive posture in order to save the company. He cut the work force 25 percent and stopped expansion into new communities, concentrating solely on existing systems. But TelePrompTer, now short of both cash and credit, continued to struggle. Although Jack's salary from TelePrompTer ran between $500,000 and $550,000 in the 1970s, varying because of bonuses, his real stake was in the stock of TelePrompTer. Larger players, like Warner, Time-Life, and the entertainment giants of the motion picture industry were all getting into cable and had much deeper pockets than Tele-PrompTer. So Jack made a pragmatic decision. He sold Tele-PrompTer in 1981 to Westinghouse Electric, Inc. for $650 million.

Jack walked away with just over $70 million for himself plus a consulting contract worth $4.65 million. It was delayed for a while by Ralph Nader, whose group claimed it "concentrated power and lessened diversity," but Jack beat Nader in the U.S. Court of Appeals. The FCC unanimously approved the deal on July 30, 1981, and the shareholders of TelePrompTer got $39 a share. When TelePrompTer was merged into Westinghouse, the firm had 1.4 million subscribers in thirty-two states.

Jack's cable era was over, for the time being. Later he would come to believe that satellite dishes would replace cable, but it was a short-lived opinion. In the decade and a half Jack Kent Cooke participated in the industry he was responsible for helping to bring cable television to nearly every state in America. He made hundreds of millions of dollars for himself and saved at least that much for thousands of TelePrompTer stockholders. He would return to it again, and on a much larger scale. But for now, he was free to concentrate on sports.

Notes

1. Ralph, Jack's oldest son, ran an ad agency in Los Angeles in 1966 called Cooke-Levitt, Inc. By this time he had married Carolyn, or Carrie, whom he had met at Scarborough Golf and Country Club in

Toronto, where she was a working model. They had three boys plus a girl, Carolyn Jean, who was born in 1961. Carrie later married NFL chief Pete Rozelle, after her divorce from Ralph. Jack's brother Hal had stopped working for Jack by 1966 and settled in Yuma, Arizona, in the real estate business. Only Donald remained with his brother, working out of New York.

2. Kahn was a nephew of the famous musical composer.

3. Andrew Jerrold "Jerry" Perenchio would go on to become a producer of major Hollywood films, most notably, *Blade Runner* with Harrison Ford and Sean Young. In 1979, he considered taking over Filmways, on the New York Stock Exchange, but after purchasing 5 percent, bowed out from acquiring the troubled moviemaker that later became Orion Pictures. Today his 11.5 acre house in Bel Air is among the most expensive in Los Angeles, estimated by *Newsweek* to be worth more than $32 million in 1991.

4. Ten years later Jack was asked the same question. This time he said, "Washington, after Paris, of course."

5. Among the "fun" Jack experienced in New York, was a personal sketch by Leroy Neiman, done at Toots Shor's. Jack had the gratis effort framed.

6. Kahn's reasoning for the bribe was that the $15,000 was cheaper than having to travel there for hearings. He figured the cost to go to Johnstown would have been $4,300 a day for him and his lieutenants.

7. Allenwood was later made famous as the "country club" penitentiary of Watergate's G. Gordon Liddy and other presidential assistants.

8. Later, Kahn, after getting out of prison, said that Schafer "didn't have a clue" when it came to running TelePrompTer.

9. Muzak, the elevator/restaurant music known as "slush" by the trade, saw some of Jack Kent Cooke's compositions spliced into its tapes in the early 1970s. TelePrompTer purchased the music system from Jack Wrather, a southern California businessman who owned the *Lone Ranger* and *Lassie* TV series.

CHAPTER
11
HOOPS AND HOOPLA

"It would be wonderful to watch a team you own play 365 days a year."

When Jack Kent Cooke paid $5,175,000 for the Los Angeles Lakers basketball organization on September 15, 1965, it was the highest price ever paid for a National Basketball Association team up to that time.[1] More surprising was the fact that Jack had written the check without ever seeing an NBA game, except for bits and pieces on television. A few months before, the Boston Celtics had been sold for $3 million and that had been a record.

Professional basketball franchises were escalating geometrically in the mid-1960s. The Syracuse franchise had been sold for $500,000 in 1963. The Baltimore Bullets had gone for $1,200,000 in 1964. But Jack's bid staggered the pro basketball community. The seller, Minnesota trucking king Robert Short, had paid just $150,000 for the franchise in 1957, when the team was known as the Minneapolis Lakers, and back when Clyde Lovellette was trying to fill the shoes of the great George Mikan. Short had moved them west in 1960. Jack's cash brought the NBA community of owners up to a level where they could now dream of prices approaching the sums paid for major league baseball teams. Jack, then, was an instant hero in the halls of the National Basketball Association, greeted by happy club owners everywhere.

Jack telephoned his son John, in La Crosse, Wisconsin, to tell him about his newest investment. "Call your mother at home this afternoon to say hello," he told John after reporting the good news. "But remember to call station-to-station. Money doesn't grow on trees you know."

Jack's burgeoning cable television franchise systems, were a great, albeit boring, way to make a lot of money. Certainly, flying into communities of fewer than 25,000 in states like Wisconsin, Wyoming, New Hampshire, and Oregon, wasn't Jack's idea of a fun time, particularly in light of his claustrophobia. Jack and Jean had far more good friends in glitzy and glamorous Los Angeles. Bette Davis was an intimate long before their move to southern California—they had entertained her at the Frybrook Road house in Toronto. Nick Mayo, Janet Blair, Jerry Lewis and, of course, Lorne Greene were usually available for dinner at the Brown Derby, the restaurant owned by old pal Bob Cobb, former owner of the Pacific Coast League baseball franchise, the Hollywood Stars. Jack and Jean also hung out with Dan and Mary Reeves, at least at first. Dan, who owned the Los Angeles Rams, lived close to Jack and Jean on Bellagio Road in Bel Air. But other than these people and a few lawyers and bankers, Jack Kent Cooke was still unknown in southern California during the early 1960s.

Unlike Toronto, where he was as well known as the mayor or the Canadian prime minister, with his name in the papers every week, he was virtually anonymous in the City of Angels. Only two small stories were published about Jack Kent Cooke between 1961 and 1965 in the *Los Angeles Times*. Meanwhile, the Toronto papers continued to headline Jack's every move as if he were the black sheep of a royal family living in voluntary exile.

Buying the Lakers changed all that. But it wasn't just a subconscious desire for attention that compelled Jack to own the Lakers' franchise. He had had the Lakers appraised at $4.5 million months before he bought them, and even though he knew he was overpaying, he felt that Los Angeles was one of the three most valuable properties in the league (Boston and New York being the other two). Sheer inflation would take care of the overpayment in a few years. But buying the Lakers was also a way to get the advantage for purchasing a National Hockey League franchise, the game Jack knew best, had played best, and loved best—at least at the time.

Jack knew that the NHL, after remaining a small fraternity of six teams for more than twenty-five years, was about to expand in a big way. In 1966 the league was scheduled to double in size and Jack, after making some inquiries around the NHL, felt he had an excellent chance when the expansion decision came up for a vote early in 1966. His friend Dan Reeves, who besides the Rams also owned the Blades, L.A.'s minor league club that was at the bottom of the Western Hockey League, also wanted an NHL franchise, as did three other syndicates. But this was business, and in 1965 Jack wanted a major league hockey team more than anything. Ownership of the Lakers legitimized him as a sports mogul and propelled him to the front of the bidding.

His speech the day after he bought the Lakers was, on one hand, a nod to basketball, but more so the beginning of a lobbying campaign for a hockey franchise. He hadn't been in a joint venture with anyone since the Roy Thomson days so he began by saying, "As usual I'm all alone.[2]

"This doesn't diminish one jot my desire to obtain an NHL franchise for the city of Los Angeles," he stated. "As a matter of fact, if anything, it increases my desire. It would make a beautiful combination of sports for the most beautiful sports arena I've ever seen in my life. When the basketball team is home, the hockey team would be on the road. It would mean for almost six months of the year we'd have control of the most important sport entities in Los Angeles. It would mean one big front office organization whose cost would be supported by two teams instead of just one."

Getting back to roundball, Jack said that "one of the first things I noticed when I moved out here was that on any street you'd see backboards and hoops. One of the beauties of this climate is they can play basketball all year round and outside. This town has been intensely interested in basketball in recent years because of the championship caliber of our college teams and of course, the Lakers" (they had just lost out to the Celtics for the world championship).

He also waxed rhapsodic about the Los Angeles Sports Arena: "It's the most beautiful building for sports you'll ever see. It's won all kinds of architectural awards on an international basis. Why, the aisles are wider than my office, and they don't even let anyone loiter in those aisles."

During the six months that remained until the NHL was expected to decide which cities would be chosen, Jack turned on the charm. He visited every city in the league and ingratiated himself with their team owners. He let the minor league Blades pick a fight with him. They tried to get an injunction to keep his proposed hockey team out of the Los Angeles Sports Arena. Jack didn't mind. The Coliseum Commission let it be known that it wanted Dan Reeves to get the NHL franchise. The commission thought that if it froze Jack out by awarding the Blades a three-year extension for the arena, Jack's team would have nowhere to play. Jack Kent Cooke didn't mind that either—he wanted his own sports palace. He took an option on five pieces of land around the Los Angeles area and prepared to build what Los Angeles Mayor Sam Yorty would later call "the most beautiful sports theater in America," a structure the *London Times* would describe as "one of the better designed buildings in the last half century."[3] Named "The Forum," Jack himself would modestly describe it as "the finest arena built since the original Roman Coliseum."

When he made his presentation to the NHL governors during the first week of February 1966, a Toronto writer described the fifty-three-year-old, former wonder boy this way: "His dark suit was open to expose a tasteful vest, a black knit tie festooned a shirt of sober blue. A skin infield is springing up where his hair used to be, but his eyes remain bluer than an Alaskan hitchhiker's thumb. His high-watt smile came from a powerhouse of confidence."

Jack's presentation consisted of a fifteen-page brief to each governor that detailed his credentials—his 25 percent ownership of the Washington Redskins, his 100 percent ownership of the Lakers, his success in the 1950s with the Maple Leafs baseball club. But what may have impressed the NHL executives most was a statement from the Security National Bank of Beverly Hills that Jack's deposits at the bank averaged in the low millions and his net worth was more than $10 million.

Part of Jack's presentation was letters of reference from a VIP network he had built up over the years. First on the list was Roy Thomson—now Lord Thomson, a second Baron of Fleet—thanks to a tap on the shoulders by Queen Elizabeth II. Lawyer friends William Shea and Edward Bennett Williams were next. Dan Rooney, president of the Pittsburgh Steelers, and John McHale, then president of the Atlanta Braves, weighed in, as did Warren Giles, president of the National Baseball League, and Gabe Paul, owner of the Cleveland Indians. Governor Edmund "Pat" Brown of California, whom Jack had backed in his election bid, also endorsed the new arrival to southern California.

Jack promised the NHL committee a new 16,000-seat arena built for hockey first and basketball second.[4] It worked. Jack Kent Cooke and Los Angeles received one of six new franchises awarded by the NHL, at a fee of $2 million per city, and a guarantee to build, get, or renovate an arena that would seat at least 12,500. Jack beat out four syndicates for the L.A. rights, which became the first NHL franchise ever to be owned by a single entity—all the rest being held by partnerships or corporations. The other new teams were San Francisco–Oakland, St. Louis, Minneapolis, Philadelphia, and Pittsburgh—all major American cities. This rankled many Canadians who thought Vancouver should have been included. Buffalo made a strong bid but was shut out because it "was too close to Toronto."

Scott Young wrote in the *Globe and Mail* that having Jack in the NHL was a reason for all Canadians to want to live a few years longer. He envisioned lively battles between the Maple Leafs hockey team and the Los Angeles club, alluding to the fact that John Bassett, the largest Toronto hockey club stockholder, was a longtime enemy of Jack Kent Cooke. Young summarized Jack's twelve-year disappointment in getting major league baseball in Toronto and cited Bassett's failure to join with Jack in building an all-purpose stadium for both the Toronto Argonauts football club, which Bassett owned, and Jack's Maple Leafs baseball team. It didn't help either that Bassett headed the group that beat Jack out for the TV license.

"I do not know why Bassett might dislike Cooke, either, except for about 100 public remarks Cooke made that I can recall offhand," Young wrote. "To quote only one, 'I would like to see how many people go to see John Bassett's minor league football when we have major league baseball in here.' "

Newspaper scribes aside, nothing was going to upset Jack on his day of triumph. "Happiest day I've ever known," Jack exulted. "I haven't slept for twenty-four hours from sheer excitement."

Less than a year after buying the Lakers, Jack now had a hockey team, was building what he promised would be the arena of the century, and was making noises about a professional soccer team as well. He had become a star in a city of stars, and suddenly his green Bentley, with the initials still scrolled on the side, was noticed.[5] Table number one at Chasen's was his virtually anytime, although Jack would often pull the elegant luxury car through a drive-in fast-food emporium and grab a hot dog.

As he had done with the Maple Leafs, Jack plunged right in during his first season as owner of the Lakers. No detail was too small to overlook. No source of revenue was too tiny to miss. Just weeks after buying the Lakers he attended a game and saw the ball boys down on their hands and knees mopping up perspiration from the floor. The new owner thought it was undignified. He solved it by having terry cloth fastened to brooms so the crew could do the job standing erect. When he sent out solicitations for season tickets by direct mail, even the postage was underwritten. An ad for Wilson Meat Products went on the back of the envelopes pushing "The Franks the Athletes Prefer." That paid for the stamps.[6] He devised community tie-ins like Pasadena Night or Long Beach Night and relied on the local media for free publicity, which eliminated the need to advertise. He installed special equipment inside the L.A. sports arena so that the fans could pick up the Laker broadcasts by Chick Hearn on transistor radios inside the concrete and steel building. This helped raise the Lakers' ratings and thus the amount of revenue the team received from radio. He dug into his past as a pop song and jingle writer and rewrote the Lakers' fight song. Jack added a little bit of the old Maple Leaf hoopla by having celebrities sing the national anthem at every home game and lead the audience in an old-fashioned pledge of allegiance. There were even poetry readings, a daring concept, to say the least, for a basketball crowd.

Jack also added to revenues by shrinking the press area. Before, the press was on both sides of the court, but now they were moved to just one side. The former press area became a "celebrities row" frequented by Jack and his entourage, which included Doris Day, Tony Curtis, Peter Falk, Walter Matthau, and Jerry Lewis. Jack's mother Nancy, who lived nearby (his father Ralph had died on

November 15, 1962), attended nearly every game and later would earn the title "Queen of the Forum" after Jack's own stadium was inaugurated. Even Jean, whose mother had also settled in southern California, now professed to be a basketball fan.

"When Jack came home and told me he had bought the Lakers, I said, what's that?" Jean loyally told the *Los Angeles Times*. "I had never seen a professional basketball game. I sat through thirteen years of baseball and it's boring, but I love basketball. It's so exciting." Jean added that Ralph and John, her two sons had given her six grandchildren. "Five boys and a girl," Jean said, "or a basketball team and a girl."

Although Jack said he would leave the day-to-day operation of the team to coach Fred Schaus and general manager Lou Mohs, that didn't prevent him from seeking out deals and talent, despite the lack of a basketball heritage. He was already studying and memorizing NBA talent and within months knew nearly every player's record in the league.

And it certainly didn't stop Jack from letting his opinions about basketball be known. He would sit with his entourage of celebrities at midcourt and heckle the players when they made a mistake, and shout encouragement when they made good plays, both in a voice so loud that virtually everyone in the arena could hear him. This behavior can be seen as a preamble to the intensity he would show in his owner's box at RFK stadium in Washington. During the beginning of Jack's second season, Laker forward Rudy La-Russo got in a fistfight with New York's Willis Reed. It turned into a melee and resulted in LaRusso being benched for the first time in his career. While Jack shouted at the players, he would also stare at LaRusso on the bench. LaRusso returned the dirty looks. A week later the forward was traded.

But that didn't end the LaRusso story. LaRusso refused to be traded and retired instead, blasting Jack Kent Cooke. "When the owner is at courtside, watching every move you make, it's difficult" he said. "The whole thing was not conducive to good basketball. There was a mountain of pressure. We were never in a position to just go out and play." And then referring to former owner Bob Short, LaRusso said, "Maybe absentee ownership wasn't that bad at all."

LaRusso began attending games as a spectator, receiving cheers from the crowd. Then two fans took up a petition in favor of reinstating him and also blasting Jack. They got hundreds of signatures. "We realize that the purchase of a ticket neither assumes a victory in a game nor gives us any managerial role. But please," the petition read referring to the aborted LaRusso trade, "if you cannot find a trader who is shrewd, at least find one who is lucky."

That did it. Jack surrendered and reinstated LaRusso to the team. "I have learned of the extenuating and unique circumstances from Rudy's standpoint," Jack said at a quickly called Beverly Hilton Hotel press conference. "I agree with Rudy on this score. In light of that and the pleasant things Rudy has said to me this morning, I accept his apology."

But although Jack may have accepted LaRusso's "apology," the defeat in the matter, was clearly his. Jack was, and still is, a pragmatist in matters of both business and play.

The Lakers were a superb team during Jack's first year as owner. Led by the University of West Virginia's best contribution to the NBA, Jerry West, who averaged thirty-one points a game and was second only to Wilt Chamberlain in league scoring, Los Angeles won the Western division in 1965–1966 and reached the finals against the Boston Celtics. In the series for the championship, the Lakers upset the Celtics 133–129 in the first game in the Boston Garden. It was memorable basketball. The match pitted Hall of Fame forwards Elgin Baylor and Jerry West against the ultimate in defensive skills, Bill Russell, who was near the end of his playing career. But Boston's coach, Red Auerbach, who was one of the best in the business, had won seven straight championships coaching the Celtics and had announced before the start of the year that the 1965–1966 season would be his last as a coach. Auerbach wasn't about to end his career as a runner-up.

Just before the start of the second game, Red Auerbach announced that Bill Russell would be the new Celtics coach. The news gave the Celtics the emotional lift that Auerbach had hoped for: Boston won the next three games, two of which were in Los Angeles. But Jack's team rose to the occasion and won the next two with Elgin Baylor scoring 41 points in one of them, forcing a final match at the Boston Garden. Although the score in the last game was 95 to 93, the Celtics grabbed an early lead and the score is not indicative of the huge margin Boston enjoyed going into the last quarter.

If the Lakers had won the NBA playoffs, Jack could have claimed two champions that season. He had also plunged into the fledgling United Soccer Association, the forerunner of the North American Soccer League that Jack himself would spearhead. The United Soccer group simply "leased" the top teams from around the world to play in the U.S. in their off season. Jack's team, the British Wolverhampton Wanderers, was renamed the Wolves in Los Angeles and won the league title. Jack paid just $250,000 for the privilege, but may have lost a little more as the season progressed. Soccer was already sending out warning signals that it would never be a draw in the U.S.

"They were the youngest team in the league," Jack recalled after the season, "and a second-division club back home. Maybe those know-it-all sportswriters should be reminded of that when they sneer at my hockey team, the youngest in the NHL, and admittedly mostly minor leaguers, until now."

Jack impetuously offered to buy the Wolverhampton Wanderers from their British owners, offering a flat $1 million. He was turned down. A member of the club's board of directors, Wilfred Sproson, told him, "There's not enough money in the world to buy the Wanderers."

Jack Kent Cooke now had a huge challenge facing him, greater than anything he had faced in Toronto. And although he publicly professed to be a "homebody," the strain of what lay ahead eventually cost him his marriage to Barbara Jean Carnegie Cooke.

Consider. He was the "hands-on" owner of one of the most valuable franchises in the National Basketball Association. He was trying to translate a lifelong dream—ownership of a major league hockey team—into a winner that could compete immediately with his Canadian rivals, Toronto and Montreal. He was attempting to get a new major league, the North American Soccer League, off the ground. He had just put himself on the line for nearly $17 million for a new sports arena, in a town that already had an indoor stadium. A commission for the L.A. Sports Authority, was actually charging him with a sports monopoly, saying it would lead to higher ticket prices. Outside sports, he was literally racing other entrepreneurs to get the largest slice of the cable television pie before the rest of the business world caught on. And he was doing all this virtually alone, without the benefit of a deeply delegated organization.

Outwardly, Jack was the proverbial darling of the L.A. press. He was the man who was daring to thumb his nose at the local government and build an indoor stadium without even a bond issue. He became the Walter Mitty fantasy of every jock in America, a man who owned four major sports teams and lusted after more—someone who said that it would be wonderful to watch a team you own "play 365 days a year."

Meanwhile, Barbara Jean Carnegie Cooke, surrounded by servants, with her own Aston-Martin (identical to the exotic car driven by James Bond in the movies), now wearing original gowns and living in a dream Bel Air mansion, would attempt suicide in 1965. It would be the first of four attempts prior to a final, bitter separation that would take place just a little over a decade later.

In hindsight, Jack was clearly headed for a heart attack. The years of several packs of cigarettes a day and hard-charging, sixteen-hour work periods were beginning to catch up with him. He was verging on obesity, fifteen to twenty pounds over his normal 160 pounds. He would go on sporadic diets, cutting out all starches until an emotional crisis hit, which was at least once a week, when he would end it on a binge of cake and ice cream. Jack Kent Cooke was on the way to a disaster—the breakup of a long marriage and a crisis that would threaten his own life.

Notes

1. Jack and Bob Short originally agreed upon an even $5 million until they quarreled about the right to $350,000 worth of advance ticket sale money that was in escrow. They split it down the middle.
2. Dan Reeves offered Jack 49 percent of the Rams for $7 million and also a piece of the Blades. Jack was no longer willing to join in

partnerships, a rule he broke just once, in 1971, when he joined with Jerry Perenchio for the Ali–Frazier fight, a necessity because of the short time frame.

3. Roy Thomson owned the London *Times* at the time and also later served on the board of directors of the Forum.
4. Jack's promise of a new arena was the clincher. Every NHL team in 1967 played in a privately owned facility and Jack's competitors for the Los Angeles franchise all were content to tell the NHL that they would put the team in the L.A. Sports Arena, which was government owned.
5. Jack paid $28,000 for the car. He still owns it today, and its value has more than doubled.
6. The first week Jack was in full control of the Redskins he complained about the player's roster being typed on several sheets of typing paper and ordered the names printed back-to-back, thus cutting paper use for the Xerox photocopier in half.

CHAPTER
12
SIX KINGS AND A JACK
"Why not call it the Fabulous Forum?"

On July 1, 1966, Jack Kent Cooke announced he had purchased a former golf course on 29.5 acres in Inglewood, California, on the south side of Los Angeles, from the White, Book, and Fisher land development company for $4,014,340.63.[1] He said he would erect his own arena on the land, and he said the building itself would take up 3.5 acres. The structure would seat 15,048 for hockey; 16,602 for basketball; 17,526 for boxing; and 14,504 for the circus. His architect was Charles Luckman, who had just designed the new Madison Square Garden. The construction company was C.L. Peck.

The budget for the building was $11 million, financed privately in part by Atlantic-Richfield Oil.[2] Construction costs would run just $1.2 million over projection. The arena was completed fifteen months after the first shovelful of dirt was dug on September 15, 1966.

The first things decided upon were the columns. Tall, simple, unadorned columns, eighty of them, each 57 feet high, weighing a ton per foot. They were the columns of Jack's boyhood home on Neville Park Boulevard in Toronto, multiplied by twenty.

The architect had first shown Jack something completely different but Jack didn't like it.

"What I want is something 6,000 miles east of here and 2,000 years ago," Jack told him. A designer started to draw Greek and Roman columns. Jack looked over the artist's shoulder.

"That's the beginning of what I want," he told him.

Jack began calling the place "The Forum." It was a perfect

circle of a building in the center of a treeless lot that would park 4,000 cars.

Jack was ecstatic. "Perhaps 200 years from now—or even 2,000—people will say that The Forum was one of the finest buildings erected during the twentieth century," he said with typical understatement. Less eloquently, he would later sputter, "It's man's greatest tribute to athlete's foot."

But it was, and always will be, the house that Jack built.

"You know," Jack Kent Cooke told the new chief broadcast announcer for the Forum, Chick Hearn, "this place needs a special adjective, something more than just 'The Forum.' "

"Well, Jack," said Chick, after thinking it over for about three and a half seconds. "Why not call it the Fabulous Forum?"

"Wonderful," said Jack, "really wonderful. And by the way, there will be a little something special in your pay envelope this week."

On Friday, inside Chick Hearn's pay envelope, besides his regular salary check, was a wallet-size photo of Jack. And everyone in the building was instructed to answer the phone, "Fabulous Forum."

As for hockey, the Kings were costing Jack a lot more than the $2 million expansion fee. He was pledged to pay a $1 million indemnity to the Blades and the Western Hockey League for usurping their territory. Dan Reeves was happy to fold the Blades, take the money, and run. Jack also bought the Springfield Indians (from NHL myth Eddie Shore) of the American Hockey League for $900,000. He changed their names to the Kings as well, and made them his chief farm club. Then there was the cost of the players.

On June 6, 1967, which the NHL termed D day, the first expansion draft of the NHL took place in Montreal. Jack's "mazel" that morning was in fine form—he won by lottery the right to choose the first player.

"Los Angeles draws Terry Sawchuk, from Toronto," Jack said, in a loud clear voice. He had chosen one of the top goalies ever to play in the NHL, a highly paid master of the nets, as his initial pick. There was one problem: Sawchuk was now in his sixteenth NHL season, was thirty-seven years old, and had more scar tissue on his body than a third-degree burn victim. His high $40,000 salary, combined with his losing more than a step or two, made him an expendable item. Jack, sensing the fading star might fill a few seats in his new arena, grabbed him from the Maple Leafs unprotected squad. The rest of Jack's picks were a bunch of young minor league players that nobody had heard of—Gord Labossiere, Bob Wall, Ed Joyal, Paul Popiel, Terry Gray, and Brian Campbell. Of these, only Sawchuk had matinee appeal.³ Dick Beddoes of the *Globe and Mail* said that Sawchuk would be safer in Vietnam than behind a line of Jack's players, and he called the new Kings, the L.A. Clowns.

That there was already bad blood between Jack and the Maple Leafs before the Kings had even played a game was evident at the draft. The Leafs hockey club had a crowd favorite, a veteran left wing and sometime center by the name of Red Kelly. Unlike Terry Sawchuk, Kelly, thirty-nine, had been planning to pack it in after playing on eight Stanley Cup winners in twenty NHL seasons for Detroit and Toronto. At his age, he didn't expect to be claimed by anyone. Jack had romanced Kelly before the draft, and let it be known that he planned to hire him afterward as his head coach. He didn't believe any of the other six teams would claim a bald, high-salaried player like Kelly.

But as the expansion draft progressed, the Leafs lost two young left wings, and on the tenth round Punch Imlach, the Toronto general manager, drafted their "retired" player to fill in. Jack was furious. He thought that Toronto had done this to him out of spite. The Leafs, for their part, complained to NHL president Clarence Campbell that Jack had worked out a hidden agenda with Kelly before the draft and charged Jack Kent Cooke with "tampering." The matter was settled a few days later with the Kings having to give the Leafs their fifteenth draft choice for Kelly's return.

The Kings' first preseason training camp was held at Guelph, Ontario, in September 1967. Jack sent his new play-by-play announcer, Ken "Jiggs" McDonald, ahead with instructions to get "a room and three meals a day for each player" at a budget of "no more than $9 a man." McDonald thought it was nearly impossible but made deals in and around Guelph, including one which had a motel removing all its TV sets and renting them back to the players to break even. McDonald made the deal work out to $9.25 per man, but Jack was not pleased. "That's my money you just spent," Jack told his employee referring to the 25 cents per man over budget. Terry Sawchuk was not above squeezing a few extra dollars from the rookies either. The team was put in out-of-the-way motels and Sawchuk, the only player with a car, charged each player he drove to the practice rink.

Jack gave Jiggs so much to do that the young announcer told him it was impossible. Jack proceeded to tell Jiggs how it could be done.

After Jiggs left the room, Jack turned to one of his assistants and said, "Well, how was that?"

"Like Churchill, Jack," the employee said.

"Hell," Jack said, "better than Churchill."

When Jack returned to Toronto a few months later, Conn Smythe, former president of Maple Leafs Garden, turned up the temperature at a Variety Club charity lunch. "I knew him before he brought Kent into the business. He was simply Jack Cooke," Smythe jabbed. "Perhaps he was thinking of royalty even then. He knew he'd become a King."

The Kings played their first two games in the NHL in 1967 at Long Beach because of the Blades dispute. The rest, prior to the opening of the now "Fabulous" Forum, were played in the Los Angeles Sports Arena, the Blades having folded after Jack paid the fee for "territorial invasion" to the Western Hockey League. Neither game was successful from a financial standpoint. The Kings drew less than 12,000 for their first two games and midway through the season were fourth in attendance among the new expansion clubs, despite having the largest population from which to draw. For the first six home dates they drew just 48,400.

But there were bright moments as well. On November 10, 1967, with the largest crowd yet present at the L.A. Sports Arena, the Kings hammered the defending Stanley Cup champions, the Maple Leafs, 4 to 1, and solidified their lead among the expansion club division.[4]

Jack was ecstatic. He kissed a Toronto sportswriter on both cheeks, kissed Jiggs McDonald, and was the first man in the dressing room, where he kissed his coach, Red Kelly.[5]

"You're the most wonderful bunch of guys in the world,"

yelled the multimillionaire, addressing the Kings players. "I wish you were all my sons!"

"So do we," piped up a brash young right wing by the name of Howie Hughes, from St. Boniface, Manitoba.

That was one of the good times. More typical was an away game that took place at Maple Leafs Garden on Jack's birthday in October 1967. Jack, putting a good face on a now difficult marital situation, had Jean with him in a front row box and when the Leafs, the symbol of what he had wanted in Toronto—tradition, respect, and adulation—took a 2–0 lead, Jack leaped into the air, turning a 360-degree arc like a bull that had just been stuck with a banderilla, and faced the Toronto crowd.

"We were down 2–0 to Chicago and came back to score four goals," he roared. "We'll do it again tonight!"

If there were any gift Jack Kent Cooke could have had for his fifty-fifth birthday, it should have come in Toronto. A win in the city that had rejected him. He had proven himself time and time again, and what had he been given in return? A major league baseball stadium? A television station? A daily newspaper? Jack Kent Cooke could have run those businesses better than anyone and either old money or Canadian bureaucrats had beaten him back too many times.

The Kings were down 2 to 1 now. It was the third period. There was plenty of time left.

"We must win. We've got to win," the *Globe and Mail* reported him as repeating over and over as he sat forward, his arms over the railings. He was completely absorbed in the game, maintaining his concentration even as he signed for the many business telegrams delivered to his seat.

The *Globe and Mail* said afterward that he was so tense and excited that many observers expected that "a doctor might have an opportunity to use his stethescope."

"Come on Brian, I mean Terry," he yelled. "I know the players by name, not by number." And when Brian Smith almost tied the game, he punched a friend in the box hard and Jean Cooke as well. After the game, she complained of a sore arm.

157

"We'll get another one now," Jack yelled with six minutes to go and his Kings behind 3 to 2. "We'll tie it up and go on to win."

The Leafs scored another goal and wrapped it up, 4–2. Jack slumped in his seat, a tired expression on his face. For all the hundreds of triumphs he had enjoyed, for all the wins he had experienced, one loss could depress Jack Kent Cooke for days.

But for every bad evening there were many more great moments. Jack would often practice with the players, living out his childhood fantasies. He would lace up his own skates and work out with the Kings. Practice after practice, he would go one on one with Terry Sawchuk, trying to put the puck past him. Sawchuk wouldn't let him score.

Jack finally figured out how. As he skated toward Sawchuk he turned his head to the left and looked up into the stands.

"Hey, Terry, isn't that your wife sitting up there?"

Terry Sawchuk looked up in the stands and as he did, the former Malvern Collegiate sports star flipped the puck past him. Jack quit while he was ahead.

The gala grand opening of the "Fabulous" Forum took place on December 30, 1967, at the private Forum Club.[6] At the club, inside the completed building, Jack had invited a thousand people, including several hundred from Toronto. It was a veritable "This Is Your Life, Jack" as far as old friends and employees were concerned and even enemies were invited, given amnesty for the night.

Torontonians included George Gooderham, of the Gooderham family who had sold Jack CKEY, Sam Shopsowitz, the hot dog king who had sold the Maple Leafs baseball team buns and sausages, Al Dubin, Lorne Greene, and even Roy Thomson.[7] Hollywood was represented by Jack Lemmon and his wife Felicia Farr, Jimmy Durante, and Rhonda Fleming.

"How are your 148 newspapers?" a reporter asked Thomson.

"One hundred sixty-eight," he quickly corrected. "I'm shooting for 200."

"Do you ever write an editorial, or anything?"

"No, writers I can hire. I spend most of my time buying new businesses—that's a full-time job."[8]

After the reception and buffet, Jack's ushers, tanned southern California toga girls, wearing copper-colored miniskirted costumes that vaguely smacked of a Cecil B. DeMille interpretation of Roman garb, gave guests a tour of the building and then led them to their seats for the first event ever held in the Forum—a 2:30 afternoon game against the Philadelphia Flyers.

Lorne Greene was master of ceremonies for the pregame show. Harve Presnell sang the "Star Spangled Banner" and a young girl, Jackie Shabassion, performed the Canadian national anthem, "O Canada." Then the giant green and gold ribbons that stretched the width of the rink were cut by Jean Cooke. A fashion writer described her as "stunning, in a parrot-green wool coat."

The Kings spoiled the day by going scoreless and losing to the Philadephia Flyers 2–0. The next night, on New Year's Eve, the Lakers mitigated the Kings' loss by easily beating the expansion San Diego Rockets, 147–118 before a good crowd of just under 15,000.

On New Year's day, Sam Shopsowitz and Al Dubin visited Jack at his Bel Air home on St. Cloud Road.[9] Jack showed them the grounds and led them in through a back door.

"Be sure and wipe your feet, Sam," he told Shopsy, the hot dog king.

"Hey, Jack," Shopsowitz asked, "How come you didn't tell Al to wipe his feet?"

"I don't have to , Sam," Jack replied. "Al worked for me for eight years. He's been trained."

But there was more to the "Fabulous" Forum than Lakers and Kings. Jack got a quick lesson in show business box-office appeal and actually became a rock and roll promoter. It is a title he probably would not enjoy today, as he travels easily with politicians and journalists whose tastes run to more serious musical fare.

"Now let's see you get me some good shows," Jack is quoted as telling his booking agents in one newspaper story in 1968. "No more Tony Bennett or the Smothers Brothers, eh?

"We had The Cream in here and they did $206,000 gross. The Supremes did $106,000. Who needs Tony Bennett or the Smothers Brothers? He did $60,000 and the Smothers did $74,000."[10]

159

Sports Illustrated later called Jack Kent Cooke the Sol Hurok of sport. For a short time at least, he could have been called the Sol Hurok of rock, a testament to his ability to adapt to any business challenge.

The "Fabulous" Forum is a great building for players and fans in terms of design.[11] Every view is unobstructed. The roof of the Forum is designed like the spokes of a bicycle wheel; forty huge cables stretch above the crowd. The seats—twenty-one inches wide versus eighteen in most arenas—on the west side of the expanse are gold, on the other side, orange. The colors of the seats gradually shift to a lighter shade the further one gets from the rink or basketball court.

Adapting to a new era of pampered players, Jack Kent Cooke thought of nearly everything. In the hockey dressing rooms the benches that the players sit on were three inches closer to the floor than in the basketball locker rooms, an accommodation to the differences in their heights. There was also a players' lounge with a color television, a house-finding service, financial planning help, and free tax assistance. Each player was given a small safe to store his valuables.

But Jack maximized the seating space, as he had done in the Los Angeles Arena, this time moving the press upstairs, seventy feet away from the action. Jack told Chick Hearn, the Forum announcer, that he alone could sit at courtside. Chick asked if the opponent's broadcasting crew could be at courtside also. When Jack said no, Chick said that he'd come down when they did.

It must have galled Jack Kent Cooke that in hockey, a game that had been a lifelong passion with him, he now had a team that was mediocre year after year, partly because of his efforts. Yet, the Lakers, who played in a sport to which Jack had come late in life, was one of the best teams in the league each season. That was also because of the efforts of Jack Kent Cooke. Jack put into motion the deal that brought Wilt Chamberlain to the Lakers in 1968. In turn that led to the chemistry that eventually won the team its first NBA championship, in 1972.

Jack had reached the conclusion in both basketball and hockey that "the draft be damned." New players didn't draw like established superstars—the only drawback was superstar salaries. Jack got Wilt by dealing Darrall Imhoff, Archie Clark, and Jerry Chambers to the Philadelphia '76ers on July 9, 1968, for the seven-foot, one-inch superstar. Chamberlain was depressed because in the 1967–1968 season the '76ers had the best record in the NBA, 62–20, but had failed to even make the finals in the playoffs. When his coach, former USC great Alex Hannum, deserted Philadephia for Oakland in the rebel American Basketball Association, Wilt was ready for a change. And Jack was willing to pay Chamberlain's salary demand, which made him the highest paid player in the NBA. Wilt's Laker contract—$250,000 a year for four years—was more than the combined salaries of the three players Jack traded.

Jack thought that with Wilt Chamberlain in the middle, his other two stars—"Mr. Outside," Jerry West, and "Mr. Inside," Elgin Baylor—would form a dream forward line that could terrorize the NBA for years. He had already bumped Fred Schaus upstairs to management and put in Butch van Breda Kolff, one of the few men to work as a coach in both the NBA and the soon-to-fold American Basketball Association. But the dream team of Baylor, West, and Chamberlain didn't gel in 1968. For one thing Baylor was thirty-four and his legs were nearly gone. Still, Jack's star line did average 72 points a game and won the division, but the 1968–1969 win–loss record was the same as Philadelphia's, the team that Jack had given up three players for to get Wilt. In fact, the Lakers were almost outdone for attention by UCLA, playing on the other side of town. The Bruins were led by a young Lew Alcindor, who had learned his skills on the playgrounds of New York City. Just before his last year at UCLA, Alcindor quietly converted to the Muslim religion and changed his name to Kareem Abdul-Jabbar. Kareem meant generous, and Abdul, servant of God.

Jack loved being a small part of the players' lives but often baffled them with his $3 words. Jack, who had puzzled his radio sales staff by reading the dictionary the night before and spouting words of wisdom they didn't understand, was by now a walking thesaurus. He baffled the ballplayers with his phrases. One time he said to Chamberlain, "the perpetual peregrinations of a pro basketball club are costly."

"What's that word again?" the basketball star asked.

"Peregrinations," Jack said.

"Oh sure," Wilt said. "I didn't catch it the first time around."

He also amazed sports writers with his choice of words. He responded to a critical column written about him, calling it "a vile blow to my groin."

In the 1969 playoff finals, once more against the Celtics, the favored Lakers and Boston went to seven games. The rubber match at the Forum was a shoot-out in which both teams scored more than 100 points and culminated in an ending that once again foiled Jack's party. Expecting his investment in Chamberlain to be quickly rewarded, Jack had suspended thousands of balloons above center court—Forum employees spent the day blowing them up individually. Orders called for them to fall from the ceiling after the Lakers won. But the balloons stayed aloft, cradled in the catwalk, and the champagne fizzled rather than fizzed. Jack had hired the USC band to begin playing "Happy Days Are Here Again" the moment the game was over, but the Trojans' trumpets stayed mute. So did the ceremony that had been arranged at center court. The bubbly celebration, with bottles on ice, ready both in the locker room and in the press lounge for the wives and girlfriends of the players, remained capped. The perennial champions, the Celtics won again, 108–106.

After the loss, Jack's face, according to one observer, was "drained, colorless." A young employee made the mistake of going over to Jack and asking, "What do we do now, Mr. Cooke?" He was fired the next morning.

Jack was of the old school when it came to players' contracts, insisting that the athletes honor them. When one of his favorites, Jerry West, asked for a raise before his contract expired, he was in a quandary. He solved the problem by giving West an interest-free loan and instructing him to put the money immediately into an investment that Jack specified. West made more money on the deal than the amount he was asking Jack for. Jack got his "loan" back and the contract was never renegotiated.

Other sports investments were not as successful. The North American Soccer League was a disaster. Jack's team, called the Zorros, didn't draw, and to make matters worse, Dan Reeves established a rival team called the Toros. Today, when a writer tries to inquire about the soccer venture, Jack usually answers, "Don't ask."

The mediocrity of the Kings continued as well. Only the Lakers were consistent winners through the season, but always a bridesmaid, never a bride in the playoffs. In the 1969–1970 season they went all the way again, only to lose the last game of the finals to the New York Knicks. In 1970–1971 they won their division but folded against the new Milwaukee Bucks led by the recent UCLA graduate now known as Kareem Abdul-Jabbar.

But if the Lakers were stellar, the Kings so-so, and the Zorros terrible, Jack's marriage to Barbara Jean Carnegie Cooke seemed most shaky of all. They had separated for a short time in 1970 and although Jean would gamely smile to all at every Lakers and Kings game she attended, a few years later her attorneys would testify, "she felt like a puppet being dragged to dinners and events at the Forum," a contradiction of her public persona.

Jack's best year as owner of the Lakers was the 1971–1972 season. It may have been the best year any professional basketball team has ever had. Jack brought in Bill Sharman to coach—he was a local hero who had played at the University of Southern California years before. Wilt Chamberlain shot field goals with a 70 percent success record. Jerry West was still contributing, but Elgin Baylor had to crawl away on bad legs. He was replaced by Gail Goodrich, a former UCLA star.

It was a season of unparalleled excellence. The Lakers won thirty-three games in a row, an NBA record that has yet to be equaled. The streak began on November 5 and continued past Christmas and into the New Year, finally ending on January 9. They were led by the "rookie" coach, Bill Sharman, and a classic combination of veterans like Wilt Chamberlain and Jerry West, and younger players, Gail Goodrich and Jim McMillian. The NBA's most valuable player award though, went to Kareem Abdul-Jabbar of an otherwise mediocre Milwaukee Bucks, who had averaged 34 points a game. It would not go unnoticed by Jack Kent Cooke.

Including the playoffs, the Lakers went 81–16 for the year, with the final series against the New York Knicks a 4–1 romp, after losing the first game. Jack could finally drop the balloons. On May 7, 1972, the Lakers were champs.

But the championship was marred before and afterward by off-the-court controversies. The first centered around the playoff telecasts. The ABC broadcasts were blacked out in southern California and Jack picked up extra cash by going to a business he knew well—closed-circuit telecasting in movie theaters. However, ABC could show the games on a delayed basis and they did. Knowing this would dilute the gate at the theaters, Jack put pressure on the local media not to announce that the games would be carried on TV until after the closed-circuit broadcasts were nearly over, and made sure that the games weren't in the TV listings of the newspapers. The practice stopped when a newspaper accused him of "flimflam." And after the Lakers won the championship, a dispute arose as to whether or not coach Bill Sharman should get a bonus. The players were to divide $224,500 in playoff money or a little more than $17,000 per man. The NBA Players Association policy excluded coaches from sharing in the playoff money, so the players thought Jack would give Sharman at least the same amount as they received. But Jack gave the players a $1,500 per man bonus and told them to make up Sharman's bonus out of that. The players, who could add, figured that after they gave Sharman his share, their "extra" bonus from Jack would amount to $61 per player. They refused Jack's money, since they had received a larger bonus the year before when they hadn't won the NBA championship. Jack said it was a misunderstanding and that "I'm as innocent as a lamb. At no time did anyone want to exclude Bill, who molded this fine team," he said. This upsetting note to an amazing season ended at a club party on May 9, 1972, with a player joking, "share and share alike." Nobody smiled.

Less than a year later, the Washington Redskins made the Super Bowl for the first time. The game was played in the Los Angeles Coliseum. Jack, the absentee owner—he now had the majority of the stock—was on hand to greet the VIP plane when it landed in Los Angeles on January 11. The first evening he spirited away club president, famed lawyer Edward Bennett Williams, with Ed and Jane Muskie for dinner.

The Williams entourage in California was a liberal Democrat's Who's Who that included, besides Muskie, Ethel Kennedy, Joe Califano, Carl Rowan, eighty-one-year-old Milton King (a major stockholder still), and PBS television newswoman Nancy Dickerson. It was not a group that Jack would normally choose to have over for dinner on Saturday night. Although Jack Kent Cooke was now the majority owner and had given the "thumbs up" to hire "the future is now" zealot George Allen as coach, it was Williams' team.[12]

It was Edward Bennett Williams to whom Carl Rowan gave his special pork chop sandwich recipe that weekend. It was Williams who decided his Washington group of Democrats would sit in the stands and skip the imperial majesty of the visiting owner's box, leaving it in the hands of injured quarterback Sonny Jurgenson. In the early 1970s, the majority of players on the Redskins didn't even know who Jack Kent Cooke was. If Jack resented Williams then, he didn't show it. Uncharacteristically, he let Ed Williams have the spotlight.

That may have been just as well. In a dull game that didn't even sell out—there were nearly 9,000 empty seats in the Coliseum, which the NFL listed as no-shows—the Dolphins running back duo of Larry Csonka and Mercury Morris beat the Redskins 14–7. Billy Kilmer, although completing 50 percent of his passes, was not a factor, nor was Washington's prime back, Larry Brown, who was shut down by an obscure Miami defensive player, Manny Fernandez. The only Redskins score was by an interception made by safety Mike Bass, on a freak play. The Dolphins' kicker, Garo Yepremian, aborted a field goal, and attempted a pass. Bass intercepted the "fluttering duck" and ran it back forty-nine yards into the end zone.

Even though his team lost the Super Bowl, Jack could still claim several laurels. He had hired both Sharman, whom he had convinced to jump ship from the ABA's Salt Lake City team, and Allen, who had been lured to Washington with a salary of $125,000 a year, a record at the time. Both men were named

Coach of the Year during their first seasons. Sharman went all the way. Allen led the Redskins to only their sixth winning record in the last thirty-one years. The next year he went all the way to the Super Bowl.

Although there was a sports triumph nearly every day, the early 1970s were full of other, more serious pressures. Jack knew that his $50 million investment at TelePrompTer could fall apart. His marriage of thirty-six years to Jean was in total collapse. His sixteen-hour days at the "Fabulous" Forum had put so much fear in the men and women who worked for him that a "Cooke watch" was established to pass the word when he was on the premises. George Wallach, who worked in advertising sales for $14,000 a year, told Dave Kindred, then of the *Washington Post,* "I'll always be grateful to Cooke for showing me how fast I could run but I'd never work for him again. He wasn't human or compassionate. He'd publicly flog you or praise you. But I learned I could perform under the most intense pressure. It's like graduating from the Harvard Business School. When you go to Jack Kent Cooke Tech, people know that you've got something."

Jack had a heart attack just over a month after the 1973 Super Bowl. It should not have surprised anyone. A half-century of endless, pressure-filled days, aided by several packs of cigarettes finally took its toll. What is amazing is that it took so long to happen.

Notes

1. The land sold by the square foot, hence the pennies. Jack tried to get them to knock off the 63 cents but the owners wouldn't budge.
2. Atlantic-Richfield later agreed to sponsor all the Lakers and Kings games for ten years for a cost of $12 million.
3. Jack would have mortgaged the ranch to get Bobby Hull, the Wayne Gretzky of his day. Speaking in a bar in Barrie, Ontario, where the Kings were in preseason training in 1968, Jack said of the Chicago left wing, "Just think of him in Los Angeles. He'd be Charlie Chaplin, Douglas Fairbanks, and Mary Pickford rolled into one!"
4. The Kings actually had the best win–loss record among the expansion NHL clubs for the first two years. But they lost nearly $2 million so Jack began trading draft choices for big names. The team was me-

diocre for the rest of the twelve years it was owned by Jack Kent Cooke.

5. When Ken "Jiggs" McDonald's father died, Jack deposited $30,000 in a checking account at the Canadian Imperial Bank of Commerce and told the young Ontarian to draw on it as needed for funeral expenses. This is typical of the charity practiced by Jack, although he has had minor involvement with the Arthritis Foundation, the Little League Foundation, and of course, Variety Clubs International, where he is still a member.

6. A Forum Club membership was initially $1,000 a year.

7. Thomson served on the board of directors of the Forum, along with Edward Bennett Wiliams and Bill Shea.

8. A year before Thomson died, a writer asked him if he had any regrets. "Yes," Thomson is said to have replied. "I had hoped to have a net worth of $1 billion. I'm only worth $800 million and I don't think I'll make it."

9. By the late 1960s Al Dubin had risen through the ranks at Warner Brothers and was vice president for distribution for Warner's motion pictures in Canada.

10. Jack promoted everything at the Forum from an all-time record for the roller derby (more than 10,000), to a record live gate of $465,000 for the second Muhammad Ali–Ken Norton fight in 1973.

11. The "Fabulous" Forum now goes by a less exciting name, the Great Western Forum, the result of a California Savings and Loan deal with Dr. Jerry Buss, a former chemistry professor who bought the Forum from Jack in 1979.

12. Etty Allen, George's wife, said that her husband's coaching made her so tense she carried Maalox to every football game.

CHAPTER
13
THE UNRAVELING

". . . you want to live forever. I once thought I might, you know."

Jack Kent Cooke underwent his annual physical in 1973 on Thursday, March 8. The various examinations took four hours and Jack passed several tests. He went to the Forum for dinner at his private Forum club. After dinner, he planned to stay and see the Kings play the western division leaders, the Chicago Black Hawks. The Kings, mired in fifth place, were fighting for the last playoff slot.

Before he could order, he experienced an unusual feeling that began in his throat, with the pain spreading to his jaw. Jack didn't know what was happening but he knew it wasn't right.

"Excuse me, I have an important call to make."

Walking as quickly as he could across the Forum Club he tapped the Lakers team doctor, Robert Kerlan, on the shoulder and asked him to follow him to his office.

"There was pain, but it wasn't excruciating," Jack remembers. Kerlan had Jack lie on his back on the sofa and removed his shirt. Then he grabbed the phone and ordered an ambulance.

"You've had a coronary," Kerlan told Jack.

Jack tried to spring into action. "Keep everyone away. Keep those bloody newspaper men out! And radio! And TV!"

"Jack, for God's sake, lie down and shut up," Kerlan said.

The ambulance took him to Daniel Freeman Hospital, the closest one to the Forum. After treatment by the hospital staff, Jack's personal physician, Keith Agre, arrived. Jack Kent Cooke would stay in the hospital two weeks.

After returning home to Bel Air, Jack was more subdued, more introspective. At first, he divided his time between Bel Air and his Raljon Ranch, the 13,300-acre spread (just over twenty square miles) he had acquired in the Sierra Nevada mountains near Glenn-ville, a three-hour drive or a thirty-five-minute flight from Los Angeles.

Jack had paid $1 million cash for the ranch in late 1969. At that time it was stocked with some Black Angus cattle and a few cottages. Most of the time, Jack and Jean would go to the ranch by driving to Bakersfield from Los Angeles on U.S. Route 99, north on U.S. 65, then east on U.S. 155. A few times they flew by private plane. At first they enjoyed the ranch. It was new and they im-mediately wanted to make improvements.

One of Jack's first tasks was to design the main lodge, a house for entertaining guests and in which he and Jean would live when at the ranch. Jack Kent Cooke has said many times he once wanted to be an architect. At Raljon he got his wish.

The two-story redwood house he created was about 6,000 square feet—4,000 on the main level. In the living room, the ceiling opened to the roof line, which was forty feet from the floor. The style was that of a modified A-frame; the high walls on the first floor slanted steeply to meet at the roof peak on the second. Jack also created a dominant feature for the main room—a chan-delier that resembled the spokes of a wagon wheel without a rim. At the end of each spoke there was a light bulb.

Jack also designed a road system through the forty acres. In this area there were five cottages, a good sized house, and Jack and Jean's lodge. The road wound around the dwellings and then went back out to the main road. He also built a small five-acre pond and stocked it with bass and blue gills. After it was finished the new Redskins coach, George Allen (whom Jack had suggested the Redskins hire), dropped by and presented Jack with two swans which Allen had already named Jack and George. The swans didn't last long; when they disappeared, Jack told visitors they had been eaten by a mountain lion.

In the early 1970s John Cooke was moved from the sunless below-ground confines of the Forum ticket-selling operation and literally elevated several thousand feet above sea level, when Jack made him ranch manager at Raljon. John (who always was more dependent on his father than his elder brother Ralph), his wife Becky, and their two sons, John and Tommy, began living at the ranch.

By this time Jack had purchased and bred nearly 2,000 head of Brangus cattle—a cross between Black Angus and Brahman—that Jack had planned to make into a profitable cow–calf operation. There was also a forest on the property, mainly California white oaks—nearly 300,000 of them.

Once, on a long walk around his ranch in 1973, Jack wistfully said to a friend, "You know, you look around on a day like this and you want to live forever. I once thought I might, you know." Although his mortality had been revealed to him, Jack didn't slow down as much as his doctors had advised. And a year later he began to sometimes deny that what had taken place was even a heart attack and would say "I'm resentful that a thing like a coronary thrombosis would have the audacity to stop me from doing the things I want to do. Mentally, there's been no impairment whatsoever. Physically, yes."

Although Jack was at the Forum less after the heart attack, he made up for it by constant phone calls from home or the ranch. Sometimes he would call as often as three times an hour. He did quit his fifty-year smoking habit. Just before the heart attack, his cigarette addiction had increased to five packs a day. At first he considered tapering down, but when advised by a doctor that it probably wouldn't work and that "he was kidding himself," Jack quit cold turkey, on March 25, 1973. Using candy as a nicotine substitute, Jack gained eight pounds in three months. He started dieting.

While it might be expected that Jack's illness would repair his marriage to Jean, it didn't. Jack wanted the relationship of forty years to remain as it was, but Jean was looking for a way out. The separations and Jean's attempts at suicide continued.

Jack wrote Jean a love letter in his own handwriting on March 22, 1976, shortly before their final separation and Jean answered it the next day. Both letters are an accurate record of the couple's feelings toward each other.

Jack's letter to Jean contained many words of endearment. In his three-paragraph note, he lamented that both their days on earth were limited and that they should make the most of their time left. He proposed that their remaining years be lived and loved to the maximum so that they could spend their final years together in perfect harmony.

Jean's reply was not nearly so romantic. She began by thanking Jack for his pledge and confirmed that she still loved him. Then she went into a number of reasons why things weren't working out. Jean said that she was less than perfect, couldn't take the tension, and wanted more lighter moments. She didn't blame Jack, saying he couldn't help it, it was how he had become. Jean said that their future was predestined but both of them had made an effort.

Jack didn't let his crumbling marriage or his physical condition prevent him from flying back and forth to New York, and saving TelePrompTer. He also found time to pull off the two biggest trades in the Lakers' and Kings' histories. Jack was responsible for both parts of this one-two sports punch.

The first came on June 16, 1975, when Jack traded the core of his basketball team—Elmore Smith, Brian Winters, Dave Meyers, and Junior Bridgeman—for perhaps the best player of the pro game in this century, Kareem Abdul Jabbar. Kareem came back to Los Angeles with a journeyman ball player, Walt Wesley.

The trade came out of necessity. The Lakers' miracle 1971–1972 performance of thirty-three straight wins and a championship was over. The next year they had gone 60–22 in the regular season again going to the finals. There they lost to the Knicks 4–1.

The team was headed down. Before the 1973–1974 season began, Chamberlain, now thirty-seven and with more than a thousand games and half the NBA record book under his belt, got one more big payday by jumping to the ABA's San Diego club as head coach. Jerry West, thirty-five, was through as well. He was now only able to appear in about a third of the Lakers' games because of bad legs. Jack shored up the team by getting the well-traveled Elmore Smith—he would eventually play for four NBA clubs—from Buffalo in a trade and Connie Hawkins from Phoenix. But neither was a "franchise" player who would put fans in the seats or dominate games. The Lakers went 47–35 in 1973–1974 and were knocked out of the playoffs in the first round. Jack, who had told the *Los Angeles Times* "the only thing that hurts more than kidney stones is when one of our teams loses," wasn't ready to accept a losing Laker team. He was ready to act and Kareem was available.

When Jack Kent Cooke put together the deal for Kareem, he made the most of it. It was very important to him that the trade be kept secret. He planned to announce it at a lavish press unveiling at the Forum. Several hundred reporters and VIPs were invited.

"If this breaks before the press conference, you're all fired," he told his public relations staff.

When the time came, the lights dimmed, and a spotlight shone on the curtains at the south end of the Forum. A policeman ripped the curtains open and Chick Hearn intoned, "And now I give you Kareem Abdul-Jabbar."

But there was no Kareem. He had gone to the men's room just before the announcement. Jack was furious. The seven-foot, two-inch center eventually showed and the day, if not the moment, was saved. Chick Hearn modestly said it was "the most dramatic and explosive moment in the history of sport," and Jack said he had reached "an impossible dream."

Many thought differently. Letters from the public and the press said that Jack had given up too much and had made the Milwaukee Bucks into a dynasty. Letters filled the L.A. newspapers criticizing the trade. Junior Bridgeman, the key player in the Lakers' package said, "I think the Bucks got the best part of the deal."

If circumstances had been different, Kareem Abdul-Jabbar could have returned to his hometown of New York and played for the Knicks. The Knickerbockers were willing to pay cash for Kareem and the Bucks asked $4 million. The deal fell through because the Knicks thought they could get the star seven-footer center George McGinnis from the ABA for much less. Unlike the Lakers, the New York team couldn't offer to trade players because they had far less of a talent pool to offer the Bucks.

Time has proven Jack right. Kareem would have been a steal for $4 million and Jack's critics in Los Angeles who decried the trade have been proven wrong. "I ignored it, as usual," Jack Kent Cooke remembers, "because I knew I had one of the best players that ever lived."

A few years later, everyone advised Jack to pick a college player by the name of Sidney Moncrief first in the 1979 draft. Although Moncrief would have a long, honorable NBA career with Milwaukee and Atlanta, Jack traded for Utah's number one pick instead, so he could get Earvin "Magic" Johnson. It would begin a Lakers' NBA dominance that would last for more than a decade. Jack's success as Lakers' owner did not include coaches. Jack would have five different coaches in the twelve years he owned the Lakers and almost as many general managers.

A few weeks after acquiring Kareem Abdul-Jabbar, Jack pulled off a similar deal in hockey when he traded captain and veteran defenseman Terry Harper and left wing Dan Maloney to Detroit for the best scorer of the day, Marcel Dionne. This move was looked on unfavorably by the Kings' coach, Bob Pulford, who believed that the hockey team had just begun to gel (they had a 42–17 record in 1974–1975 with twenty-one ties and finished second in their division). Pulford believed that trading away their captain for a selfish, though unarguably great, freewheeling player like Dionne was not in the best interests of the club. And Jack's signing Dionne to a $1.5 million contract over five years led to grumbles from some of the players.

The Dionne deal didn't turn out as spectacularly as the trade for Kareem. While one man, particularly one like Abdul-Jabbar, can immediately change the fortunes of a basketball team, a single hockey player, no matter how great, has to depend more on teamwork and reach a greater merging of "chemistry" with the other players, so that a forward line eventually acts as one when they skate down the ice. The Kings, much to Jack's consternation, continued to be a mediocre team, both on the ice in the arenas of the NHL, and in the stands as a draw. When Jack Kent Cooke first bought the NHL club, he boasted that nearly 400,000 former Canadians lived in the Los Angeles area and would form the nucleus of the Kings attendance. Years later when he was reminded of the transplanted Canadians, Jack replied, "Yes—and they all moved down here because they hate hockey, apparently."

Jack certainly tried everything with the Kings and Lakers. Besides always looking for the big deal that would assure a winning team, Jack went through sixteen different general managers and coaches in the dozen years he owned the teams. In the early days at the Forum, Jack made everyone in the front office, including himself, hustle season tickets. Jack sold sixteen tickets to Frank Sinatra, as well as two each to Cary Grant, Danny Thomas, Bob Hope, Danny Kaye, Dean Martin, and David Janssen. In the late 1960s, his son John, back from cable pioneering in La Crosse, Wisconsin, worked out of the subterranean Forum ticket offices. John headed the sales force there, designed flipcharts, traded for merchandise which he used in contests, and let groups like the YMCA and the Boy Scouts sell tickets on commission. John even had the Kings mail out playoff ticket information when the Kings were in last place in 1969 with a 10–63 record. John did it on purpose, proving he was learning from his father. "We got our money's worth in publicity," John recalled in a newspaper interview.

Still, while the Lakers were at near capacity, the Kings played to an arena that was sometimes less than 50 percent full. Overall though, the "Fabulous" Forum, operating under a holding company called California Sports, Inc., was profitable because of the Lakers and continual fill-ins of pop concerts, circuses, and special events like a Jehovah's Witnesses Convention that drew a one-day record of 22,598.

By 1975 Jack was spending half his time at the Forum in Los Angeles and the rest at TelePrompTer in New York. Jean was still at Jack's side for nearly every Forum event. Jack insisted that she be there. Jean couldn't handle it. She fled to Hawaii and rented a unit at the Kahala Condominiums near Diamond Head on Oahu. From there she called Edward Bennett Williams for help in saving their marriage. She believed Ed was not only a friend of Jack's, but of hers as well. Ed, who talked to Jack daily, promised to do whatever he could to keep them together.

After a month Jack flew to Hawaii and convinced Jean to

174

return, no mean feat. It was difficult for Jack to fly such distances with his claustrophobia and since his heart attack; he generally used sedatives and a large glass of white wine just before he flew.[1] Later Jack would testify under oath that, according to his own medical records, between October 1973 and January 1976, he had purchased the following sedatives: 800 tablets of phenobarbital, 200 tablets of Nembutal, 200 tablets of Dalmane, 100 tablets of Amytal, and 100 tablets of Triavil.

Jack would also say that in 1975 he and Jean had orally agreed to a separation distribution of assets while in Hawaii. Under the terms Jean was to get $100,000 a year for the rest of her life, her mother Bernice was to get all her living and medical expenses paid for until her death, and Peter and Helen Carnegie—Jean's brother and sister-in-law—were to get a house that Jack owned at 60 Evans Street in Toronto, rent-free for the rest of their days. But Jean said such an agreement never took place and there were no other witnesses.

So Jean returned with Jack to the house in Bel Air. By now, the Venetian villa seemed like a pink prison.[2] Jean's new Mercedes, with the vanity plates BJKC, stood parked in the driveway for days. Ginny Mancini, wife of the Hollywood musical composer, would later tell friends, after the final separation, "I don't understand it. Jean is one of the nicest women in Los Angeles."

That Jean was headed for either another suicide attempt, a breakdown, or worse, was evident in her written communications to Jack in 1976. On January 11 she wrote a letter to her husband in which she detailed some of her faults. She mentioned her inability to speak words correctly, her jumping in when others were speaking, her forgetfulness, and her weakness for luxury possessions such as mink coats and diamonds. But she talked about her pluses as well. She wrote that she told the truth and was never underhanded. And she said she would never hit anybody. Jean concluded by stating that maybe it would be best for her to just keep quiet.

Jean's distraught mannerisms culminated in a handwritten list of twenty-eight faults which she wrote out by hand on March 11. The list is full of both basic and obscure flaws Jean felt she had. She talked about her stubbornness, her temper, and how she didn't listen well to other people. She wrote about how weary she was of managing the household help and the appearances she was expected to make on behalf of Jack. She berated herself for being overweight and having a short attention span. Jean said she was quick to make judgments and was often forgetful. And in her most bizarre statement she bemoaned how she couldn't learn to master a knife and fork in the continental manner.

The list clearly shows a personality about to short-circuit. Jean was tired, unhappy, and fed up with the responsibilities of entertaining and managing a complicated household. But she still loved her husband.

This is evident in another letter she wrote to Jack on March 23, 1976. In it she talked about Jack's perfection and her imperfections. She ended the note by concluding that perhaps that's why they were a good match. It was signed with the most basic of all endearments.

Weeks later, in April, Jean attempted suicide again and this time was hospitalized. Meanwhile, on the surface at least, Jack's public life—making deals and making money—went on as usual. There was TelePrompTer, the Lakers, the Kings, the Forum, the Redskins, real estate in Phoenix, and Raljon, the 13,300-acre working ranch in the Sierra Nevada foothills.[3] Jack owned it all and it was pretty much a one-man show too, with little delegation except for the Washington football team.

Was Jean Cooke just another team to Jack, another investment? The answer is a loud no. Jack, a romantic always, still loved Jean—but in a way a newer generation probably wouldn't understand. He had scrapped and fought for more than forty years to give her the riches she now enjoyed, beginning with the battle to get $5 out of the high school principal in Verigin so she wouldn't go hungry. But Jean didn't enjoy the pressure of business like Jack. She didn't like having to show up at every game, every event, and smile at strangers.

The marriage between Jack and Jean, now in its forty-second year might have gone on for several more. But it ended the evening of July 1, 1976, when Jean hit Jack with his mother's car, nearly killing him.

Notes

1. Jack had become a connoisseur of fine wines by the early 1970s. Once while riding in a limousine with someone, Jack opened a bottle of white wine. When his guest, who thought the wine was not cold enough, tried to add ice, Jack said, "Nobody puts ice cubes in my white wine."
2. Jack convinced Paige Rense of *Architectural Digest* to feature the house in the March–April 1974 issue. Titled, "An Affair of the Heart" and subtitled "My 40-Year Affair with Antiques," the article gave Jack both pride and pleasure. He still has copies of the piece and proudly shows it to intimates.
3. Raljon is a combination of Ralph's and John's names.

CHAPTER
14

COOKE VS. COOKE

"You can't be serious. I wouldn't kill Mr. Cooke or anyone else."

It had been a star-spangled summer for America, the adopted homeland of Jack Kent Cooke. The country had been planning for 1976, its bicentennial, for years. There were tall ships in New York's harbor, mammoth fireworks on the mall in Washington, and parades in every large and small city throughout the land. But as jubilation spread from coast to coast, a deep sadness enveloped Jack and his family.

It began on April 21, when Jack's mother Nancy, died. Jack's father Ralph has passed away fifteen years earlier. Shortly afterward, Jack's chauffeur and longtime servant Eddie Parr had also died.[1] He had been with Jack for twenty-seven years, since the CKEY days, following him to the brown-gold land of southern California from the blue-green terrain that characterized their Toronto homeland next to Lake Ontario. Both men's deaths were a further reminder of Jack's own mortality.

While a public pretense prevailed, Jean and Jack's marriage was dead as well. Jean had fallen apart. The pressures that Jack faced daily, and on which he thrived, were something that she could no longer handle, no matter how diluted when thrust upon her. Jack's constant calling upon Jean, asking her to be part of his team, was too much. She now wanted just to get out.

Still, here in the low Sierras, at Raljon, one could feel tranquility, at least for short moments. Jack had come here some fifteen to twenty times since his heart attack in 1973. And on this morning of July 1, 1976, just days before his adopted country's celebration, one felt that life could go on forever. The weather was clear, without wind, and the temperature at these higher elevations would stay in the seventies. There would be a full moon tonight, but now, early in the morning, the sun had not yet come over the mountains to the east. There was a busy day planned. John and Becky would be over with their two boys for dinner. Chick and Marge Hearn were coming up for the long weekend ahead. The air was filled with the promise of happiness.

Jack had a bad knee. He thought it was caused by arthritis. Jean disagreed and thought it had come from horseback riding. Jean would later say it made Jack "crabby" all day.

Jack and Jean took the new blue Cadillac limousine to Porterville, a small town of 8,000.[2] It was a 35-mile drive from the ranch but Jean wanted to shop at Smith's Groceries for food and special treats for the Hearns.

Jean said later that Jack was "very cranky, cross, and miserable" at Smith's because of his bad knee. "He was hard to handle," Jean said at a deposition, "whenever I bought something special, Jack would take it out of the cart and put it back."

Later, at the dinner table, with John, Becky, and his two grandsons present, Jack sat at the head of the table and read aloud testimonials from friends and famous people who knew his deceased mother and had written to him after her funeral. Jean said Jack "was very morbid about his mother's death and read testimonies from people John and Becky didn't know. One of the little boys fidgeted and Jack got very angry. It was a very upsetting dinner."

Jack saw Becky, John, and the two boys out. He came back in and Jean, who was sitting in a chair, started to say something but Jack spoke, interrupting her.

"I don't want to talk with you, woman," he said according to a statement by Hernando Gutierrez, their houseman, and the only person present in the lodge besides the two.

Jean felt that this comment was the "last straw" as she later put it, so while Jack was changing into a robe, she went into her dressing room, changed into slacks, put a few personal effects into an overnight bag and left the house, intending to drive back to their house in Bel Air.

179

She started to drive off the property in a Chevy Nova that had belonged to Jack's mother. The Nova had a broken muffler and made a lot of noise. Jack, hearing it, ran out of the house in his robe, and raced ahead, blocking the way and Jean's escape. He stood in the road with his hands raised.

There are three different versions of what happened next, as Jean's car came toward Jack.

Jean said that Jack ran toward the side of the car when she passed and that she heard "a little thump" and looking back, saw Jack lying in the road.

Hernando, the houseman, who had witnessed the accident, ran out to help Jack.

Jean backed the car up and rolled down the window.

"How is he—is he alright?" she asked Hernando.

"He's broken his arm," Hernando said.

"Is that all that's wrong with him? Is he alright other than that?"

"Yes."

"You take him to the doctor's. I'm leaving."

According to her deposition, Jean said she drove to Porterville, distraught, and checked into a motel. She called John and Becky from the motel, and Becky answered the phone. John wasn't there. He had driven Jack to the hospital.

Jean said to Becky, "Becky, what is it that caused all these things? What do I do wrong?"

Becky said, "Jean, it isn't you. You don't do anything wrong. And I love you."

Jean said, "Would you please tell John I said for you two to go on your vacation no matter what Jack says. You go and don't let him spoil it this time. I'll call Johnny in the morning."

In the morning Jean called again and John Cooke said, "Mother, what happened?"

Jean told him and asked, "Johnny, should I go back to the ranch or go home?"

"Mom . . . look, you've got to do something. You can't go on like this any longer. Why don't you go home."

So Jean drove back to Los Angeles.

*　　*　　*

Jack's version is slightly more dramatic.

"The car came towards me at forty to fifty miles an hour," Jack said in his deposition. "The roar sounded like a Ferrari. When I finally realized, with horror, what was happening, to protect my life I leaped aside or leapt aside, whichever you prefer. Thank God I did.

"I lay on my side and she drove on. Hernando put ice on my arm. It was the first broken bone of my life."

Jack then said, "Call Mr. John."

When Hernando called John and asked him to come back. John said, "Why, what happened?"

Hernando said he couldn't tell him over the phone.

After ten minutes, Jack said, "What the hell is taking so long." Finally, John, who had been filling up the car at the ranch's gas pump, arrived and took Jack to a hospital in Bakersfield. Jack Kent Cooke was treated there for a broken wrist.

Hernando, the houseman, who would later play a pivotal part in the divorce and settlement, at first signed a description of the event that was similar to Jack's. But later he recanted, saying he didn't know what he was signing, and sided with Jean Cooke's version of the event. To buttress Jack's version, a statement was solicited from Jerry Perenchio, who said that Hernando had told him that Jean had "tried to kill Mr. Cooke" when Hernando drove him to the airport after a meeting with Jack.

Jerry said he was shocked. "What!" he testified saying. "I thought he had broken his arm playing with his grandchildren."

Jerry said Hernando answered, "No—that's what he tells everyone but Mrs. Cooke speeded up the car and knocked Mr. Cooke down."

When Jean drove back to Los Angeles, she said, she was afraid to go back to the Bel Air house. She stayed at the Beverly Wilshire Hotel for almost two weeks, then moved into the home of Los Angeles attorney and family friend Fred Nicholas for a few days. Finally, she decided to go to New York City, where she felt she would be safe from Jack. In New York, Jean checked into an apartment at the Carlton House. Not knowing how long she'd be staying, Jean signed a one-year lease at $1,500 a month because she said management told her that she'd be saving $200 a month and that they could easily sublet for her if she left before the end of the year's lease. Jack's team of attorneys later used the lease agreement to attempt to prove that Jean had given up her California residency and no longer qualified under the community property 50–50 laws. But Jean was able to produce a roundtrip plane ticket which negated most of that argument.

In New York, Jean visited with Carrie Rozelle, her former daughter-in-law who had been married first to her oldest son, Ralph, but later had married Pete Rozelle, the National Football League Commissioner. Carrie had met Ralph when she was a Toronto model at a Canadian Golf Club. She had met Pete at an American tennis club tournament.

Ralph and Carrie's daughter, Carolyn Jean, then known as Jean, lived with Carrie now, as did Ralph's other sons. She was Jack and Jean's only granddaughter.

Jack left the ranch and drove to Reno, Nevada, where he hired a lawyer by the name of Virgil Wedge and tried to get a quick divorce. When he found out that wasn't possible, he drove back to the ranch, picked up a few belongings, and then drove to Las Vegas where he first took up residence at the Tropicana Hotel.

He soon found a house at 4 Crescent Drive that had been designed by Frank Lloyd Wright. The house had a circular living room, a built-in wine cellar, a pool, and a greenhouse attached to one side. There were oleander and other tropical plants and Jack installed a piano as well, spending his free moments gardening and picking out tunes.

Not that there was much free time. Jack formed three Nevada corporations and transferred joint assets to them. And when he learned that Jean was in New York he sent a Bekins moving van to the house on St. Cloud Road in Bel Air and stripped the pink palace, which *Architectual Digest* in its 1974 article had called "An Affair of the Heart," clean. Gone to Las Vegas were the Georgian and Louis XV furniture, the Japanese antiques, the paintings by Georges Roualt and Goedike—Jack even had the stereo speakers ripped out that were built into the walls. Except for the carpeting and curtains, the house was stripped bare. After Jean retained legal representation, she got a court order for return of the furniture until the divorce was settled. Everything was returned. Jack's moving bill for the furnishings' roundtrip was more than $20,000.

Although the day-by-day sparring of the long divorce battle would take an emotional toll on Jean, Jack saw the pending court settlement as war, and he had five different law firms working for him. In a deposition, Jack said his legal group was made up of Los Angeles lawyers Arthur Groman, Alan Rothenberg, Howard Soloway, and Joe Ball. Virgil Wedge worked for Jack in Nevada. Bill Shea advised from New York, and Edward Bennett Williams from Washington.

Jean's attorneys were Arthur J. Crowley and his assistant, Douglas Bagby.

Jack prepared meticulously for his divorce, as if it were a major business deal. From his exile in Las Vegas he talked daily with his legal lieutenants. Outside of his California employees and his immediate family, Jack only had two major visitors during his Nevada years. One was the political reporter Lou Cannon, of the *Washington Post*, who wrote a favorable feature story about him for the newspaper's sports section (ten years later he would be invited to the 1988 Super Bowl as Jack's guest). The other was attorney Bob Schulman, who told a writer he only discussed the Redskins and taxes with Jack.

In mid-1977, Arthur Groman took a deposition from Jean and attempted to break her down in order to facilitate a fast settlement. Groman's strategy was to threaten Jean with criminal charges and intimidate her because she had hit Jack with the car. When Groman, who had been entertained by Jack and Jean at the Forum and in their home, tried the tactic, Crowley adjourned the deposition but not before this exchange took place:

183

ARTHUR GROMAN: Isn't it a fact, Mrs. Cooke, that Mr. Cooke was standing in the middle of the road and that you saw him and drove the car directly at him at a high rate of speed?

JEAN COOKE: Arthur, you can't be serious. I wouldn't kill Mr. Cooke or anyone else. That's ridiculous. He is lying to you if he told you that. He hit me—I didn't hit him.

ARTHUR GROMAN: Mrs. Cooke is guilty of unconscionable conduct and unclean hands which bars her from this court.

ARTHUR CROWLEY (interjecting): That's the most ridiculous statement I've ever heard in my life.

ARTHUR GROMAN: We have two witnesses who will testify.

JEAN COOKE: I would have hit him head on . . .

ARTHUR CROWLEY: Just a minute, Jean.

JEAN COOKE: Oh shit. I'm sorry.

At this point Arthur Crowley adjourned the deposition. However, this conversation between Crowley and Groman is in the transcript:

ARTHUR CROWLEY: In almost thirty years of practicing law, I've never seen such disgraceful conduct in my life.

ARTHUR GROMAN: This is serious. We have two witnesses.

ARTHUR CROWLEY: You could have filed a lawsuit. The statute of limitations is one year.

ARTHUR GROMAN: There is no statute of limitations on assault as far as I know.

Jean visited a psychiatrist in an effort to have any further questions from Groman as written interrogatories. According to a letter to the court by Alvin E. Davis, M.D., on October 19, 1977, "The sitting blood pressure in her left arm was 130 over 90 . . . she became tearful in minutes."

Jean told Dr. Davis: "I'm here to see if I can face the deposition. My husband wants me to be intimidated by questions so I'll give up but I won't. I know Mr. Groman and Mr. Rothenberg socially— at games and at our house, so it was terribly embarrassing to answer questions like 'Isn't he stronger than you?' and 'Do you look up to your husband?' "

Jean said that during the deposition, "My heart pounded and I cried and my lawyer stopped it and the court said I could have a written deposition."

She described herself as "feeling fine since away from my husband" except for the "heart-pounding of the deposition." She told Davis that she felt any further pressure by Jack's lawyers might cause her injury—"a stroke or a heart attack."

Jean told the psychiatrist that she had always been loyal to her husband and did not want to attack him in front of people she knew socially. She also described her marital relations as stressful since the inception of the marriage. She described her four suicide attempts as a result of "wanting to get out of a box."

Dr. Davis ended his description of his meeting with Jean by saying, "Thank you for this interesting referral."

Attempts to take depositions from Jack were getting nowhere. Jack's lawyers raised the argument that his health was so precarious that he could not come to Los Angeles from Las Vegas. Jack's business friends introduced statement after sworn statement attesting to his failing health and his bouts of claustrophobia, telling of the many times he had been either sedated for travel or had a chartered plane stopped on the runway.

Theodore Jacobs, M.D., a Las Vegas physician, gave a sworn statement as to Jack's health at the time in which he described Jack as "ashen in appearance, with a systolic rate of 146 over 88, an irregular heart rate," and suffering from "instable anginal syndrome." He concluded that a divorce trial would be too much of a strain on his health.

Jean retorted that Jack had flown to Hawaii to get her after the 1975 separation and had no problems in getting places when he really wanted to go. She also detailed a week in June 1974 when they had driven to a resort called Rancho Murietta in Sacramento where Jack had taken a week of lessons for riding Tennessee walking horses. She said it had been nearly 100°F every day, and that they had traveled back by a longer route, through Carmel and Monterrey.

If Jack's attorneys believed that Jean would crumble under pressure they were mistaken. Jean, or at least Jean's attorneys, fought every charge and action by Jack's legal group with aggressive moves of their own. It was as if a fast-moving chess game were taking place, with each side calling "check" at each turn.

Meanwhile friends and members of the family were forced to

choose sides. There is no question that John Cooke, who had worked for his father for more than a decade, came out firmly allied with Jack from the beginning. He started by sending back a gift that Jean sent to him and Becky for their wedding anniversary in March 1977. The rejection was intended, as he expressed in a letter to her, to let her know his feelings. Then on March 12, 1977, the exact date of the wedding anniversary, Jean testified that she had this conversation with her son:

> JOHN: "Dad's going to accuse you of manslaughter if you don't settle with him."
> JEAN: "What do you mean?"
> JOHN: "The accident at the ranch."
> JEAN: "That's ridiculous. I didn't hit him. He ran into the car."
> JOHN: "It doesn't matter, Mom. That's what he's going to do anyway and he'll take the case to the Supreme Court if you don't settle."

A month later, after one of Jack's attorneys, Bill Shea, had offered Jean $2 million on behalf of Jack, John called and told Jean, according to a sworn statement by Jean Cooke, "My God— $2 million. You can't help but live well on $2 million." Later, John said that Jean was "possessed by greed."

Ralph, Jack's oldest son, who was running his own business at the time, tried to remain neutral. For not choosing sides—at least not his father's—he was disowned after the final settlement and made a nonperson. Jack's profiles in the early 1980s make a point of saying, "one son" or "one son by first marriage."[3]

Not that Jack didn't try to enlist Ralph's support. A sworn statement made on January 16, 1978, by the houseman, Hernando Gutierrez, contains this information:

> On November 23, 1977, Mr. Cooke asked me to go to the airport to pick up his son, Ralph. Mr. Groman [Arthur Groman, Jack's attorney] and I went to the airport to pick up Ralph. Before we left for the airport, Mr. Cooke was talking to Mr. Groman and to me quite normally. He was talking in a loud voice as he usually does. I did not see anything wrong with him at all. He was in bed working and talking to Mr. Groman and to Mrs. Anderson [Peggy or Margaret Anderson, his Las Vegas secretary]. Mr. Cooke has for years worked while he is in bed.

Before Mr. Groman and I left the house to go to the airport, the curtains in his bedroom were open and the room was bright and Mr. Cooke was talking with Mr. Groman. When Mr. Groman and I and Ralph returned to the house, the curtains in his bedroom were all closed and the lights were turned down very low. The room was almost dark.

Before we left the house, I heard Mr. Cooke say to Mr. Groman: "On the way home, you prepare Ralph. Tell him how sick I am."

When we returned to the home from the airport, Mr. Cooke was alone in his bed with a lot of medicine on the table beside his bed. The medicine was not on the table before we left for the airport.

When I arrived in Mr. Cooke's bedroom with Ralph Cooke, Mr. Cooke spoke in a very soft voice from his bed as if he were very ill. After Ralph Cooke left the home, Mr. Cooke's voice returned to a normal volume at it had been before Ralph's visit.

Outside of the immediate family, others were asked to choose. Jack and Jean's friend, the distinguished trial attorney, Edward Bennett Williams, took Jack's side. As president of the Washington Redskins, he talked with Jack on a daily basis. In a letter he wrote by hand on his personal stationery on October 10, 1977, Williams said this from his office in the Hill Building in Washington, D.C.:

Dear Jean,

I thank you so much for your kind and gracious letter. I'm glad to report that I've fully recovered and up to speed [Williams had been operated on for cancer].

I hope you are well. I'm deeply troubled by what's happening between you and Jack. If only I could help to bring it all to an end! It would be a first priority.

Please stay in touch and let me help if there's any role for one to help two old friends.

Ed

But Edward Bennett Williams never helped Jean. He did, however, unofficially advise Jack. According to Jack's own deposition, the famous criminal lawyer advised Jack to "pop the assault charge" on Jean. Williams said the case could be "stage-managed" and that Jean would come to terms. Williams said not to accuse Jean directly but just to bring it to her attention. He felt that the charge would upset her and cause her to settle.

Bill Shea, another friend of Jack and Jean's was also brought into the fight. He was dispatched by Jack to Los Angeles from New York in a last attempt to negotiate an "amicable" settlement.

Shea arrived in Los Angeles on January 31, 1977, and checked in at the Beverly Hills Hotel. Jean, Shea, and Arthur Crowley met at Jean's house from 5 to 11 P.M. in a long, no-holds-barred informal session.

At the meeting, Jean and Crowley said that Jack was worth at least $50 million. Jean said, "I don't want $25 million [referring to California's 50–50 community property rules] but I'm willing to settle for $7 million."

Bill Shea said that Jack wasn't liquid and his assets were frozen. Crowley retaliated, "He has only to sell his TelePrompTer stock— it's $9 a share." Crowley said former USC chemistry professor-turned-entrepreneur, Jerry Buss, was willing to pay $25 million for the Forum. Arthur Crowley also gave his opinion on the state of the Washington Redskins. He said that Edward Bennett Williams and George Allen were paying out too much money. He also said that the Lakers and Kings were doing better than the Redskins financially.

At this point, according to a summary written by Arthur Crowley's associate Doug Bagby, Bill Shea asked for an offer "and I'll take it back to Jack. It's up to him to accept."

Crowley asked for $7 million again.

Shea said: "It's preposterous. Jack is now willing to double his offer of $1 million to $2 million."

Arthur Crowley treated Shea's offer with contempt and Jean said, "Your offer is insulting. It is a pittance. I thought you wanted to settle properly."

Bill Shea answered, "We've worked very hard to get Jack to make this offer. It's very fair. As a matter of fact, it's generous."

But there were no takers. Crowley, trying to be the host, gave Shea a tour of his new house in Beverly Hills and both men congratulated each other on keeping the case "out of the newspapers." Shea flew back to New York City on February 1, 1977, empty-handed.

A few weeks later, Jack Kent Cooke made his "final" offer to settle with Jean and end the marriage on a semipeaceful note. In his proposal, he offered the following: The "pink palace" at 310 St. Cloud Road, which he valued at $1 million; all the furniture, art, and fixtures, which he estimated to be worth $1.5 million; he allowed that Jean could keep her jewelry, which he said was worth $500,000; he said she could keep her 1973 Mercedes (with the BJKC vanity plates), which he priced at $20,000; he offered her $1 million cash; and finally he offered her alimony at $65,000 a year for twenty-one years. The package was now more than $5 million.

Jack also offered Jean some financial advice and a few bonuses. He advised Jean to take the $1 million and invest the money in triple-A tax-free municipal bonds at 5 ¼ percent, which would give her an income of $5,000 a month or $60,000 a year after taxes. He also included the rent-free offer again on the house in Toronto for her brother. He promised that both Ralph and John would get $100,000 a year for life plus cost-of-living increases, adding that Ralph and John would also get $100,000 cash upon his death plus the right to ask the trustees of his estate for more money if they had a valid reason. The rest of the estate would be divided among the grandsons after they reached the age of thirty, and Carolyn Jean, his granddaughter, would get her share upon reaching the age of twenty-one.

Jack said in the offer to Jean that the trustees of the estate would be the Trust Department of the Bank of America, Ralph, John, his chief lieutenant Jim Lacher, and two of his attorneys, Arthur Groman and Alan Rothenberg.

He also reminded Jean that the now late Dan Reeves had only left his widow, Mary, a house in Bel Air, furniture, and a car, with the rest in trust for the children, implying that Jean should feel fortunate.

Jean refused and the battle continued.

Back in Las Vegas, Jack was already taking a financial beating. Besides the $20,000 for the Bekins Moving Company, he had already been ordered to pay $80,000 to Jean's attorneys on January 19, 1977, plus $8,000 a month. By September 1977 Jean's attorney alone had run up legal bills of $462,000 in legal discovery—a figure that Jack Kent Cooke was obliged to pay. In addition, Jack had been ordered to pay Jean $9,800 a month in

189

living expenses plus rent-free use of the Bel Air house. Jack struck back by having his second-in-command, Jim Lacher, write Jean and inform her that Jack would be filing his income tax separately from now on, thus making Jean's support payments taxable. The move infuriated Jean Cooke and made her even more determined to fight on.

The Las Vegas sojourn wasn't a total loss for Jack. It was there he met Jean Maxwell Williams Wilson. An attractive blonde in her early fifties, she was the widow of Edward E. Wilson, who had been the son of Charles Wilson, a former secretary of defense and CEO of General Motors.

Jean Wilson, who later was referred to by Jack as Jeannie II, to differentiate her from the first Jean Cooke, worked as a public relations person for the Sands Hotel and was a nationally known sculptor. By late 1977, according to a sworn statement by Jack's houseman, Hernando Gutierrez, Jean Wilson was spending nearly every weekday evening with Jack Kent Cooke, and living with him on weekends.

Jean Wilson was a change of pace for Jack. She was petite, blonde, and slender—the opposite of Jeannie I. According to Hernando, Jack Kent Cooke, who was being portrayed as too ill to travel to Los Angeles for a deposition, took weekend bicycle rides with Jean Wilson of five to six miles.

Jean Wilson also sculpted a bronze bust of Jack which he decided to give to his son John and daughter-in-law, Becky. Prior to their visit in August 1977, Jack wrote them a letter dated August 5, 1977, praising the bust. Jack, writing on Raljon stationery, talked about looking at Jeannie II's sculpture of him with both a critical and an uncritical gaze. Jack said that it held up to any criticisms and came away on top. He boasted about Jean Wilson's bust of him, saying that it would last eternally. He described Jean Wilson as one of the best sculptors in the country.

Jack then got serious and talked (obliquely) about his mother's death, saying that the Cooke household had become smaller but had expanded in emotional caring for each other. He told John and Becky he had no misgivings over what had happened during the past year, but was upset that such unhappiness had surrounded the family.

Jack concluded with an admonition to celebrate the days ahead because the black shadow over the family would eventually disappear.

Jack listed his net worth on September 20, 1977. His statement (at which Arthur Crowley looked with a skeptical eye) said he was worth "just" $18,757,000. According to the document, his interests in California Sports, Inc. (Lakers, Kings, Forum) were worth $9,098,000; TelePrompTer, $4,912,000; the Washington Redskins, $3,186,000; Raljon, $940,000; the house on St. Cloud road, $765,000; and the furniture, art, etc., $652,000. The total came to $19,553,000 but Jack listed liabilities of $1,296,000. But Arthur Crowley was able to find a financial statement of Jack's dated January 20, 1975, in which his fortune was estimated to be $73,341,755.

The financial figures that were produced regarding the Washington Redskins are particularly interesting. A statement reveals that the Redskins lost $340,000 in fiscal year 1975, made a $50,526 profit in 1976, and a $400,000 loss was projected for 1977. It also revealed that a Richard Thigpen, Jr., a Charlotte, N.C., attorney had offered $9.7 million for the Redskins in 1976 and agreed to assume a $6.8 million loan the Washington Redskins owed American Security and Trust, a District of Columbia bank. It also detailed how Jack purchased Milton King's fifty shares from his estate on October 21, 1976, for $1,375,000, bringing Jack's share of the Redskins up to nearly 86 percent. Jack paid $800,000 down, borrowing $300,00 of the $800,000 from the Union Bank of California. He agreed to pay the estate of Milton King $575,000 more over a five-year period.

Jack and Jean were divorced on October 20, 1977. But the war between the two raged on. The settlement—the division of Jack and Jean's accumulated wealth—had yet to be agreed upon. For that matter, Jack Kent Cooke was still avoiding making a deposition.

Finally it was agreed that Jack would depose on November 21, 1977, to Arthur Crowley in Las Vegas. According to a sworn statement by Hernando Gutierrez, the houseman, the days before the deposition were spent removing documents from Jack Kent Cooke's house at 4 Crescent Drive.

Hernando testified that he took nine boxes of documents to Jean Wilson's garage. "I asked Mrs. Anderson [Peggy Anderson, Jack's Las Vegas secretary] why are we taking all these documents over to Mrs. Wilson's house?" According to Gutierrez, Mrs. Anderson said, "The less you know, Hernando, the better for you." Hernando also testified that Jim Lacher had also removed documents from Jack's Las Vegas house. He said that Jack had told Lacher, "Be sure you put those documents where they will not see them."

Gutierrez made all these sworn statements later on because even though he was working for Jack Kent Cooke as a houseman at $700 a month, he was voluntarily calling Jean Cooke and giving her information about Jack's strategy. In addition, he was photocopying documents and mailing them to Jean. In the best tradition of a John Le Carré spy novel, Hernando Gutierrez was a mole, a double agent, and the $700-a-month servant may have eventually cost Jack Kent Cooke nearly $50 million.

Jack finally deposed on November 21 and 22, 1977, but became ill on the third day. Still, the deposition ran just under 100,000 words.[4]

Hernando Gutierrez left Jack's employ in Las Vegas on January 8, 1978, going to Jean's house in Bel Air and telling her "everything." Jack first tried to hire Hernando back at $1,200 a month, but Hernando stayed with Jean for $1,000 a month plus room and board, living on the premises of the Bel Air mansion.[5]

Gutierrez said he could "no longer work for Mr. Cooke because of the lies he told about Mrs. Cooke. One of the lies was that Mrs. Cooke had tried to run over Mr. Cooke. I told Mr. Cooke that this was a lie and that he knew it was an accident."

Hernando also admitted calling Jean "many times" since he had been in Las Vegas with Jack and sending her documents and eavesdropping on Jack's conversations with his lawyers. Hernando stated that he never discussed the documents with Jean's lawyers.[6]

Trying to make good come from bad, Jack's lawyers sought to disqualify Arthur Crowley from the case. They said he had received "stolen goods" (the documents Hernando had sent to

Jean), had interfered with attorney-client privilege, and that Hernando was an agent for Crowley.

Crowley countered by having his assistant, Douglas Bagby, try to remove Arthur Groman. Bagby said that because Groman was an executor of Jack's will and since he had also done a will for Jean, he couldn't work for Jack.

Both motions were dismissed.

Jack Kent Cooke's attorneys then came up with a list of novel arguments why Jean didn't qualify for half of Jack's estate. The first was that California's community property laws were unconstitutional—they violated the Fourteenth Amendment by "impinging" on one's right to travel. The second was that he had lived in Nevada long enough that he didn't have to abide by the California community property laws. Another was that Jack had made the bulk of his fortune in Canada and that amount didn't count in southern California.

Meanwhile, Arthur Crowley tried to "shop" the Kings, Lakers and the Forum in the *Los Angeles Times* by calling and implying to reporters they were for sale. Jim Shirley, the *Times* sports editor, and Charles Maher, a writer for the *Times* and an attorney, told Alan Rothenberg about the matter. Rothenberg tried to get an injunction against Crowley, saying that such a story would force a "distress" sale, affect the morale of the players, and lower the teams' values.

And when Douglas Bagby tried to hire the American Appraisal Company to put a value on the Kings and Lakers (their previous credentials included estimating the value of the New York Yankees, the San Francisco Giants, and the Julius Schmid Corporation—a condom maker), Jack's attorneys said that American Appraisals' estimate fee of $65,000 was too high and that $25,000 to $30,000 would be more in line. Since the total for both sides in attorneys' fees was now in the millions of dollars, the disputed figure seems paltry, but the objection is indicative of how every proposal, every expenditure, was scrutinized, with each side hoping to gain a small advantage.

Two judges, Marvin A. Freeman and Julius M. Title, disqualified themselves. It then was left to Judge Joseph A. Wapner, who would later find fame on television's *The People's Court,* to force the two sides to reach a settlement. The common sense used by Wapner was not unlike the logic he uses today to settle a $129 property dispute on daytime TV.

Wapner told Jean's and Jack's attorneys to reach an agreement or else the case would go to trial. After eight days, the two sides finally agreed on a division of the huge fortune that had been accumulated over nearly a half-century. Among the assets Jean got was the Bel Air house; 1,529,000 shares of TelePrompTer, worth $16.12 a share on the day of the settlement, or $24,655,125; and 28 percent of Raljon Corporation, the new Nevada company that controlled the Kings, Lakers, the Forum, the Raljon ranch, Videotape Enterprises—a company Jack owned—and another 180,000 shares of TelePrompTer. Jack got the house in Las Vegas, kept his 86 percent ownership in the Redskins, and got a controlling 72 percent of Raljon Corporation. It was pretty much an even split worth about $42 million each. Later, reporters would note that the $42 million figure was a million dollars for every year of Jean's marriage to Jack Kent Cooke.

Final salvos were fired. Crowley claimed victory by noting in an eight-column banner story that was the lead story in the Los Angeles *Herald-Examiner* on March 6, 1979, that "if it's not the largest settlement, it's certainly one of the largest." He was correct. The amount was dutifully recorded in the 1981 *Guinness Book of World Records* as the largest divorce settlement ever.[7]

Jean called Jack a "tyrant" who made her attend as many as eighty sporting events a year. Jack—who had seemed taken aback, at least publicly, when Jean had filed for divorce, saying, "It was my understanding that we both had religious scruples against divorce"—had no comment. When the two passed each other in the corridors of the Hill Street courthouse, there was no eye contact, let alone a greeting. But years later, Jack would tell friends that the divorce was "the biggest mistake of my life."

The final divorce documents ran more than 12,000 pages and were divided into sixteen volumes. The case had run nearly three years. Thus it was only fair that on the day of the decision, another Hollywood show trial, the Michele Triola Marvin and Lee Marvin "palimony" case, was relegated to second billing in the Los Angeles newspapers.

Jean lived in the Bel Air house for a few years and then moved to a southern California beach community. She later married a commercial and graphic artist. She is Jean Carnegie Berwald today, living a quiet, anonymous life.

Many people thought Jack would return to California and reclaim his throne at the Forum, sitting behind his large Chippendale desk in his genuine Biedermeier chair. But California is for sunsets. Jack was still beginning. So, in June 1979 he sold the Forum, the Kings, the Lakers, and the ranch to USC chemistry professor Jerry Buss for $67 million and headed east.

It was time, as he told friends later, "to start my third life."

Notes

1. Roy Thomson, now Lord Thomson, would die on August 4, 1976.
2. The blue Cadillac limousine is the same auto that is mentioned in the first sentence of the first chapter of this book.
3. Other published descriptions of Jack disowning Ralph say that Ralph sided with Jean. The author's review of the entire court file shows no evidence that Ralph sided with either parent. The author's inference is that he tried his best to stay out of the battle.
4. A complaint was made by Jack about Arthur Crowley running a tab of $1,615.12 for his two days in Las Vegas for himself and two associates. Jack said Crowley turned the visit into a "holiday." Much was made of the trio's stay at the MGM Grand Hotel where Arthur Crowley had rented a suite. Crowley said he needed the extra room to work in and that Jack's complaints were "grossly exaggerated."
5. Jack called Hernando and said, "Do you know you are going to ruin my life?" Hernando fired back, "What about Mrs. Cooke's life?"
6. A letter was introduced into evidence by Jack's attorneys from George Holt, the Las Vegas district attorney, who said that if Hernando had taken papers from Jack, he had committed a felony—to wit, burglary.
7. The Guinness entry contains many errors, which would seem to call into question its accuracy. Jack is called "James Kent Cooke," and his birth date is given as 1913. Jean is only referred to as "Mrs. Jeannie Cooke."

WASHINGTON

CHAPTER
15

LIFE THREE

"The guy with the gold makes the rules."

Jack Kent Cooke's presence in the capital of the United States marked the end to the decades of mediocrity of Washington football teams. Between 1980 and 1990, the Redskins would appear in three Super Bowls, winning two.[1] Washington would own the best win–loss record of the twenty-eight teams in the league, with the exception of the San Francisco 49ers.

There is no doubt that the success of the Washington Redskins can be attributed to the stewardship of Jack Kent Cooke. Jack's huge passion for winning was underscored by his willingness to pay for it by hiring the best talent in the league, on and off the field. It made the difference between good teams and great ones. This is not to say that Jack Kent Cooke was a blank check. In fact, the opposite was true. The days of loose expense accounts were over. Edward Bennett Williams, whose presidency of the team was marked by high player salaries and, except for the 1973 Super Bowl appearance, only better than average field performance, had paid George Allen $125,000 a year, beginning in 1971, a mammoth salary then for a coach and the highest in the NFL. A short time later Williams quipped, "I gave George an unlimited expense account and he exceeded it in the first month." It was Jack who had lobbied for Allen. In 1970, they were frequent dinner partners at the Forum Club and at one time Allen had sold Jack on the physical conditioning plan that he required of his football players. Jack tried it with the Kings, but because hockey players use different muscle groups, it only resulted in shinsplints and other minor injuries.

Under Jack, scouts were made to fly coach instead of first class and every expenditure was scrutinized.² Taking a note from the Forum days, Jack even had advertising put on the Redskins season schedule cards, a trifle, but one that marked the difference between Jack Kent Cooke and Edward Bennett Williams. Pro Football, Inc., the team's corporate name, was now a tight ship.

Jack Kent Cooke moved to Washington as one era was ending and another was beginning. The 1970s—a decade of Watergate scandal followed by the administrations of two "good guys"—the lackluster Gerald Ford and Jimmy Carter—were ending. Carter was a Redskins guest in 1978, before Jack arrived. Now, the decade of "I've got mine" was nearly over and the "We can do anything" 1980s were beginning. Jack Kent Cooke was about to give the Redskins, and himself, a new identity.

When Jack took up residence, in the summer of 1979, he owned most of the team. He had reached that figure by a series of sales and purchases by himself and others in the Redskins' hierarchy. C. Leo DeOrsey, who had been willing to sell his 13 percent to Jack for $910,000 but had been prevented by George C. Marshall's guardian, had died. His family sold the shares back to the Redskins, who retired all but 50, or 5 percent, giving them to the man they thought would establish a coaching dynasty, Vince Lombardi, as part of the deal to coax him away from Green Bay on February 7, 1969. Two days later, Marshall died and his estate, which had been disputed for years by his children—he left nearly everything to charity—was up for grabs. To settle with the estate, the Redskins, as a corporate entity, bought 260 shares from the heirs for $3 million. Jack, Edward Bennett Williams, and Milton King bought the other 260 shares for $5.4 million and retired them. Then, when Vince Lombardi died of cancer on September 3, 1970, less than two years after joining the team, the Redskins (which had the right to do so) purchased his shares from his widow, Marie, and retired them as well. And when Milton King, the last stockholder other than Jack and Ed, died on January 23, 1975, Jack purchased those shares. The final two stockholders were Jack Kent Cooke, 350 shares, and Edward Bennett Williams, 50.³

Williams, one of the nation's premier attorneys, could see the future. At the club's homecoming lunch on August 23, 1979, Williams said he and Jack had agreed to work together under the golden rule of sports.[4]

That rule, said Williams, is, "The guy with the gold makes the rules," meaning the one who controlled the organization—Jack—was now in charge. Not willing to play second fiddle, Williams completed a deal in October 1979 that made him the new owner of the Baltimore Orioles. His days of leading the Redskins were over.

Jack, who might have chosen the glitz of Georgetown or the newer but close-in, upper-crust suburbs of Potomac, Maryland, or McLean, Virginia, settled instead in the "old money" bastion of Middleburg, Virginia, a rural paradise populated by the gentrified second and third generation corporate masters of American business. Middleburg, although technically a town in Loudoun County, is really a state of mind that also envelops nearby Fauquier County and the communities of Upperville, Delaplane, and The Plains. The area's signature feature is mile after mile of waist-high fences made from loose stones that had been dug out of pasture and farmland over the centuries. In Middleburg, a farm of thirty acres would be considered modest. Here, there were estate names, rather than street addresses. A family bred thoroughbreds or jumpers. Others raised cattle—Black Angus were a favorite. They rode to the hounds. They were surrounded by servants. F. Scott Fitzgerald described Daisy in *The Great Gatsby* as having a voice "full of money"; the women of Middleburg had that voice. Their men did too, the accents overlaid with forgotten past generations of piracy and plunder.

Jack's first house was a twenty-room stone Georgian manor house in Upperville. "It's 6.3 miles beyond Middleburg," Jack would tell his few guests, "then 1.3 miles after the turn." Jack named the estate of fifty-one acres Fallingbrook, after the area of Toronto that was near his first home on Neville Park Boulevard and where he had once aspired to live. He paid $1,338,298 for the property. John, the loyal son, and his family were set up nearby in The Plains on a 362-acre farm called Byrnley, while Ralph was left to flounder in Los Angeles. One of Jack's corporations owned the Byrnley estate.

Fallingbrook was a place where Jack could, at least for a few years, focus on a single endeavor, the Redskins. With Tele-PrompTer nearly sold to Westinghouse, Jack had little to do except to concentrate on the team and some real estate holdings. For him, this was virtually treading water. He puttered around the grounds, rode horses, and continued his romance with his Las Vegas sculptor Jean Maxwell Williams Wilson. On his estate, topiary sculptures, something many Americans associate only with Disney World, were fashioned in the shapes of dogs and pheasants. Jack got back into horseback riding, buying a few Tennessee walking horses. He became involved in steeplechase racing, which was popular among the Middleburg horsey set. His most successful entry was a bay gelding named Lithograph. But he was considered a little too "new" by some of the conservative dowagers of Middleburg. One society woman labeled him a "little light in the loafers" in a 1988 *Dossier* magazine article.

He concentrated on every aspect of the Redskins, putting his mark on the team at every opportunity. When he first took his place in the owner's box on September 2, 1979, he had already ordered it remodeled. And when a reporter asked him how Edward Bennett Williams liked sharing the owner's box with him, Jack answered, "Is Mr. Williams having a good time sharing *my* owner's box with *me* is more the question." Jack was surrounded at that first game by friends of Williams—columnist Art Buchwald; Ben Bradlee, then executive editor of the *Washington Post;* lawyer and cabinet officer Joe Califano; Motion Picture Association President Jack Valenti; PBS television doyenne Nancy Dickerson; and baseball immortal Joe DiMaggio. The Williams group of liberal Democrats was soon gone, along with Williams, who was quietly given a smaller box on a lower level of the stadium. After that, Williams rarely attended football games at the stadium, turning his box over to members of his law firm. Jack began to form his own coterie of regulars, particularly writers with a national reputation and politicians of a conservative bent. On the literary side, one now saw Aaron Latham, author of *Crazy Sundays, F. Scott Fitzgerald in Hollywood,* a book about Jack's writing hero, and columnist George Will, novelist and playwright Larry L. King, wordsmith William Safire, and ambassador/writer Carl Rowan. And of course, the crusty Morrie Siegel. If a journalist wrote a favorable story about Jack, he would sometimes be invited for a Sunday or a series of Sundays in the owner's box. Jack had become a Holden Caufield of sorts, except now he really could call his favorite authors to talk about the book.[5] Robert Pack, a writer for *Washingtonian* magazine, who had written a generally favorable profile about him in 1982, was a guest several times, as was Redskins beat reporter Christine Brennan. But when the writers crossed Jack (both Brennan and Pack eventually did) and wrote things he didn't like, he would summon them to the box, accuse them of lying, and dismiss them. In the case of Pack, who had written another article about Jack, harping on the question "Does money buy happiness?" Jack warned him never to set foot in RFK Stadium, a public facility, again.

Other box regulars included the former Republican senator from Nevada, Paul Laxalt; Reagan appointee and secretary of agriculture John Block; neighbor and conservative Republican John Warner; and moderate-to-conservative Democrat and then Virginia governor Charles "Chuck" Robb.[6]

At Redskin Park, where the team's training facility and offices were located, about forty-five minutes from Fallingbrook, a new, imperial presidency developed. All employees (and reporters) were told in no uncertain terms that Jack could only be addressed as "Mr. Cooke." When Bobby Beathard, the team's general manager, and next in command after Jack, made the mistake of first speaking to the new owner as any casual Californian would, calling him Jack, he was dressed down vociferously. But although most of the radio and TV kowtowed and called him "Mr. Cooke" as well (Jack even insisted he be sent copies of each television interview including the outtakes), some of the tougher media did develop a first name relationship. Tony Kornheiser, the *Washington Post* columnist told a writer it was always "Tony and Jack" no matter what he wrote, which was not always complimentary.

Jack also was sure to let the front office know it was dealing with a man of wealth and power. Once, when talking about an available player, an assistant coach tried to lighten the mood by saying, "After all, Mr. Cooke, you can afford it. You're a millionaire."

Jack stared at the coach and corrected, "No, I'm not. I'm a billionaire."

On another occasion Jack tried to explain to a group of coaches the value of money. "Why I bet not one of you even has $100,000 in a savings account," he told the coaches prior to leaving the meeting room.

After he was gone, one of the coaches stood up and shrugged. "He's sure right on that one," he said.

But it was the coaching that may have made the team one of the 1980s NFL powerhouses. The Redskins often carried fourteen assistant coaches, nearly twice as many as some clubs. Each coach was well paid. In 1985, the average was more than $100,000 a year per man.

Jack Kent Cooke's eccentricities were soon the source of new anecdotes. A Saturday dinner in a Chinese restaurant at a Dallas shopping center before a Cowboys game generated countless howls. Jack, not liking his dessert of lichee nuts, had thought of sending it back, but general manager Bobby Beathard, at the table along with Morrie Siegel and Redskins public relations chief Charlie Dayton, had told Jack he couldn't.

"I don't think you can send them back Mr. Cooke, you've eaten nearly half."

"You didn't eat yours either?" Jack said to the general manager.

"No, Mr. Cooke, I didn't like them."

Jack took the two orders, spooned one dessert into the other and made one full dessert. Then he sent it back and saved $1.95.

But unique owners are the norm in the National Football League. Jack was joining a fraternity of owners which, if it didn't share the same level of wealth with him certainly had uncommon traits.

In Los Angeles, the Raiders were owned by Al Davis, who dressed mostly in black and silver and (although Jewish) once said, "I didn't hate Hitler. I was captivated by him. I knew he had to be stopped. He took on the whole world." In San Diego, Gene Klein, who had hawked used cars by the pound, saying they were "cheaper than hamburger," sold the team to Alex Spanos. Spanos once spotted a receptionist with a cold, half-finished cup of coffee (she had set it down to take a phone call). Spanos told her, "If you're not going to drink a complete cup, only take half a cup." In Phoenix, Bill Bidwill, owner of the "road show" club that was formerly the St. Louis Cardinals, and prior to that, the Chicago Cardinals, was the son of a dog track owner who had associated with Al Capone. Now, he was straitlaced to the point of wearing bow ties and requiring a dress code for the players on road trips. Robert Irsay had moved the Baltimore Colts to Indianapolis by backing up moving vans and loading up equipment at midnight to avoid lawsuits. In New England, the Sullivan family, which had nearly gone broke promoting Michael Jackson concerts even though "the gloved one" was a sellout in nearly every outdoor stadium in America, would give way to electric shaver king Victor Kiam. In 1990, he would refer to a female sports reporter as "a classic bitch." In Los Angeles, Carroll Rosenbloom's widow, Georgia (Carroll had died in a tragic, mysterious ocean drowning), had taken over, the first and only female NFL owner. Georgia Rosenbloom, a former nightclub singer, had shown up nearly an hour late for her husband's funeral and had to be talked out of singing at it. Instead, comedian Jonathan Winters presided, doing his routines.

At Redskin Park, Jack set new standards on player contracts. John Riggins, the team's dominant running back of the early 1980s, was the first to feel the Cooke power. Riggins had signed a five-year, $1.5 million contract with the team but had wanted the contract redone in 1980, with the final two years guaranteed. Jack refused to change the deal, citing his belief that a "contract is a contract." Riggins played his cards a little too close to his chest, and rather than lose face, sat out the 1980 season and gave up his $300,000 salary plus endorsements. Jack wouldn't negotiate with the players' agents either, no matter how large the salary, leaving that to Bobby Beathard, his general manager. Even Beathard himself had to negotiate directly with Jack, and when an impasse was reached, Beathard would go outside and telephone his Los Angeles attorney and agent for advice, then go back inside and negotiate further, using his attorney's counsel.

205

There is no question that Jack often took a paternalistic interest in his players, similar to the way he dealt with his employees in Los Angeles. As he had advised Jeannie I on how to invest the funds, when offering a $5 million cash divorce settlement in 1977, he also advised quarterback Joe Theismann to insure a just-signed multiyear $4.5 million contract in 1985, even to the extent of suggesting companies and agents. Theismann grudgingly took the advice and later, when his leg was snapped in half by Lawrence Taylor of the New York Giants on November 18, 1985, was glad he did.

Midway through the 1980 season Jack married his lover of three years, Jean Maxwell Williams Wilson of Las Vegas, on Halloween afternoon, Friday, October 31. Jack gave Jean, the sculptor, a six-carat diamond wedding ring. The ceremony was performed by U.S. District Judge John Sirica in Washington.[7] As he had done nearly half a century before with Jeannie I, Jack had the marriage resolemnized in the Episcopal church a few days later.

Two weeks afterward on Saturday, November 15, 1980, Jack unveiled the dimunitive, blonde Jeannie II in his box at RFK Stadium. There was a champagne party at halftime with a wedding cake designed in the burgundy and gold colors of the Redskins. Footballs were etched on both the top and sides of the cake. During the game, the Redskins magic message board flashed "Jack and Jean" over and over complete with hearts and flowers surrounding the names.

Jack made his first major decision on the future of the Washington Redskins on January 5, 1981. The team had gone 10–6 during the 1979 season under George Allen's replacement, coach Jack Pardee, but had failed to make the playoffs and in the 1980 season had slumped to 6–10. Jack Kent Cooke summoned both Beathard and Pardee to Fallingbrook for a discussion of their futures. Beathard was better in articulating himself than Pardee and was able to get across his belief that Pardee was a poor communicator, particularly with the younger players. As the talks progressed, Beathard, a veteran front-office man who had observed football politics with three other NFL clubs—Miami, Atlanta, and Kansas City—was easily able to get his other major points across. The club was too conservative and too old. Pardee, who had played on the Redskins' 1972 Super Bowl entry was on the defensive throughout and after three series of talks, his future with the Redskins was behind him. He was summarily fired. After he was let go, Pardee aimed some weak jibes at Beathard, but it was too little, too late.

"I believe each coach should have control and not have to worry about being shot down from other angles," the ex-coach said, "Everything that affects the record on the field should be under the coach's control. They don't print the general manager's record in the newspaper."

But it was a poor harvest of sour grapes. Beathard was already on the road interviewing potential replacements.

Beathard's first choice for Pardee's replacement was John Madden, the former Oakland Raiders coach who was now becoming a media sensation. Madden and Beathard had played college football together at California State Polytechnic University at San Luis Obispo, a small college nearly halfway between San Francisco and Los Angeles. Madden's dorm room was across the hall from Beathard's. But Madden wasn't about to give up the high pay and relative security of television for the vagaries of coaching NFL children-in-adult-bodies again. He had also developed a fear of flying and now went from city to city on trains or buses, something that was impossible in the NFL.

When Beathard told Jack this, the owner became insistent. "Call him and ask him," Jack ordered Beathard. "You never know until you ask."

Although John Robinson, the coach of the University of Southern California was mentioned, as were assistant coaches Tom Bass of Tampa Bay, George Perles of Pittsburgh, and Dick Coury of Philadelphia, Beathard's first choice, after Madden proved unobtainable, was Joe Gibbs, the offensive coordinator at San Diego.

Gibbs, a deeply religious man and a native of Mocksville, North Carolina, had moved to southern California as a teenager and had spent his life in football, either as a high school or college player, a college coach, or as an NFL assistant coach. Other than his church activities and racquetball (he was a national champion in that sport in 1976), Gibbs lived, ate, and breathed life on the gridiron.

Jack summoned Beathard's choice to his suite at the Waldorf

Towers in New York City. Over the weekend of January 12, 1981, Jack met with Gibbs for several hours. Gibbs' messianic devotion to the game (he would later admit to having "no idea" who Madonna or Oliver North were) was apparent, and when Jack Kent Cooke was told that the offense platoon of the Chargers, under Joe Gibbs, had just become the only squad in the NFL to average more than 400 yards a game, he was sold. Gibbs was in no position to bargain for a high salary, but when Jack let slip that he had recently bought the seventy-seven-story Chrysler Building a few blocks away, the new coach raised his salary sights accordingly.

Jack tossed out (for Jack) toned-down rhetoric in praise of his new employee in a press conference: "I have confidence that Joe will provide the Redskins fans with a team that will stir the imagination, win or lose. And I believe his abilities match his ambitions. He's a pioneer in the game in as much as he recognized before others, the perceptible change in the character of the game."

After Jack welcomed Joe Gibbs to the Washington Redskins, it was goodbye to Jean Maxwell Williams Wilson. They separated on July 14, 1981, and were officially divorced on August 28, 1981, after ten months of marriage. Jean Wilson, who should have seen it coming when the halftime "wedding cake" had footballs on it, didn't like the East Coast or football. She received $30,000 a year from Jack and a 50 percent interest in their Las Vegas house. The yearly stipend amounted to just under $700 for each week they were married, as opposed to the $1 million a year that the first Jean Cooke gained.

Unlike his two other former wives, Jack Kent Cooke has remained friendly with Jean Wilson to this day. Two of her sculptures—those of John Cooke's two sons, Tommy and John—remain on prominent display in his Upperville home, and her sister, Helen Banks, has been his guest at a Redskins Super Bowl. In 1989, many of Jean Wilson's sculptures were shown at an art show in the Washington, D.C., area. Jack purchased one of the pieces, "the least expensive," according to one attendee.

With the advent of the 1981 season there were high hopes, if not realistic expectations, for the new Beathard–Gibbs duo. But under Joe Gibbs the Redskins lost their first five games and Jack, who began the season telling the guests in his box that he had discovered a bright new coach, was reduced to muttering and barking at Beathard, a command-performance guest in his box.

"You've done this to me," Jack fumed at his general manager when the team was 0–5. The club finally won its sixth game of the year, against the Chicago Bears, 24–7, and from then on were virtually invincible, winning eight of the last eleven games.[8] They continued winning in the strike-shortened 1982 season, going 8–1, and were victorious in the Super Bowl in Pasadena. The reinstated and colorful John Riggins dominated the game, which the Redskins won 24–17. Riggins won the game on an off-tackle run the team had named "70-chip." Before the Super Bowl, he showed up at Jack's pregame party in top hat and tails. The next year, the Redskins were again nearly unbeatable with a 14–2 record. However, they badly lost the Super Bowl in Tampa Bay to Al Davis's Raiders.

A major league baseball team was still a goal lusted after by Jack Kent Cooke. When the San Francisco Giants and the Pittsburgh Pirates were up for grabs in 1985, Jack considered writing a check for one of the teams. But each sale stalled because the deals were contingent upon the clubs staying in their respective cities.

A new Jack Kent Cooke with little real business on which to concentrate in the early 1980s seemed to enjoy life, as well as the success of the Redskins. "Girlfriends," after the departure of Jean Maxwell Williams included a European countess, Agnetta Bonde; a West Virginia businesswoman, Anne Pallie; as well as dozens of eligible moneyed women in the Middleburg horsey set.

There were times when Jack Kent Cooke began to show a gentle side, even a new trait, self-deprecation. He once broke an awkward after-dinner silence at Boiling Springs Tavern near the Redskins training camp in Carlisle, Pennsylvania, following a marital breakup with, "Perhaps you've all noticed my recent success with women . . . ," his voice trailing off inaudibly. And Redskins front office veterans still like to tell Jack's Lord Nelson story:

During the early 1980s, when the Dallas Cowboys were one of the premier teams in the NFL, the five days prior to the bout with the Texans were known as "Dallas Week."

Jack, who had just read a biography of Viscount Horatio Nelson, the British naval hero who had defeated Napoleon's fleet in 1798 and the Danes a few years later, spent a half-hour with Joe Gibbs and the assistant coaches creating an analogy between Nelson and the Redskins' game plan. After lecturing the coaches on Nelson's secret—it was, according to Jack Kent Cooke, preparedness and organization—Jack concluded with an exhortation to fight like Admiral Nelson.[9]

On the way out, he gave a quick glance at Joe Gibbs and winked.

"Now, if the Dallas Cowboys would only arrive by boat," Jack whispered to Gibbs.

But Jack could still be tough. When Mel Krupin, the owner of one of Washington's more popular steak and bake power restaurants (named, of course, Mel Krupin's) hung the banner of the competing United States Football League team in his restaurant, Jack cut the restaurateur off in the blink of an eye. Krupin, who had hung the new Washington Federals insignia because the owner, attorney Berl Bernhard, was an old friend, instantly became persona non grata as far as the Washington Redskins were concerned. His parking privileges at RFK stadium were revoked, the weekly cake that he brought out to Redskins Park was refused, and the word was passed that loyal Redskins shouldn't go there. The restaurant, which had been a mainstay among downtown Washington's power eateries, went downhill from there and folded six years later.

Jack began acquiring some choice chunks of hunt-country real estate as well. In addition to Byrnley and Fallingbrook, which totaled 412 acres, Jack bought: Heronwood in Upperville, which also featured a stone house on fifty acres; The Retreat, a 180-acre farm in nearby Loudoun County that had belonged to Harold Runnells, a Republican congressman from New Mexico; and an office on Liberty Street in Middleburg that had been the home of the widow of the well-known horse trainer, Preston Burch.

Jack Kent Cooke wanted one other piece of real estate. It had to contain enough acres of land to put a new 78,600-seat football stadium on it, complete with parking and the infrastructure necessary to get the paying customers in and out in a minimum amount of time. Haggling with the District of Columbia began in earnest in 1987. At first Jack wanted Mayor Marion Barry to build it with government funds. Later, he recanted and said he'd build it but the D.C. government should provide the land. At first it was to be a domed stadium but Jack changed his mind on that too. He also kept encouraging various northern Virginia municipalities to make a deal but didn't get any takers of consequence. By mid-1991, with the D.C. ex-mayor facing a six-month sentence on cocaine possession, and a new straight-arrow Sharon Pratt Dixon replacing Barry in a recession, the resolution of Jack's new stadium remained elusive.

But it was in the 1980s that Jack Kent Cooke reached full frenetic stride in acquiring wealth. He joined with a high-profile group to take the media giant Metromedia private in 1983.[10] He bought the famed Kentucky thoroughbred breeding farm, Elmendorf, in 1984. He made an abortive try for Multimedia, a conglomerate of newspapers, television and radio stations, early in 1985. He purchased the *Los Angeles Daily News* late in 1985, a 9 percent piece of a cable network, The Nostalgia Channel, in 1986, and McCaw Cable in 1987. They were new toys for a growing toy chest that would catapult his wealth from nine figures to ten.

Notes

1. In 1990, Jack Kent Cooke was asked to recount the "saddest moment of your life" in a deposition. Jack answered, "losing to the Raiders in the Super Bowl at Tampa Bay."
2. Jack ordered frequent-flyer awards given the scouts turned back into the front office. But Bobby Beathard went to John Cooke and made a case for the scouts, saying they were away from home for weeks at a time, and were relatively low-paid. This was the only way, Beathard said, that the scouts could afford to take their families on vacation in June. John Cooke relented, with the final words, "But don't tell Dad."
3. When Edward Bennett Williams finally sold his shares on February 28, 1985, he said he owned 14.7 percent of the team, which would be a small contradiction of 1 percent. The figure for which he sold it was reported to be $8 to $10 million; a former Redskins executive said it was closer to the lower amount.
4. At the lunch, a new, outspoken quarterback for the Redskins, Joe

Theismann, stuck out his hand and introduced himself. Cooke knew with whom he was dealing. Reaching into his literary bag of tricks, Jack said, "Remember what Robert Browning said, 'A man's reach should exceed his grasp, or what's a heaven for?'"

5. In J.D. Salinger's *The Catcher in the Rye*, the narrator, Holden Caulfield, says, "What really knocks me out is a book that, when you're all done reading it, you wish the author that wrote it was a terrific friend of yours and you could call him on the phone whenever you felt like it."

6. Jack put Warner on the board of directors of Pro Football, Inc., aka the Washington Redskins. Warner sold Jack the acres that comprise most of his current estate, Far Acres.

7. Sirica was the judge most closely associated with Richard Nixon's tragedy, known as "Watergate." He sentenced many of the defendants.

8. After Washington won its first game of the Beathard–Gibbs regime, Beathard had a picture framed of himself and Gibbs embracing after the victory, and hung it in the kitchen of his Vienna, Va., home.

9. Admiral Nelson wasn't infallible. He was killed at the Battle of Trafalgar in 1805.

10. The backers of the $1.45 billion buyout included lots of Jack's friends: Jerry Perenchio, Marvin Davis, Rupert Murdoch, Gene Klein, and Norman Lear. They were led by John Kluge, who by 1990 had earned the title, "America's richest man."

CHAPTER
16
ACQUISITIONS FOR THE MODERN MOGUL

"I'd like to win a Kentucky Derby for Elmendorf."

As soon as Jack Kent Cooke made his first million dollars in the early 1940s, trips to New York City became a part of his life. A man of habit and tradition, Jack at first stayed at the Waldorf-Astoria Hotel, but later switched to a suite next door at the more exclusive Waldorf Towers at 100 East Fiftieth Street, an elegant mass of suites that sits on top of the main hotel, fifty-five stories in the sky.

Manhattan offers the best and worst of Western civilization on an island of vertical masonry. From the beginning, Jack Kent Cooke, made an attempt to sample the best of the most prominent city in North America. His weekends in Manhattan usually included an afternoon being outfitted at Brooks Brothers, or watching the action at Belmont Park, long before his own thoroughbreds raced there. A sampling of restaurants visited by Jack in the 1980s includes the top layer of New York gastronomy: La Petite Marmite, La Cote Basque, La Caravelle, La Grenouille, Lutece, Laurent, The Palm, and a table near Bobby Short at the Carlyle Hotel. But to Jack, the dining room where he has always felt the most comfortable, the one that always told him he had "arrived," is the '21' Club, a public, yet seemingly private restaurant at 21 West Fifty-second Street.

The '21' Club, which was begun in Greenwich Village in the 1920s by the Berns and Kriendler families, moved to its present location in 1938. In 1940, the owner of a small Bermuda air service asked if he could suspend a model of his company plane from the ceiling. The manager granted this request, and within a week executives from Pan American and American Airlines asked for and received permission as well. Within a year, the ceiling became filled with toys—models and replicas that were in actuality symbols of corporate America. Jack's most visible corporate symbol, the Washington Redskins, is represented at the '21' Club by a helmet that hangs over his regular table by the wall, near the front of the main dining room, to the left of entering patrons.

Before one even enters the interior of the restaurant, there is evidence of Jack Kent Cooke. Years ago, a customer's horse won a big race and he celebrated at '21.' The next day he presented the restaurant with a metal jockey painted in his stable's colors. The manager placed it outside. That attracted many thoroughbred owners and soon the entrance to the restaurant was lined with jockey figures from many famous horse breeding enterprises. Jack's name and the name of his wholly-owned Elmendorf Farms is printed below the yellow and blue colors of his Kentucky thoroughbred organization. In the days before his troubles began, it was his and Jean's favorite restaurant, the place they would go to celebrate special occasions when in New York.

But as one who appreciates and looks for beauty in all things, human or otherwise, it might be expected that for years Jack Kent Cooke's love affair with New York could be epitomized by the city's most beautiful skyscraper, the Chrysler Building, at 405 Lexington Avenue, between Forty-second and Forty-third streets. The large window in the bathroom of his suite at the Waldorf Towers looks directly on it, and there is the occasional evening, after showering and dressing, that he will look out the window and admire the grandeur of its architecture.

When the building came up for sale in the summer of 1979, Jack Kent Cooke knew he had to have it. The New York real estate market had just finished bottoming out—the Chrysler Building was a great value. He purchased it for $87 million from Massachusetts Mutual Life Insurance, which had acquired it just a year before by foreclosing on an unpaid mortgage. The cost to Massachusetts Mutual was $35 million, but the firm immediately began a $58 million renovation program. It had no choice. The building had fallen on hard times and was worn out, shabby, with occupancy below 50 percent.

Construction on the skyscraper had begun during the last heydays of the 1920s and was completed while the nation was falling face-first into the Depression. When the seventy-seven-story edifice was in its final construction stages, another, the Manhattan Bank Building on Wall Street, topped its projected height by 22 inches, at 925 feet.[1] That's when William Van Alen, the architect who created it, added the graceful stainless steel spire that rises to pencil thinness, surrounded by a crown of art deco triangles. The finished structure rose 1,048 feet into the air and descended 69 feet into the ground, surpassing Manhattan Bank.

The Chrysler Building was New York's tallest skyscraper for just over a month. It was surpassed by the Empire State Building, which held the title for more than four decades until construction of the World Trade Towers.

The Chrysler Building is not just another tall warehouse of people. It is perhaps this century's most enduring example of art deco. The highly detailed three-story entrance brings one into a lobby of marble and granite that was imported from five countries of Europe and Africa. The large Edward Trumbull mural on the ceiling catalogs the history of transportation. The thirty-two elevators are made from stainless steel and four different types of wood; no two elevator interiors are alike. There are 200 flights of stairs, 391,381 rivets, and miles of brass strips embedded in its terrazzo floors.

Built for Walter P. Chrysler, the soaring structure has Chrysler automobile hubcaps and radiator tops built into its walls. Chrysler himself was originally supposed to live in a penthouse there, but never moved in when he discovered his wife was afraid of heights. Jack Kent Cooke has a slightly different problem. His claustrophobia makes him extremely panicky in enclosed spaces. Because of this, he has never been to the top of the building, and rarely visits the executive offices on the thirty-ninth floor.

Walter Chrysler envisioned the building as a showplace for the Chrysler Corporation. He established a showroom on the second floor and brought cars in by crane through the windows. He built an observation deck near the top and put a display case close to its entrance that features the tools he once had used when he was a nickel-an-hour teenage metalworker.

After the grand opening in May 1930, Walter Chrysler opened a three-story private club near the top of the building called the Cloud Club. It contained special liquor lockers for each member (Prohibition was still in force), a barbershop, a Turkish bath, a library and a twelve-foot walk-in cigar humidor. Even though its earliest members had names like Vanderbilt, Whitney, and Firestone, it lasted about as long as Jack did selling encyclopedias in Saskatchewan—closing about the time young Jack was beginning his western Canada tour. Nothing lavish lasted too long in the Great Depression.

Outside, on the salmon-pink brick exteriors, are many more examples of twentieth-century art deco style—stainless steel eagles, gargoyles, and a frieze of automobiles on the twenty-sixth floor. Inside the building, many innovations for comfort and convenience were installed that are still rare today in commercial structures. There is a central vacuum cleaning system, self-cleaning central air conditioners, concealed radiators with individual thermostats, and wiring ducts under the floors.

When Jack bought the Chrysler Building there was still much renovation work to be done. So he added more than $30 million to complete the insurance company's plans, which included new windows and new metalwork framing. But his biggest contribution was adding the 580 pieces of zigzag neon tubing that frame the finial at the top of the skyscraper. Until Jack installed the seven tiers of tubing that form the tiara of the tower, it was lit for decades by floodlights.[2] It took more than six months, in 1981, to install the neon crown, the strips framing the triangular shaped windows near the pinnacle.

When asked how much the neon had cost him, the answer was a typical Jack Kent Cooke reply to the press: "I don't know how much it's costing me. And I don't give a damn." The lighting, looking like carefully arranged pick-up sticks, was switched on at dusk on September 17, 1981, fading to darkness at midnight. It has operated continuously that way ever since.

When the lights were turned on, Jack said, "I've spent $31

million getting this building back in the shape it was in when Walter Chrysler first turned the key in the lock. It's 98 percent rented already. People love that address." Pragmatic as always, Jack certainly had a profit motive. And that too has succeeded. His leveraged $87 million investment, aided by a booming Manhattan real estate market, was estimated to be worth about $550 million ten years later. Jack refinanced the Chrysler building in July 1982, doing what's known in commercial real estate terms as a "consolidation modification and spreader agreement." At that time, the terms called for Jack to pay interest only, at the rate of 10.5 percent a year in twelve equal payments of $552,887.20 a month on a mortgage of $60,567,127.29. Jack also refinanced the building in 1987, for $250 million. Wanda Wiser, who now ran Jack's staff of thirty-eight in Middleburg and was his most trusted employee except for Jim Lacher, signed the documents.

Jack reasoned that the building would be a success partly because of its location. Situated just two short blocks from Grand Central Station, it is an ideal destination for workers to arrive via public transportation. And because of its prime east side midtown site, it is more in demand than, say, the Empire State with its lower midtown spot near Herald Square, and thus is able to command higher rents per square foot.

When Jack bought the Chrysler building, he actually bought, for all practical purposes, the block. The other large building on the block was known as the Chrysler Building East. A more pedestrian structure in both size and style, its thirty-five stories are topped with two levels of concealed heating and air conditioning. It is located on the east side of the block, at Forty-second Street and Third Avenue, fronting on Third. After Jack bought it, he renamed it the Kent Building.

Today the Chrysler Building is one of the most tangible symbols of the Jack Kent Cooke business empire. Its position on the New York skyline, looking from its northwest corner into Jack's suite at the Waldorf Towers, must give the former door-to-door Depression salesman an emotional lift every time he sees it. Perhaps Jack's friend, the popular Canadian author Morley Callaghan, said it best in a letter to the aging entrepreneur shortly after it opened.

Callaghan wrote to him saying that the skyscraper and Jack

217

were an incredible tale. He said that the steepled apex of the building had always represented Manhattan to the young Canadian
entrepreneur. The building had possessed Jack Kent Cooke, Callaghan wrote, and it was fitting that Jack had finally possessed the
structure. The writer concluded by prophetically writing that Jack
and the Chrysler skyscraper would flourish together. Jack, years
later, probably couldn't agree more.

The elevator ride always gave Jack a rush. And although
he trembled and fretted every time he went up to the top of the
Waldorf, it was worth the suffering.

He looked out from his suite at the Waldorf Towers, staring
at the neon-lighted spire of the Chrysler building. The beauty of
it gave him a lift. This weekend—October 27–28, 1990—could
have great fortune ahead. But then again, as the mogul had said
many times, "You win some, you lose some." It was an expression
Jack often used, but as the weekend progressed, it was never more
apt.

First there was the Renaissance Ball matter. The annual event
was to be held Saturday night next door in the Starlight Roof
Ballroom of the Waldorf Astoria Hotel. Jack called to reserve a
table, but he was told Suzanne/Susan was a chairperson and since
she would be there, Jack wouldn't.

Next it was off to Belmont Park on Saturday afternoon for the
Breeder's Cup. His horse, Flying Continental, was in the Classic,
the most prestigious race of the day. Two weeks before it had
earned $503,100 by winning the Jockey Club Gold Cup at Bel-
mont, bringing its career winnings to $1,486,350, and Saturday it
was one of the favorites. But alas, it wasn't to be. The colt ran a
poor eleventh and was never in the running. Coming back in the
limousine, Jack shrugged it off. "We lost because Marlene wasn't
here to kiss the colt," he told his friend, Orator Woodward, the
Jello heir, referring to a new tradition he had begun some weeks
before with his fourth wife. Marlene had chosen to stay in Washington.

But there were always the Redskins. The team would play the
New York Giants Sunday in a four o'clock game and if the club

were to win, they'd still have a chance to win the NFL Eastern Division title.

That was a disaster as well. With the Washington team poised to go ahead and just minutes to go in the game, running back Earnest Byner bobbled a pass in the end zone, and it bounced out and into the hands of a Giants' defender for an interception and the ballgame. Bill Parcell's team added another score for insult and Jack left the Meadowlands a 21–10 loser.

Publicly, Jack shrugged it off—it was just predestination. Privately, although he never let it show, he brooded about the losses for days.

Lexington, Kentucky, has little in common with New York City, but Jack's other major real estate acquisition of the 1980s occurred on an eleven mile stretch of narrow, two-lane, tree-lined road the locals refer to as "the Park Avenue of the Blue Grass." In fact, Elmendorf Farms, the 505-acre property, with a population of 373 thoroughbreds on the premises when Jack bought it, is, like the Chrysler Building among New York skyscrapers, undoubtedly one of the most beautiful and prestigious of the twenty-seven farms that line the road called Paris Pike, just outside Lexington.[3] Running out from Fayette County and into neighboring Bourbon County, it is also the oldest thoroughbred breeding farm in America, having operated continuously since 1874.

Jack paid $43,323,000 for Elmendorf, substantially more than the $65,000 C.J. Enright, the first owner, got for the 140-stall, 544-acre farm when he sold it in 1897 to James Ben Ali Haggin, a California copper mining baron. Haggin, who had a 44,000-acre horse farm in California and another farm with more than 400,000 acres, quickly pushed Elmendorf up to 10,000 acres, which included most of northern Fayette County. James Ben Ali Haggin grew tobacco on 350 acres of the property—a prime Kentucky crop at the turn of the century. Haggin, who at one time owned 375 broodmares and fifty stallions—the largest breeding stock of thoroughbreds in the state—maintained Elmendorf as a pristine showplace. His masses of retainers swarmed over the property, building cottages and stone bridges over North Elkhorn Creek,

219

which ran through the farm. Haggin commissioned the stone lions that are seen at various points on the property.

Haggin died in 1914 at the age of ninety-three and much of the farm was sold. Greentree Farms, owned by the widow of John Hay "Jock" Whitney, and Spendthrift Farm, owned by Leslie Combs II, were one part of Elmendorf.[4] After Haggin, Elmendorf had a succession of owners. The next, John E. Madden, set a new record by selling a thoroughbred called Hamburg Place for $40,001—one dollar above the then-highest price ever paid. The Widener family of Philadelphia made the farm the leading American breeder in 1940. Two Cleveland horse fanciers, Tinkham Veale II and Sam A. Costello, were the next owners. They were succeeded by Jack's predecessor, Maxwell H. Gluck, who purchased Elmendorf in 1952. Gluck's life story was similar to Jack's. He had risen from being the owner of a dress shop to clothing manufacturer to United States Ambassador to Ceylon.

Under Gluck, Elmendorf gained even more stature. It was the country's leading breeding stable in 1973, the second leading breeder in 1974, and maintained a leading position for the three decades it was owned by him. The former rag king's horses won more than 100 stakes races during his Elmendorf tenure.

When Gluck died, on November 21, 1984, at the age of eighty-eight, it was put up for sale by his widow, Muriel. Jack had been talking to Max and Muriel about buying Elmendorf for three years and had also tried to buy nearby Greentree Farms, which was owned by the Whitney family. Muriel Gluck now formed a committee of three—herself, a real estate attorney by the name of Leonard Marx, and a financial advisor, Don Riefler. The three put Elmendorf up for sale via a sealed bid process. The bidders for the property were Fred Sahadi of California's Cardiff Stud Farm, who bid $34 million; Kinghaven Farms, an Ontario, Canada, corporation, which bid $43,111,000; and Jack, who bid $43,323,000.

At a news conference held in Lexington on December 20, 1984, to announce his victory, Jack Kent Cooke promised no staff changes and said he hoped "my family will keep control of Elmendorf for at least the next 100 years."

Muriel Gluck said, "Maxwell Gluck built a superb establish-

ment at Elmendorf. . . . I'm sure Jack Kent Cooke will carry on
the tradition and that Jack Kent Cooke will ride with the great
Elmendorf colors."

A week later, on December 28, 1984, Kinghaven Farms filed
a lawsuit against Jack Kent Cooke for $25 million in punitive
damages and $5 million in compensatory damages alleging that
Jack's bid for the farm was invalid and that Elmendorf should be
awarded to Kinghaven. The Canadians claimed that an "add-on"
bid of $212,000 had been allowed Jack Kent Cooke and that the
add-on violated the bidding rules. They alleged that a secret agreement enabling Jack to purchase the farm had been made between
Jack and Arthur Groman, an attorney for Elmendorf, and that it
constituted fraud.[5] Also alleged was that the committee failed to
accept the highest bid, which, without Jack's add-on, was Kinghaven's.

In his defense, Jack said that Kinghaven had received a confidential appraisal of Elmendorf's worth from a former Elmendorf
employee prepared by the Keeneland Association and that Kinghaven's receipt of the appraisal constituted "inequitable conduct,
sharp practices, fraud and unfairness." Finally, James Park, Jr.,
Jack's Kentucky attorney, said that the Gluck estate had "the right
to reject any and all bidders, according to the instructions."

The case was dismissed in May 1986 by U.S. District Judge
Henry Wilhoit, who ruled that the committee had the right to
accept Jack's bid. But Kinghaven wasn't quite through. It appealed
the ruling to a federal appeals court where the case was dismissed
on July 10, 1987. Jack was now officially (as Kentucky horse farm
owners sometimes designate themselves) "Master of Elmendorf."

Jack Kent Cooke immediately made plans to make Elmendorf
the leading horse breeding farm in the country. For all its more
than a century of glory, Elmendorf was lacking a major jewel in
its crown. An Elmendorf horse had never won a Kentucky Derby.
In fact, it had never even been in the money there, the best being
two fourth-place finishes.

"I became the major owner of the Washington Redskins and
they won the Super Bowl. I'd like to win a Kentucky Derby for
Elmendorf," Jack told a writer for the *Los Angeles Times,* shortly

after purchasing the farm. Jack's first opportunity came in 1989, but the Elmendorf entry, the chestnut colt, Flying Continental, finished sixth.[6]

Jack's other chief task was to find a new star stud horse. Elmendorf's mainstay, Verbatim, was twenty years old when Jack took over in 1984. It had sired 515 foals by late 1990 including forty stakes winners, at a fee of $15,000 per service. Of its foals, 247 had been sold as yearlings at an average price of $35,281. This outstanding record would be hard to beat. Jack's decision, made with farm manager James Brady, was to bring in Juddmonte Farm's Alphabatim in 1987, a son of Verbatim, to stand at stud. The stallion had won more than a million dollars on the track. Jack also decided to push the stud services of Super Moment, a stallion that had won the Bay Meadows Handicap three straight years.

Buying Elmendorf also helped resolve a messy personal family matter. Jack's oldest son, Ralph, had made the mistake of not supporting his father in Jack's bitter divorce from Barbara Jean Carnegie Cooke. After the decree Jack had disowned Ralph, even deleting his name from his *Who's Who* listing. Ralph had then tried a number of businesses, most notably advertising services, on his own without much success. His most prominent failure was a Los Angeles independent motion picture distribution company he had taken public under the name of Cardinal Productions, at $2 a share. Cardinal's "top" two cinematic hopes in 1985 were *Hot Moves*, a teen T & A exploitation film, and *Creature*, a horror movie that starred Klaus Kinski. Neither was a success and Ralph's days as a movie producer, at a salary of $125,000 per year, ended in bankruptcy, with Cardinal Productions delisted from the National Association of Securities Dealers stock tables in the daily papers.

Jack took Ralph back in and made him the titular head of Elmendorf. Not that Ralph's new job was without penance. Ralph lived for more than a year in a small, unglamorous 1,000-square-foot cottage on the property. His father then built him a new modern home. Its vaguely Spanish Californian look jars the traditional surroundings of the other parts of the farm. Haggin's original mansion, which cost $300,000 when it was built in 1901, was lost to fire. Its four columns, like classic Greek ruins, still stand dramatically silhouetted against the sky behind the new house.

The Lexington press said Jack would begin a tradition of naming all his horses after Italian sculptors and artists when Elmendorf was bought. But Jack Kent Cooke promised to name his Elmendorf horses after American Indians. He said he already had three examples of that in the fillies Goleta, Amdala, and Capay. "I've discovered that when you name horses this way, the Jockey Club never turns you down," Jack told the Lexington community.

The mogul's third major trophy of the decade was his purchase of the *Los Angeles Daily News*, on December 10, 1985. Jack paid $176 million for the newspaper, then based in Van Nuys, California, a Los Angeles suburb in the San Fernando Valley. Most experts say that Jack Kent Cooke overpaid for the media property, which was then owned by the Tribune Company of Chicago, owner of the *Chicago Tribune*, the *New York Daily News* (which the *Tribune* sold in 1991 to Robert Maxwell), and a scattering of other newspapers, television stations, plus syndicated programming.

The Tribune Company was forced to sell the *Los Angeles Daily News* because it was buying KTLA-TV in Los Angeles, and federal regulations had been changed to prohibit owning two major media properties in the same city. The Tribune Company also sold its Los Angeles cable operations at the same time to Jones Intercable, giving it a total of $413 million. But the company paid $510 million for KTLA and Jack's high bid was an unexpected windfall.

Jack Kent Cooke had been looking for a newspaper for five years. He had considered making an offer for the *Washington Evening Star* and the *Los Angeles Herald-Examiner*. He had made a serious offer for the *Detroit News* but had lost out to Gannett, publishers of *USA Today*. And his bid for Multimedia, which had thirteen small newspapers in its diversified empire, had gone awry, though still netting him $25 million.[7] The *Los Angeles Daily News* was a triumphant return to southern California, albeit at a high price.

"Cooke has paid at the high end of the range," a media analyst, John Morton, told the *Los Angeles Times*.

"I thought $100 million was reasonable. It looks like he wanted to get it badly," said George Keiselmann, of the securities firm of Morgan, Olmstead, Kennedy, and Gardner.

Jack paid $1,100 per subscriber for a newspaper that had an annual profit of $12.5 million on yearly revenues of just under $100 million. The 13 percent operating profit was well under the industry average of 18 percent.

There were three other bidders for the *Los Angeles Daily News*, but they had all bid $80 to $101 million—about half of what Jack paid. They were the two corporations that owned, respectively, the *San Francisco Chronicle* and the *Dallas Morning News*, and an employee group from the *Los Angeles Daily News*.

"I want to return to my first love, newspapers," Jack said at the time. "This paper has a shiny future."

It had taken Jack Kent Cooke more than thirty years since he had bid for the *Globe and Mail* in Toronto to acquire a major daily newspaper. At that time the editorial staff had been apprehensive— to say the least—when it learned he was a possible buyer. But this time the staff welcomed him. "The fact he spent so much money is a vote of confidence in the newspaper and the staff, too," said one reporter.

When Jack took over, the publisher was Byron C. Campbell, a career Tribune Company employee. He had been there for less than three years, but had moved the *Los Angeles Daily News* from a yearly profit of $7 million to $12.5 million in that time and had changed it from a suburban San Fernando Valley daily to a full-fledged metropolitan newspaper. But it was still a gnat compared to the area's largest paper, the *Los Angeles Times*. The *Times'* circulation at the end of 1987, for example, was 1,113,459 daily, 1,384,857 on Sunday, compared to the soon-to-fold *Herald-Examiner's* 238,811 and 195,009, and the *Daily News'* 159,348 and 174,767.

By the end of the year, Campbell resigned, as did the marketing director, the vice president of circulation, and the manager of the resources department, although Jack had vowed to keep the management on, "lock, stock, and barrel."

Campbell said that his decision to leave "basically related to differences in management style. There are different philosophies in operation and neither one is right or wrong. I have to be comfortable with the way I was operating."

Jack agreed with Campbell. "There was perfectly understandable disagreement between the two of us. He may be right or I may be right. Who knows?"

Campbell was known to be in disagreement with Jack's dismantling of the human resources department that he had instituted. The section enveloped personnel, training, and employee benefits.

But Jack cleaned up the *Los Angeles Daily News* as well. He moved the "dump" (as employees like to call it) to a spanking new complex in nearby Woodland Hills and bought a new fleet of trucks for delivery, a new phone system, new computer system, and new presses that gave the paper the capacity to run off 300,000 copies per edition. And with Jack's demonstrated commitment behind it, the paper's circulation and advertising continued to climb each year until 1990, when a slowdown in media advertising all over the country cut advertising revenue at the *Daily News* 10 percent.[8] Jack, as many other owners would do, reduced the staff 4 percent.[9]

The improvements to the newspaper were funded in part by the high-yield (also known as "junk") bond department of the Drexel Burnham Lambert securities firm, originating in the Beverly Hills office, which was the headquarters of the king of "junk," Michael Milken.[10]

Jack's "junk" bond offering, executed on April 10, 1987, encompassed both the refinancing and expansion of the *Daily News* and a much larger purchase (and also a return to his roots), a $755 million acquisition of McCaw Communications. This major cable operation had 464,311 subscribers in forty-two communities, mostly in the western United States, although the two largest markets served by McCaw were Syracuse, New York, and Tucson, Arizona.

Jack paid nearly $1,800 a subscriber for the cable operation, six times what he had paid for his first system in 1964. He now owned the twentieth largest cable system in the country. "Broadcasting has been called the fifth estate," Jack Kent Cooke told the press. "I believe cable will become the sixth estate."

The acquisition—$755 million for the cable system, $160,000 for the *Los Angeles Daily News* refinancing, and $36 million in fees, expenses, and working capital—totaled $951 million, a far cry from the days when Jack ran around Toronto begging $25,000 from investors to buy CKEY for $500,000.

The $951 million came from the following lenders: $300 million from a syndicate of banks led by Bank of America and including the Bank of California, Security Pacific National Bank, Provident National Bank, Wells Fargo Bank, Canadian Imperial Bank of Commerce, Sovran Bank, and Seattle First National Bank; $251 million in 11 ⅛ percent senior subordinated deferred interest notes with a final maturity of 1997; $300 million in 11 ⅝ percent debentures with interest paid semiannually until maturity in 1999; and $100 million from JKC, Inc., which was 90 percent owned by Jack, with the other 10 percent under the name of his son John.[11]

Jack went into the cable deal believing that, because the U.S. Congress had just deregulated cable, he would be able to raise rates enough to create a cash flow sufficient to carry the debt service, which was substantial. By the end of 1987, the deficit of the cable operation was more than $100 million a year. The company was highly leveraged.

Nevertheless, his expansion continued. In mid-1987, Jack announced he was buying First Carolina Communication's cable television system for another $300 million. This time there were 156,000 subscribers—mainly in the south—and Jack paid $1,900 per subscriber. He was now the fifteenth largest cable operator in the country.

Cable's new growth didn't last long. The public rebelled against the higher deregulated cable fees and the growth of homes wired for cable slowed. By 1990, Congress was threatening to reregulate cable systems. Cable was no longer a growth industry—it had matured. Premium pay services, such as HBO and Showtime, were slowing down as well.

But Jack Kent Cooke had moved ahead of the market again. In mid-1989 he agreed to sell all his cable holdings to a consortium of buyers for $1.6 billion or $2,300 per subscriber. Jack's real profit was probably about $400 million. And since he had long learned the principle of leverage, his own investment of less than $200 million had more than doubled in less than three years. By May 1990, only half the deal had gone through and it was said Jack might have to lower the price on the remaining properties. If he did—$2,100 per subscriber was the rumored figure—Jack would be back to "just" 100 percent profit in three years.

Jack Kent Cooke made one other acquisition investment deal in the 1980s, a deal that went bad. His marriage to Suzanne Elizabeth Szabados Martin, a vibrant young woman who gave him a daughter, should have given him great joy. Instead it created a final fall from mass public popularity that even the mighty Redskins couldn't resurrect.

Notes

1. When the owners of the Eiffel Tower learned they were about to be beaten by a New York skyscraper, they considered adding on to the famous French structure.
2. The neon framing was in Van Alen's original plans, but not implemented.
3. In 1982, Jack had a small string of five thoroughbreds at his Kent Farms property in Middleburg, Virginia. He appropriated the Redskins burgundy and gold colors for his racing silks. The thoroughbreds cost him nearly $2 million and Jack hired the famed trainer LeRoy Jolley to make them ready for the track. The partnership ended in rancor and after buying Elmendorf, Jack moved the horses to Kentucky.
4. Across Paris Pike from Elmendorf Farms is the highly regarded Gainesway Farm, the world's largest stallion station. Gainesway was begun by John R. Gaines, who made it big in the dog food business (those Gainesburgers). Losing horses, contrary to local jesters, do not find their way into the pet food cans.
5. Arthur Groman was one of Jack's lead attorneys in his divorce from his first wife, Barbara Jean Carnegie Cooke.
6. Flying Continental did have a successful career. By late 1990 the colt had won more than $1.5 million for Jack Kent Cooke.
7. The last mogul was somewhat embarrassed by the Multimedia windfall, and feared he would be typed as a "greenmailer." There was no evidence however, that the money was given away or donated to charity.
8. By early 1990 *Los Angeles Daily News* circulation had grown 39 percent

to 202,000, partly due to the demise of the *Herald-Examiner*. Although the *Los Angeles Times* purchased the subscriber list of the *Herald-Examiner* for "a small fortune," the *Daily News* outflanked the *Times* by paying *Herald-Examiner* circulation managers $150 each to attend a meeting at the *Daily News*. Many were offered jobs.

9. Jack bought a plethora of small papers as well. One was the weekly Steamboat Springs, Colorado, *Pilot*, where he gave his grandson John a job as a reporter. Four others, all in New Mexico, include the Deming *Headlight*, the Valencia *News Bulletin*, the Ruidoso *News*, and the *Defensor-Chieftain*. In all, there were seven by early 1991, in Colorado, Arizona, and New Mexico.

10. Drexel Burnham earned between $15 and $20 million in fees from the bond sales.

11. Jack's junk bonds were owned by several savings and loans. After the S&Ls went under in 1989 and 1990, they became assets of the Resolution Trust Corporation, a government organization set up to solve the S&L mess. Jack bought his own junk bonds back in mid-1991 for pennies on the dollar.

CHAPTER
17

SUZANNE/SUSAN

"I want to flush that piece of shit out of this city."

When the direct descendants of the Mongol ruler Ghengis Khan swept down from the north into India in A.D. 1526 they were called Moguls or Mughals, which are the Arabic and Persian forms of the word Mongol. The Moguls, as the rulers came to be known, ruled India for nearly 300 years.

Jack Kent Cooke swept down from Canada in 1959, conquering Los Angeles first, and Washington second. His empire became a series of glittering business and sports holdings. Like the Mongolian rulers, he too established dynasties (the Lakers and the Redskins), built structures of lasting merit (the "Fabulous" Forum), and certainly created fear in those who stood in his way. In modern times a mogul has come to be defined as a man of power, importance, or influence, a term that could certainly describe Jack Kent Cooke.

In 1987 Jack listed his favorite recreations as "working, riding, music, reading, and *working*" (his emphasis). Few people in their mid-seventies would make such a statement. But then few of us would spend our golden years in high-stakes business deals with such relish. Certainly it has been profitable and raised Jack's wealth quotient. But it has come at great personal expense. Jack's past half-dozen years are the tales of tabloids, of circuits shorted. They too are part of his life and legacy, however painful.

*   *   *

Suzanne Elizabeth Szabados Martin, who became Jack Kent Cooke's third wife, had a difficult youth. Her silver spoon childhood was taken away at an early age and she was jolted into reality through tragedy and family misfortune.

Diane, her mother, called Suzanne Elizabeth her "groundhog baby," when she was born on February 2, 1956. Suzanne was the third and last child by Nicholas Szabados, Diane's first husband. Stephanie was the eldest, and John had been next. John, Diane's only son, born on January 25, 1955, was a year and eight days older than Suzanne. In 1960, Diane divorced Nicholas Szabados and in 1962 married John Martin. They had two more children, Mia and Julie. John had fathered five children in a previous marriage, but they were much older. In total, there were ten children from three different marriages after the Szabados-Martin marriage vows.

Of the ten, Suzanne and John Szabados Martin were especially close. John, who was into sports, played football and hockey. Suzanne, the tomboy, tagged behind John and his peers, but would often bicycle and slide down snow-covered hills on sleds just with him. The two were a grade apart at Lafayette Elementary School in Washington, D.C. Later, Suzanne attended Ursuline Academy in Bethesda, Maryland, and John was sent to Denis Hall in Alfred, Maine. John Martin, Diane's husband, was leading the company he headed into a new growth spurt by snagging some big contracts in the Middle East. The corporation, E.C. Ernst, a giant electrical contracting firm under John's control, was now listed on the American Stock Exchange. By the early 1970s, when the stock ran to 21, John and Diane's paper net worth would hover between $25 and $30 million.

When Suzanne was born, the family lived in a town house in Park Fairfax, a then fashionable community of colonial homes in northern Virginia near the Pentagon. Richard and Pat Nixon lived there, as did Al and Charlotte Van Metre. The Van Metres would become one of the Washington area's more successful real estate developers in the seventies and eighties. As the Martin family's success continued, they moved through a series of houses, first in Georgetown, then two larger houses in the fashionable suburb of Bethesda, where they joined the nearby Congressional Country

Club, one of Washington's prestigious private places. Congressional was the home of an annual professional golf tournament, the Kemper Open.

When Suzanne was fifteen and her brother John, sixteen, a tragedy occurred during Thanksgiving weekend, 1971. It changed her life. She had gone to a party with John and he had become involved in an argument. Because of the dispute, John left the party and began walking home.

He was less than two miles from the family house, walking on a heavily traveled street called River Road. It was dark and raining on the narrow artery that runs between Potomac, Maryland, and Washington, D.C. There were no sidewalks. John was struck by a hit-and-run driver, and hours passed before his body was discovered by a Hungarian woman walking her dog. He survived on a respirator for five days before he was pronounced dead. It was the type of tragedy that changes a family forever. Suzanne's mother blocked the event from her mind for years, and Suzanne blamed herself.

The family moved from Bethesda after John's death to an estate in The Plains, Virginia, called Old Whitewood. A few years later they moved to Catesby, a larger mansion—12,000 square feet on 405 acres. There were 100-year-old boxwoods, servants, and horses. That was the height. After that, John's electrical contracting company began to lose money. The tensions in the Middle East, where many of E.C. Ernst's contracts were located, caused a lot of deals to fall apart and others to go unpaid.

The Martins listed Catesby for sale in 1976 for $1.6 million. It was purchased in 1978 by Bahman Batmanghelhidj, an Iranian who had made a fortune developing real estate in the United States.

The death of her brother combined with the virtual disappearance of the family's fortune had a huge, negative effect on Suzanne. She felt guilty and began to drink. Later she started to use drugs. By 1982, when she was arrested for "illicit use of a telephone to sell cocaine" to a drug enforcement agent, she was using five grams a day. The U.S. District Court in Baltimore gave her probation after her family paid nearly $30,000 in legal fees to defend her.

Suzanne entered the Psychiatric Institute of Washington in an effort to "get clean." Later, she would tell a writer, "It was helpful, but you have to really do it yourself."

After recovering from her cocaine addiction, Suzanne tried a number of jobs. Among them was an internship at Sloan's, an auctioneer of estates and antiques in Maryland. But Suzanne, now in her mid-twenties, wasn't ready for a career.

On Halloween of 1983, there was a private party inside La Fleur Restaurant, which was located at the corner of Wisconsin and Massachusetts avenues in northwest Washington. It was there that Suzanne met Marlene Ramallo Miguens. Marlene's boyfriend was soon to be Christopher van Roijen, the son of a prominent Fauquier County family whose estate, St. Leonard's, is one of the better farms of the Middleburg hunt set. Marlene met Chris at Desiree, a popular after-midnight club for jetsetters and Eurotrash inside the Four Seasons hotel in Georgetown. Since Suzanne knew of Chris from her silver spoon days at Old Whitewood and Catesby, the three found common ground and, as they say, hit it off. Suzanne was fascinated with Marlene and her exotic South American looks and thick Bolivian accent.

Suzanne told a writer that she didn't know of Marlene's drug past until early 1987. When Marlene went to prison in 1986, Suzanne said she told her and others she was going to visit her father in Bolivia. And when Suzanne later found out, Marlene said she had "been used" by others.

But by the middle of 1985, Suzanne didn't have much time for Marlene. She had entered a new world, one in which she at first thrived but later was nearly destroyed.

Suzanne emerged from the swimming pool at Miami's Palm Bay Club dripping with chlorinated water, her hands pushing her long blonde hair back on her head like a squeegee. Her five-foot six-inch frame had a thin coat of bronze, the beginning of a suntan. She was wearing a black one-piece swim suit and the fabric shone like a seal's, with a bright, metal zipper down the front. It was cut high, but not obscenely so, on the leg.

Suzanne was staying at the Palm Bay Club on Northeast Sixty-

Ninth Street, in Miami on this fifth day of February, 1985, as part of a deal. She was helping her mother set up a company called Crown International in southern Florida. Crown represented foreign nationals who were visiting or settling in the area, finding them homes or temporary lodging, for which Crown received commissions. The Palm Bay Club was a private resort where Suzanne and her mother had a commissionable arrangement.

That February afternoon was the sort of day that would make anyone glad to be in Miami in the dead of winter. Although cloudy, the temperature was in the mid-seventies. Washington, D.C., was in the mid-twenties.

The subject of the hour, in both Miami and Washington, was still the Redskins, who hadn't played in more than a month and had been knocked out of the playoffs in the first round by the Chicago Bears. Their outspoken running back, John Riggins, was featured in all the papers after drinking too much at a dinner, accosting Supreme Court Justice Sandra Day O'Connor, telling her to "loosen up Sandy baby," and then falling asleep on the floor while speeches were made from the head table. The birth of defensive end Dexter Manley's son was also at the top of the *Post*'s Style page in still Redskin-daffy Washington. None of this mattered to Suzanne. She was neither a Redskins devotee nor a fan of any pro football club.

Suzanne, who was staying in a small Palm Bay Club studio apartment, sat down on a chaise lounge. From two lounges away, a small, white-haired old man, nearly a half-century older, began talking to her, peppering her with questions.

"Who are you? Where are you from? Do you know who I am?"

Suzanne told him who she was and that she was from Washington and Middleburg.

The man said: "You're kidding. Do you know who I am? I'm Jack Kent Cooke, and I own the Washington Redskins."

Suzanne said, "How nice for you."

Suzanne later told a writer that the name Jack Kent Cooke didn't mean anything to her but she had certainly heard of the Washington Redskins. They did have one thing in common—Jack had a new Middleburg farm and Suzanne used to live on a Middleburg estate.[1] So when he asked her out to dinner she thought it was just that—a harmless way to spend the evening.

Jack was staying at the Palm Bay Club as well. But he didn't have a small studio apartment. As a professional courtesy, he had been given the penthouse suite of Joe Robbie, owner of the Miami Dolphins. It was one of the best units in the resort.

Suzanne went to Jack's twenty-first-floor penthouse apartment, and Jack greeted her in a rather unusual manner. He was only partially dressed, wearing a shirt, nylon underbriefs, socks, garters, and shoes. He then made a phone call and talked about the communications company in Florida he was thinking of buying. In the elevator on the way down, Suzanne got her first taste of Jack's claustrophobia. He became very nervous and grabbed her hand. They went to dinner with a friend of Joe Robbie's—Tony Sweet—and another woman who Suzanne thought was "coming on to Jack."

At first, Jack didn't make any moves. It was a kiss on the cheek and a chaste, "Goodnight, dear." But the next day there was a trip to Gulfstream Park where Jack had horses running. Jack would give Suzanne $100 to bet on a race. And then there were more dinners. And flowers. Suzanne, who at first thought Jack "a lovely old man," was being overwhelmed by the combination of Jack's charm, wealth, and power. Those three elements transcended the nearly forty-five-year age gap. They became lovers.

A short time later, Jack returned to Middleburg and began sending love letters, albeit tame ones at first, to Suzanne. One is dated February 19, 1985, just two weeks to the day after they had met. It is a dictated message, signed by Jack, and has the code JKC/mt in the left-hand corner.

Jack began by addressing Suzanne with an endearment that would be more typical in a love-struck teenager. He said that although he had just sent her a snapshot of him, he was now mailing her two more instead of a single large photograph. One of the snapshots was taken at the Redskins' training facility. The other was from a steeplechase race near Middleburg. Jack had written a message on each picture but he told Suzanne that if that bothered her, he would send plain ones. He ended the letter with a florid embellished pledge of love that clearly showed his infatuation.

Now Jack began sending presents as well. There was a Seiko alarm clock. Jack also sent Suzanne a 1983 Super Bowl ring that celebrated the Redskins' win over Miami.

In April 1985 Suzanne began staying at what Washington Redskins front office personnel sometimes referred to as "the safe house," an apartment on the eighth floor of Sutton Towers, a posh building at 3101 New Mexico Avenue, near American University, in the far west corner of the District of Columbia. Shortly after, she moved to Jack's estate in Middleburg.

That month, Suzanne became pregnant by Jack for the first time. Jack gave her money and she went to the Washington Hospital Center, had an abortion, and came home.

Jack brought Suzanne a tray of food the evening after the abortion and Suzanne said she couldn't eat. Jack said she was ungrateful—he had prepared it himself. Suzanne ran to the bathroom, threw up, and returned to the bed saying, "Now you know why I can't eat."

Jack met Suzanne's family. Her mother at first was shocked. She told a writer that Jack Kent Cooke was too old for herself, let alone her daughter. Her sister Julie said that she heard Jack talk harshly to Suzanne and didn't care for him either.

Besides having a very young, attractive woman as his new and constant companion, Jack now had a woman to whom he could play mentor and impress her with his wealth and power. Unlike Jeannie I and II, here was a woman who hadn't read F. Scott Fitzgerald, hadn't met his four-star cronies in the Redskins box, and would be impressed that he owned one of the world's most beautiful skyscrapers, the Chrysler Building, in New York City.

Jack provided money and a car for Suzanne Martin. He put her on the Redskins payroll at $20,000 a year as a "public relations" person although Suzanne didn't do anything for the money. After taxes and social security, Suzanne got $1,625 a month. He gave her a $2,000 bonus at Christmas and a slightly used silver Mercedes convertible sports car.[2] It was the same car that Jeannie II had driven three years earlier. Suzanne was also given "Mid-

235

night," a Tennessee walking horse to ride. That too, was a former possession of Jeannie II. He bought her some clothes, a few pieces of good jewelry, and let her charge meals at restaurants. By May 1985 she had moved permanently into Far Acres, in Middleburg.

Jack Kent Cooke clearly played Pygmalion with Suzanne Martin. He'd spend hours telling her how to address people ("Never use a first name—it's always Miss or Mrs. Doe"). He gave her books to read. Suzanne would read a novel such as *Tender Is the Night* and discuss it with him. Sometimes he would reward her with a gift. Suzanne's education extended to clothing as well. Jack wanted her in tweeds and blazers—the understated Grace Kelly/Dina Merrill look. Jack also wanted her by his side on his business trips. Suzanne was taken to his recently purchased Elmendorf Farms in Kentucky, where she witnessed Jack chew out a bunch of bankers, at one time hearing Jack say, "I could buy all of you before breakfast." There were trips to New York, to California. Jack, at first, showed Suzanne a new world.

But if Jack expected a docile, grateful and pliable young girl who would only thank him, he was soon surprised. Suzanne, was not, like Jack, a son or daughter of the Great Depression. She was far from uneducated, and, unlike Jack's other women, was a daughter of Woodstock and of Gloria Steinem. As she became entrenched in the world of Jack Kent Cooke she also began to make demands for which Jack had not bargained. She asked him to loan her money to start her own business. Suzanne wanted a store that sold original art in Georgetown, and she drew up organizational plans. She spoke out to Jack's business friends, offering her own opinions.

Now Jack and Suzanne's private moments were verbal battles. Jack called her dumb and stupid. "You'll never make anything of your life, Susan" (he wouldn't call her Suzanne), and Suzanne would cry and Jack would say, "Come here my princess, darling" and try to make love to her. Jack had Suzanne keep his daily journal of where he went and what he ate. If she forgot, he would scream at her in a rage.

There was always a business deal in the works. Once Jack told Suzanne: "I don't know why I struggle. I don't know why I try so hard at my age. Why do I need more and more? But if I stop working I'll die. I can't stop." Suzanne got pregnant again in January 1986, but didn't have an abortion until early March. Suzanne used the same doctor as before, John Berry.

During the autumn of 1986, Jack found out about Suzanne's cocaine past. Suzanne had an old admirer whose name was Sam Dandy.³ Sam Dandy was obsessed with Suzanne and would sometimes spend the night outside her old apartment, looking up at her bedroom window. Sam Dandy called Pete Rozelle, the NFL president, and told him about Suzanne's drug conviction.

Jack confronted Suzanne. He had called CIA director William Casey and had him in turn call the FBI. Suzanne's arrest record was on his desk within twenty-four hours.

Suzanne said that Jack waved the report at her and said, "It's over." But it wasn't.

When Jack continued to berate Suzanne she swallowed almost an entire bottle of Valium in a suicide attempt. In October 1986 she committed herself back to the Psychiatric Institute in Washington, D.C.

Jack wasn't faithful to Suzanne. One rainy night, Suzanne went into Washington to have dinner with her good friend Susan Webster. She left the dinner early, drove back to Middleburg, and arrived on the farm to find Jack in bed with another woman.

The woman was a free-lance writer working for *Town and Country* magazine, who lived in Georgetown, "a hard, not really attractive woman," Suzanne told a writer. The woman had been assigned to write a story on thoroughbred horse breeders that would include Jack's Elmendorf Farm.

"The act had been completed," Suzanne said. "They were lying on the bed, hair askew. Jack was drunk, wearing a robe and nothing underneath. She was wearing my robe. I told her to get off my bed and get out of here. They had drunk a bottle of wine."

Afterward, Suzanne said, Jack faked a heart attack. Suzanne used the opportunity to buy herself a mink coat, later giving him the bill. A friend of Suzanne's called *Town and Country* for her and

237

gave the publication a piece of her mind. The article was never printed.

Suzanne and Jack continued to fight and in late 1986, separated. She went to stay at Jack's Sutton Towers apartment. Then she visited Jack's one-time friend, lawyer Edward Bennett Williams, on November 26, 1986, and asked him to help her. Williams suggested suing Jack for $2 million—$1 million for each abortion. Edward Bennett Williams, who now hated Jack, was more than willing to help Suzanne Martin. Williams, who had advised Jack on the Jeannie I divorce, had served on the board of Jack's California sports operations, and had been Jack's adviser and friend for nearly a quarter of a century now told Suzanne, "I want to flush that piece of shit out of this city once and for all." Williams felt that Jack had moved too smoothly and too fast in getting him out of the Redskins hierarchy when Jack came to town in 1979, thereby humiliating him. And he felt he had been at Jack's mercy when he sold his Redskins stock back to Jack in 1985 and that Jack Kent Cooke had been less than generous in paying him a proper price for the stock.

On the other hand, friends of Jack Kent Cooke would claim that Jack had loaned Williams $3.5 million to buy the Orioles with the agreement that Ed would allow him to quietly buy in at some future time. Ed Williams, it was said, reneged on the deal.

Williams assigned Suzanne Martin's case to his best litigator, Brendan Sullivan. Because they had been partners in the Redskins at one time, Ed Williams told Suzanne they would attempt to get Jack to settle with her for the $2 million, charging her a 25 percent contingency fee. They would not, however, initiate a lawsuit. If that were necessary, Williams said, he would suggest another law firm. Suzanne met with Williams and Sullivan, who was introduced as "the ice man" on November 27, 1986. Williams told her, "I'm not sure if I can take your case because I once represented JKC but if I can't, I will find some cutthroat son-of-a-bitch who will take your case."

A letter was sent to Jack and Brendan Sullivan talked to him. Jack Kent Cooke thought Ed was attempting extortion on behalf of Suzanne, or Susan as he still preferred to call her.

But the potential lawsuit became meaningless when Jack and Suzanne reunited on Valentine's Day in 1987. Jack, the incurable romantic, broke into his Sutton Towers apartment on Valentine's Day when Suzanne was present. A locksmith opened the door. Then he asked her to marry him. A paid engagement notice was placed on the *Washington Post*'s Weddings and Engagements page on March 5, 1987. A few weeks later, Jack's friends, Randy and Michele Rouse, gave a party at their estate, Hillcrest, to celebrate both Jack and Suzanne's engagement and Michele's success as a leading woman horse rider in steeplechase and point-to-point races. Michele, like Suzanne, was at least three decades younger than her husband (he was formerly married to Audrey Meadows, Jackie Gleason's TV wife). Jack formed his own band that night, playing the Rouses' new piano with Randy on the saxophone. John Block, the former secretary of agriculture, played his guitar and sang.

Always the proper gentleman, Jack called Suzanne's mother Diane and asked for her hand in marriage. "I want to marry her," Jack said. "Do I have your permission?"

Diane answered, "You certainly do."

Jack said, "I'm nuts about the girl and love her, Diane. We're getting married and I want you to go out and find the best place for a reception that you can find. Go over to Marshall Coyne's— it doesn't matter.⁴ Anywhere you want to do it."

That was in early March 1987. Suzanne had a big engagement luncheon for twenty women friends.

Jack changed his mind.

"Jack, when are we going to be married?" Suzanne asked.

Jack said, "Susan, you haven't changed. You're the same person. You're having hysterical fits and we're not getting along. It doesn't seem to be working. I'm going to California."

And Jack flew to California in May 1987, leaving a jilted Suzanne on the farm.

But before Jack went to California, he made love to Suzanne once more. According to Suzanne, she became pregnant by Jack for the third time on May 2, 1987. It was the day of the Middleburg Gold Cup steeplechase races at the Great Meadows course in The

Plains, always an occasion for drinking and revelry. Jack impregnated Suzanne early that evening. Then he flew to California.

When Suzanne missed her period she called Jack from the Sutton Towers apartment on June 1 and told him, "I'm pregnant.[5] And I'm not giving up this child."

Jack said, "Oh dear girl, I love you and we're going to be married. Stay there in the apartment and I'll be there by 5 P.M."

Jack went to the Van Nuys airport, got on his private Hawker Siddley jet, and flew back to Washington. He told Suzanne that he would marry her immediately, but first she would have to have another abortion.

Suzanne, who had been raised in the Catholic church, already had guilt feelings about the first two.

"No way. I'm not giving up this child. I killed two. I'm not going to get rid of another."

One evening Suzanne began bleeding. Jack, believing she had suffered a miscarriage, celebrated by giving Suzanne a four-strand pearl necklace with a large heart-shaped diamond clasp. He begged her to have the abortion. He offered her more jewelry, a big diamond ring. And he promised marriage and happiness everlasting if only she would have the abortion. Jack's reason for insisting on an abortion, according to him, was that he wouldn't be around to see the child grow up.

Jack's combination of charm, threats, and browbeating wore Suzanne out. She agreed to the abortion and Jack, pleased, agreed to marry her. Suzanne went to Lee Cross Jewelers in Middleburg on July 22, 1987, and purchased a fourteen-karat white gold wedding band for $38.67, including tax. She used her own money.

The next day Suzanne was sent to attorney Plato Cacheris' office at 1914 Sunderland Place, just off Dupont Circle in Washington, to sign a prenuptial agreement. Suzanne was told not to tell Plato about her pregnancy or the required abortion. The agreement between Jack and Suzanne can be summarized as follows:

1. Suzanne was to get $100,000 cash within five days of the marriage.

2. Suzanne was to get a 1987 Jaguar and a new Jaguar every five years as long as they were married.
3. Suzanne was to get $50,000 a year from Jack for as long as she was married to him.

In the event of Jack's death, divorce, or annulment of the marriage within twelve months, Suzanne was to get:

1. $50,000 a year for three years.
2. $100,000 cash within 60 days.
3. Rent-free use of the Watergate apartment for five years.

If the marriage lasted more than a year, Suzanne was bumped to $75,000 a year, $150,000 cash, and the apartment for seven years. And for two years or more, there was a boost to $100,000 a year for five years, $200,000 cash, and the Watergate apartment for 10 years.[6]

There was a lot more in the prenuptial agreement. Jack agreed to leave $1 million in trust to Suzanne in his will providing they were married when he died. He also agreed to give her Far Acres and the five acres around it, but not the hundreds of acres he owned bordering it known as Kent Farms. He also agreed that his estate would pay for taxes and utilities at Far Acres. This would be permanent until Suzanne remarried or died. The prenuptial agreement ran nine pages on long, white legal paper. There was no mention of children or any contingencies to provide for either the natural birth of a child, or adoption.

On Friday, July 24, 1987, Suzanne and Jack were married by Judge Daniel O'Flaherty in Alexandria, Virginia. Suzanne wore a Chanel suit and Jack brought along the official Redskins photographer, Nate Fine, to record the moment. Nate Fine was the only witness present. Then they went to dinner at the Palm restaurant with Mo Siegel.

After the two-hour dinner, Jack and Suzanne went back to the Watergate apartment and consummated the marriage. The next morning, Suzanne left early to go to the hospital for the abortion. She first prepared some coffee, leaving it and some danish pastries for Jack, along with this handwritten note:

7-25-87

My darling husband,
   The coffee maker is working just fine and I have left some danish for you. I will call you later this afternoon when I get back to Watergate.

Your new bride,
Susan Kent Cooke

Jack, who, Suzanne said later, wanted to get out of there because "he didn't want to be around the messy details of the abortion," responded with a romantic missive to Suzanne.

Calling her his angelic spouse, Jack apologized for leaving the wedding leftovers. And he admitted to being a little worn out from their nuptial night lovemaking. Jack, for the first time, signed the note as Suzanne's husband, capitalizing the spousal term. There was a P.S. as well, asking Suzanne to telephone him when she returned from her abortion procedure. Then he signed it with repeated endearments.

But Suzanne, her Catholic heritage creating guilt every time she had destroyed a child, couldn't and wouldn't go through with this abortion. She went to Sibley Hospital, with the $1,500 in cash that Jack had given her and laid down on the gurney. But as Dr. Achim Heintze was about to put her to sleep with a sedative, administered by injection, Suzanne became hysterical.[7]

"I can't go through with this," Suzanne said to Dr. Heintze. And she started to cry.

"I can't do something if you don't want an abortion. Come back later if you feel different," Dr. Heintze said.

Suzanne, who had been driven to the hospital by Diane, had her mother come into the room.

She told Diane, "Mother, I was on the table. They were getting ready to put the needle in my arm. I just couldn't kill this baby."

Suzanne and her mother left the hospital and went to a restaurant for brunch. There would be hell to pay when Jack found out.

Notes

1. Far Acres, Jack's second Middleburg home, was designed by an architect of the Frank Lloyd Wright school and built at a cost of $1.8 million.
2. Jack gave several Redskins wives (the ones he liked) $2,000 "bonuses" for Christmas even though they weren't on the payroll.
3. Sam Dandy died of Hodgkin's disease in 1989.
4. Marshall Coyne owns the Madison Hotel, one of the nation's capital's more elegant hostelries.
5. Suzanne did not give up the taking of birth control pills as Jack later accused her of doing, although she may have skipped a few. She was taking several antibiotics for bronchitis at the same time. There is a common belief—though medically the evidence is still considered anecdotal—that certain antibiotics negate the efficacy of the pill. Suzanne said that she got frequent bronchial infections living with Jack because of his penchant for turning the air conditioning on all year long, with the temperature kept below 50°F.
6. It was like a typical Redskins contract. The team's standard operating procedure is to give a player a moderate salary and then load it with incentives based on his performance on the field. Suzanne's prenuptial deal was based on her longevity in marriage.
7. In an ironic twist, Dr. Heintze was the doctor who delivered Jacqueline Kent Cooke six months later.

CHAPTER

18

COOKE VS. COOKE, II

"Wait until you see what we have in store for you, young lady."

After Suzanne left the hospital she was afraid to face Jack. They were supposed to go on their honeymoon the next day so she called him and said she'd meet him at the airport where Jack had scheduled his Hawker Siddley jet to take them to Lexington and Los Angeles.

"I'm tired," she told him.

Jack understood. Or thought he did.

They flew to Kentucky where Jack reviewed the state of Elmendorf; they flew to Los Angeles where Jack met with Jim Lacher about the *Los Angeles Daily News*, real estate, and cable television investments. They had dinner with Jim Lacher. Every night. It was like after the wedding at the Palm with Mo Siegel. Except Jack didn't talk football with Jim Lacher and ignore Suzanne. He talked business with Jim Lacher and ignored Suzanne.

Everything was scheduled. Jack always wrote agendas five to seven days in advance. They were typed by his staff and later refined. Jack also planned daily itineraries that detailed how his time was to be spent. These were distributed to key members of his staff. In addition, Jack kept his own personal diaries and then had Suzanne keep his daily journal. And when he arrived home in the evening, Suzanne's job was to always have a requested passage of music—usually orchestral—playing when he came through the door. If Suzanne forgot, Jack would blow up.

Organization. Preparation. Like Lord Nelson of the British Navy.

When they returned to Washington, Jack and Suzanne were driven to the Redskins' training camp in Carlisle, Pennsylvania, by Harry Turner. She had gone before, but as Suzanne Martin, or S.E.M., as she was listed on Jack's agenda and was referred to by the front office of the team. But now there was a new deference. She was Susan Kent Cooke this time.

On the way back from training camp, Jack said: "Boy, you're getting fat, Susan."

Suzanne began to cry. She didn't know how to break the news.

The next evening, Suzanne got up the courage to tell Jack. With her mother present, Suzanne called Jack from the Watergate apartment.

"Jack, we have to talk. I think we should meet and talk in person."

"No—just tell me on the phone."

"I didn't go through with the abortion."

"Oh shit! Oh no!"

And Jack slammed down the receiver, but he called back five minutes later and got Suzanne's mother on the phone.

"Diane, I'm on the way. Hold her there."

Suzanne packed a bag and fled with two of her closest girl-friends who had arrived after the phone call, Marlene Ramallo Miguens, now Chalmers, and Susan Webster.[1]

Jack arrived at the Watergate in a rage. "Why didn't you keep her here, Diane?"

"I can't hold her down. She was frightened and ran."

Jack said to Diane, "If she doesn't have the abortion, I'll ruin you. No one will want to associate with you or anyone in your family."

Diane was selling real estate at the time.

"I'll get you a listing. An expensive listing—more than $2 million."

Diane said, "Suzanne's over twenty-one. I can't do anything but tell her that you're upset."

Jack started to calm down. But he didn't give up.

Suzanne later told a writer she first believed Jack's reluctance to have a child may have been due to a belief that a mentally retarded child could be born due to his advanced age. Later she

245

said that it may have had something to do with Jack's will or a possible living trust Jack was said to have put in effect.

When Suzanne brought sonograms home from the doctor, Jack looked at the pictures and said, "That's not a real person. It's not too late. We can still do something about it."

He talked to Diane about taking Suzanne to a clinic for advanced terminations in Europe. Although he now seemed to be resigned to the birth of the child, he didn't give up his hope that Suzanne would go through with the abortion.

Jack was a bundle of contradictions. He talked about adding a wing onto Far Acres for the child. Then he told her he wouldn't be around to see the baby grow up. "I'm going to die before this child reaches six years of age."

And when Suzanne came home one night and said the doctor predicted twins, Jack dropped his wine glass and seemed to go into shock.

"I'm just joking," Suzanne said.

Jack wasn't amused.

He worked on Diane, trying to get her to take Suzanne to Europe to terminate the pregnancy. At one point, he went on a walk with Diane outside the ultramodern Far Acres mansion.

He took Diane's hand and squeezed it. "If only I'd met you before Susan," he said to the married woman. "You know what I mean, Diane."

In late August, Jack went to New York without Suzanne and met with his attorneys at Shea and Gould. When he came back his agenda called for him to go to California on business and to the season opener for the Redskins, an away game against the Los Angeles Rams.

"You can't go, Susan."

"Why can't I go with you, Jack?"

"Because I'm going to be working."

"But I want to be with you. We've just been married. You are my husband. I want to be by your side."

"No, you're not going."

Before Jack went to California, Suzanne wrote him this letter on August 27, 1987:

Dear Jack:

I am saddened and puzzled by your behavior over the past week. You seem very cold and distant when we are alone. Since my return to Far Acres, when you finally accepted the fact that I am going to be the mother of your child, your behavior has not been that of a loving husband.

Your plans are to leave for California on Sunday the 30th of August and I feel I'm being abandoned. I was always included before we were married on your business trips and I don't understand why I am not included now. I want to be a help to you during the day time when you are in meetings, after all, we have a large project ahead of us.

Your loving and
devoted wife,
Susan

Jack gave the annual Redskins "Welcome Home" speech on August 28, 1987, threatening to move the team to the suburbs if he didn't get the new stadium he wanted. Afterward, on the way back to Middleburg, he picked up Suzanne at the Watergate. Harry Turner took the fast route, over the Theodore Roosevelt Bridge out of Washington and on to Interstate 66. On the way there, Suzanne and Jack began fighting again. As they passed the town of Marshall, Jack stopped the car just before the country road he lived on, route 713, between Middleburg and Upperville. He told her to get out of the car. "Wait until you see what we have in store for you, young lady," Jack said, as he slammed the door of the limousine shut.

Suzanne, four months pregnant, wearing a black knit maternity dress with a pleated red plaid skirt and new low-heel black patent shoes, began walking. It was five in the evening. She was offered rides by "good old boys" in pickup trucks and hooted at by others. Jack sent Harry back alone, but Suzanne, angry and upset, refused the ride.

After several hours, Suzanne arrived back at Far Acres on feet covered with blisters from her four-mile trek. She called her mother from a guest cottage and told her what happened, then laid down and rested.

After dark, between ten and eleven, Suzanne went to the main house. All the doors were locked. Suzanne knocked on the door and on the windows. She went to Jack's bedroom window and banged on it. She could see Jack in the room. He was sitting up in bed watching television. He tried to ignore her. Suzanne said she banged on the pane for more than half an hour.

"Let me in, Jack. I want something to drink. It's not for me. I want some milk for your child. Something cool."

Jack said, "Get out of here."

Suzanne went back to the guest house and telephoned her husband. Jack had the answering machine on and wouldn't pick up. Suzanne slept in the guest cottage. Jack called her mother at six the next morning. "Come and get her, Diane," he said. "She's having a nervous breakdown."

Suzanne awoke at nine and went back to the main house. Diane was there with Jack.

Suzanne walked in and said, "Mother, you don't know what he's done. He's horrible."

Jack said, "Susan, you're a very sick young woman. Diane, get her over to the hospital, to the Psychiatric Institute. She's not well."

Diane said, "Don't get hysterical."

Suzanne and Diane told a writer that Jack came at Suzanne and pushed at her stomach. Suzanne pulled off his glasses. She protected her abdomen with one hand and grabbed Jack's hair with the other.

Jack yelled for his maid. "Mildred, help me. She's attacking me."

The maid hurried in.

Suzanne said, "Mildred, I didn't attack him. I was trying to protect the life of my unborn child."

Jack said, "I'm sending all your things to Watergate."

Diane said, "I'm taking you to the hospital for an examination."

Diane took Suzanne to George Washington Hospital near Georgetown and had her examined. The status of the unborn baby was fine. She returned to the Watergate apartment and stayed in bed for two days, crying and letting her blistered feet heal.

Jack went to California.

He called from Los Angeles. "Susan, it's not too late. You only have to get rid of this child. We'll stay together. We'll stay married. I can send you to Europe. You can terminate it there."

"I can't do that, Jack. It's too late. I want this child very much. There's no way."

Jack went off on a tirade again.

Suzanne didn't know which Jack would call, which Jack she would see now—Jack the charmer or Jack the terrible. She was now more than five months pregnant. She still loved Jack, and with the birth of the baby less than four months away, she still hoped for a reconciliation.

When Jack telephoned and told her to get to the home opener against Philadelphia, she balked. Jack wanted her to get there on her own—drive herself or call a cab. He called the day of the game, one hour before the kickoff.

Suzanne went when Harry Turner came to drive her and the charade continued for another day. But that was the end of it. Suzanne had crossed Jack and decided to have a baby she had promised to abort. To Jack, it was a simple breach of contract—a business deal gone bad.

Suzanne felt that Jack was up to something. She thought that Jack was going to leak her drug past to the newspapers. He wouldn't answer the phone when she called the farm. And he wouldn't return the calls either. Suzanne had news too. She wanted to tell him about the amniocentesis that had been done. Jack was going to be the father of a healthy daughter for certain.

Suzanne decided to give a television interview. She chose the NBC station, WRC-TV and its "sob-sister" reporter, Barbara Harrison. Harrison specialized in getting women like Suzanne to let it all out: Len Bias' mother, when the Maryland University basketball star died of an overdose of cocaine; Washington Mayor Marion Barry's wife, Effi; and Elizabeth Morgan, the plastic surgeon, whose child custody fight with her husband was making international headlines. Suzanne played hard to get. It took a week for Barbara Harrison to convince Suzanne to talk.

Jack tried both honey and vinegar in order to get the interview stopped. He schmoozed Jerry Nachman, general manager of the television station by taking him to lunch at Duke Zeibert's.[2] Mo Siegel and Larry "Whorehouse" King, as Nachman called the author of *The Best Little Whorehouse in Texas*, to differentiate him from Larry "Radio" King ("Radio" King watched the show from a nearby table) were present. After lunch "Whorehouse" King offered to give Nachman a ride back to the station, but Jack pointedly let everyone know that he'd take Nachman back in his limousine.

Inside the limousine Jack said: "Susan's crazy. Please take that into consideration. I'd like you to be a guest in my box."

Jerry Nachman refused to stop the airing of the interview and told Jack he was a Giants fan anyway.

Jack said. "Then you'll fly up with me next week to the Meadowlands. I have a jet. You'll be my guest there. I'd be very disappointed if you ran this interview."

Jerry refused again.

Barbara Harrison got her interview and ran it. Actually, it was softball all the way. Harrison didn't ask about Jack putting her out of the car or the other abortions.[3] And Suzanne didn't volunteer it. After the interview ran, Jerry Nachman got a note from Jack disinviting him to the box even though he never had accepted an invitation. And the WRC sports director, George Michael, got the cold shoulder from Jack for the next three years.

Still Jack sued for divorce. The papers were filed on October 5, 1987, the same day as Suzanne's interview with Barbara Harrison. He wasn't about to let Suzanne make the first move, as he had with Barbara Jean Cooke. And this time, Jack Kent Cooke didn't intend to lose.[4]

The idle gossip in Jack's box during the 1987 season centered on the paternity of Suzanne's child. Jokingly, it was suggested: Quarterback Jay Schroeder? Sack specialist Dexter Manley? Among the bluebloods of the box, the talk usually involved a Redskins player. It couldn't be Jack. "My God, the man's seventy-five years old!" one regular noted.

Even Suzanne felt the gossip directly. Arriving at a dinner party given by Washington socialites Don and Debby Sigmund, Suzanne joined a group just as a woman said, "Isn't it strange that men like Cary Grant and Groucho Marx can father children at their age?"

"Yes," said another woman, "but if you think that child is Jack Kent Cooke's, you're crazy."

Suzanne spoke up. "Excuse me," she told the woman, "but I'm Suzanne Cooke and I can assure you the child is Jack's."

Mortified by her *faux pas,* the woman left the party before dessert was served.

Suzanne didn't give up easily. Even after Jack filed for divorce, Suzanne wrote him this letter on October 23, 1987, just before his seventy-fifth birthday:

> Dear Jack,
>
> I am sorry our relationship didn't work out, but regardless, fond memories of you will always be with me.
>
> October twenty-fifth is an important date on my calendar and I am sorry both last year and this year you have not wanted me around to spend the day with you. As I recall, last year you were in N.Y.C attending the performance of "Me and My Girl" with friends. I sincerely hope you enjoy your birthday as much this year by beating the New York Jets Sunday afternoon.
>
> I pray for you to have many, many more healthy years ahead of you so that our daughter "Jacqueline" can grow up during her formative years to know and love her father. I see how loving and kind you are to other children, for example the children living at "Far Acres."⁵ Since this is going to be your only daughter I hope you can chanel [sic] your love and affection as I know she will return it to you one hundred times over.
>
> Your loving wife,
> Susan

The personal turmoil swirling around Jack Kent Cooke's personal life didn't prevent his beloved Redskins from having their best year yet. In a strike-shortened season, the club went 11–4, won its playoff games against the Bears and Vikings, and headed to a Super Bowl showdown in San Diego against the Broncos on January 31, 1988.

Jack chartered a Boeing 747 for the trip to San Diego. For the

moment at least, Jack Kent Cooke was no "miser."⁶ Besides the
players' wives and cheerleaders, the "who's who" on the plane
included figures from Jack's life, past and present, such as Ed and
Jane Muskie, Mayor Marion Barry, the owner of a local business
magazine, Bill Regardie; Carl Rowan, Randy and Michele Rouse,
Bill Shea, Eugene McCarthy, D.C. Congressman Walter Fauntroy,
Watergate Judge John Sirica, who had performed Jack's second
marriage; Renee Pouissant, a local TV anchor who had allowed
Jack to dominate a series of interviews with her in 1984; Lesley
Stahl and Aaron Latham; John Hechinger, whose seventy-five-
store hardware chain was named after him; and Lou Cannon of
the *Washington Post*, who had written the complimentary article
about Jack when he was undergoing his divorce from Jeannie I.
Jack's date for the game was supposed to have been Mary Rubloff,
a former model who had been married to a Chicago real estate
king, but they had a fight a few days before the game and Jack
showed up at the Super Bowl with David Susskind's widow, Joyce.

Jacqueline (rhymes with queen) Kent Cooke was born on
January 25, 1988, six days before the Redskins' one-sided 42–10
Super Bowl victory over Denver. Even more remarkable, the
daughter of Jack and Suzanne was born on Suzanne's deceased
brother's birthday. Suzanne had a pain killer and epidural anes-
thesia and was awake during the delivery. Jacqueline weighed in
at eight pounds, thirteen ounces, and had the same large birthmark
as Jack, at the same place—where the back ends and the buttocks
begin. Present for the arrival in the room were Suzanne's friend,
Cathy Gilder, Channel 4's Barbara Harrison, and Suzanne's youngest sister, Julie Martin. Suzanne's mother, Diane, wanted to come
into the delivery room as well, but Suzanne said she "would have
felt a little strange with her mother there" so Diane stayed outside.
Jack, by this time, was on his way to the Super Bowl, but his old
friends Ron and Nancy Reagan sent a special message to the hospital that said, "You have been truly blessed and we share your
joy." There was no message from Jack.

Suzanne had Jacqueline christened in a Catholic ceremony
eight months later at the Church of the Epiphany, in Georgetown.

Her friend Cathy Gilder was the godmother. William Cushing Paley, son of the CBS television pioneer, was godfather.

It would be nearly three years before Jack would acknowledge his daughter's existence. Like Ralph, she had become a nonperson—this time beginning at birth.

Suzanne demanded that Jack submit to blood tests to determine the paternity of the child. Jack fought them. He had the first test thrown out because of a breach of confidentiality. Both times, a vial of blood had to be drawn from Jacqueline and the baby would scream in pain. But the blood grouping tests showed that there was a 95.3 percent probability that Jack Kent Cooke was the father. When Jack finally admitted the paternity on April 5, 1988, the *Washington Post* ran this headline on the front page of its Style section: "Yessir, That's My Baby."

Jack said he had a lot in store for Suzanne. He did. His lead attorney, the venerable Milton Gould, Bill Shea's partner at Shea and Gould in New York, did everything he could to paint Suzanne Martin Cooke as an unsavory person. Apparently borrowing Jack's thesaurus for the trial, Milton Gould called Suzanne Cooke at various times, "a tramp . . . an adventuress . . . a woman with a lurid past . . . a courtesan . . . a trollop," and "an odalisque."[7]

Milton Gould said, "She got pretty well paid for what she delivered on a piecemeal basis."

Suzanne's lawyer, the flamboyant Arnold Weiner, answered, "Your honor, do we have to get into the fact that this man is a customer for the kinds of things that Mr. Gould is speaking about?"

Milton Gould shot back, "Yes. As a customer, we don't usually prosecute the customers. We do prosecute the vendors. Here we are rewarding the vendor."

Suzanne was stung. She had never thought of herself as that kind of woman. She cried, dried her tears, and tried to fight back. She began by countersuing Jack for a $15 million cash settlement instead of the comparatively paltry prenuptial agreement. Suzanne's lawyers chose the $15 million figure because they said that since Jack Kent Cooke's net worth was $1.5 billion, a one percent payout of Jack's fortune was appropriate. But this wasn't California where a liberal attitude and community property laws held sway. In the conservative Virginia court of Judge W. Shore Robertson, a different code prevailed and it was in Jack's favor. And even though they had lived together for more than two years, the marriage had lasted just seventy-three days between the wedding date and Jack's filing for divorce. The only item in Suzanne's favor was the child, Jacqueline, now the exact image of her father, yet Jack still had not acknowledged Jacqueline's existence.

The most damning evidence during the proceedings against Suzanne Cooke came via her friend Marlene Ramallo Chalmers. A close friend of Marlene's, an attorney of Cuban descent, Juan Chardiet, was there to testify against Suzanne. Chardiet had previously represented Marlene when she was threatened with deportation. Later he was identified as her attorney by the *Washington Post* when she faced a bad check charge, which was later dropped. Chardiet told a writer that was an error as he is not a member of the Virginia bar.

Chardiet said in court that Suzanne had told him that her baby was "her ticket" to extracting a large settlement from Jack Kent Cooke. He also said that Suzanne had told him she had discontinued taking birth control pills on purpose in order to get pregnant by Jack.

On cross-examination, one of Suzanne's attorneys, Rodney Page, was able to establish that Marlene had been a client of Chardiet's and that he had "heard" that she was by now both an employee of and living with Jack Kent Cooke. But Milton Gould was able to get the "heard" remark struck from the record. The exchange went this way:

Q: Isn't it true that you know that Marlene Chalmers, Marlene Ramallo Chalmers, has been living with Jack Kent Cooke?
A: I don't know that.
Q: You have heard that, haven't you?
A: Yes, I have.
MR. PAGE: I have no further questions.
MR. GOULD: I will move to strike out the last answer, he has heard it. I have no further questions.

After Juan Chardiet left the stand, Judge Shore Robertson heard the arguments. Again, Milton Gould's experience showed:

MR. PAGE: I don't know why it should be stricken, your honor.
MR. GOULD: What he heard, your honor. He might have heard
it from Mr. Page for all I know.

THE COURT: What he heard in terms of showing a state of mind
or his bias or animus may be relevant, but it is very tenuous. I will
sustain the objection.

Suzanne's request for a $15 million cash settlement was de-
nied. Her request for $140,000 a year in child support, retroactive
to Jacqueline's birth was sneered at by both Milton Gould and
Jack, who stated on January 5, 1990, that he found "this proposal
abhorrent. I would not raise the little girl this way. I don't want
her to be a poor little rich girl." He said that his two sons never
had a nanny, had gone to public schools, and "earned their liv-
ings." He did not say that they both worked for him and that they
lived in houses owned by him or drove company cars supplied by
him.

Milton Gould got in more jabs. He complained that Suzanne's
request for child support was "more than we pay justices of the
Supreme Court. This is a case where a young woman makes a
meretricious connection with a rich old man and she contrives to
make the pregnancy an instrument of profit."

They brought up Suzanne's drug conviction for illegal use of
a telephone to distribute cocaine, for which she had received three
years' probation. Suzanne snapped, "I didn't go to prison like Mr.
Cooke's girlfriend for drugs."

In the end Suzanne lost. The court ruled on January 25, 1990,
Jacqueline's second birthday, that Suzanne would not get the $15
million and she would not get the $140,000 a year retroactive to
the child's birth. What Suzanne did get from Judge Robertson was
a judgment for $29,000 a year child support, but not retroactive,
with Jack not having to pay for the first year of Jacqueline's life.
The judge did not require Jack to pay Suzanne's legal fees, leaving
her with unpaid bills that she couldn't meet.[8]

Jack Kent Cooke had won, at least on a dollar and cents basis
although opinion in the Washington press ran against the ruling.
Judy Mann's *Washington Post* column on March 9, 1990, said,
"Robertson was more concerned with protecting the squire of

Middleburg and sending messages to gold-digging women than he was with the child's best interest. The judicial system conspired with a billionaire to steal $29,000 from a two year old." Lou Cook, writing in the *Fairfax Journal*, said, "Mr. Jack Kent Cooke will not be heading for Sweden to collect the Nobel Prize for child support."

Four months later, Jack Kent Cooke married the woman who had done the most to help him win his battle against Suzanne Szabados Martin Cooke, the mysterious Bolivian, Marlene Ramallo Chalmers, once her good friend.

Notes

1. Susan Webster's family owns Sloan's, a prestigious auctioneer of antiques and art in suburban Maryland.
2. Jerry Nachman is now the editor of the *New York Post.*
3. In November 1990, Barbara Harrison was assigned to do a series of profiles on Redskins players. She was denied the right to interview players at Redskin Park and was refused press credentials for a Redskins home game. Jack Kent Cooke has a long memory.
4. John Kent Cooke, Jack's son, filed for divorce against his wife Becky at about the same time, ending their twenty-one-year marriage. The joke among Redskin insiders was that Jack and John were going to get a double divorce in order to save money.
5. Many of Jack's servants live on the Far Acres grounds in cottages with their families.
6. Controversial defensive end Dexter Manley called Jack "a miser" over Washington radio station WAVA when he was attempting to renegotiate his contract in 1986.
7. An odalisque is defined as "a female slave or a concubine in a harem."
8. Jack wouldn't even pay the baby's birthing costs. Jacqueline developed hyperbilirubinemia, a liver ailment, and received treatment in the hospital. Jack kept refusing the bill sent to him by the child's pediatrician. After two and a half years, he arbitrarily deducted it from his child support payments, an act for which the courts had not given him the right. The amount was $407.

CHAPTER
19
MARLENE/MARLENA
ET AL.

"Find me a rich husband."

Depending on the decade in which you were born, or whether you view him as a friend or an enemy, you might call Jack Kent Cooke either an incurable romantic, or a ruthless womanizer. One thing is certain as Jack approaches the December of his life. If he's not currently chasing a business deal, he probably is pursuing a woman who has fascinated him.

In 1988 Jack Kent Cooke told Canada's *Domino* magazine: "I'm the God damnedest romantic you'll ever meet."

Warming to the subject he continued, "I like women in bright sunlight. I like women at all times of day and evening. I just plain like women.

"They are one of the best things the Lord ever thought of . . . they may have been an afterthought following the creation of Adam, but even as an afterthought they are highly desirable. Life without them would be a dirge."

The number of women with whom Jack was linked in the 1980s—famous public women or private, publicity shunning socialites—far exceeds the number of his business deals. And women who have talked out of school will say that Jack's skill as a lover even outdistances his business acumen.

One can only speculate whether Jack's lifelong fascination with the opposite sex is an old-fashioned macho "thrill-of-the-hunt" mentality or a true love for women. There is no doubt that

Jack Kent Cooke feels a little lost without a woman by his side. For Jack to attend a public social event alone, without the company of a woman companion, is rare.

It is a puzzle to many that Jack Kent Cooke would marry his "Bolivian bombshell," Marlene Ramallo Chalmers, the former close friend of Suzanne Martin Cooke, just a few months after agreeing to child support payments for the daughter he had just fathered. Particularly in light of Marlene's disturbing past.

Marlene Leonora Ramallo Miguens Chalmers Cooke, who married Jack on May 5, 1990, was born in Cochabamba, Bolivia, on December 23, 1952, although the wedding certificate issued after her marriage with Jack says December 23, 1955, and on an application for a Mexican tourist card in 1986, Marlene swore under oath that her birthday was December 23, 1954. On the Mexican tourist application she also swore that she was born in the state of Virginia and that she was a citizen of the United States, both factually untrue.

During the past decade, Marlene has spelled her first name Marlene, Marlen, Marlena, and Marleen. She has been known under the last name of Miguens, Neves, Chalmers, Chalmes, Ramallo Chalmers, and various combinations of the first and last names.

Marlene once used Suzanne's sister Stephanie's birth certificate to get back into the U.S. from Mexico after taking it from Diane Martin's home without permission. When Suzanne's mother found out and expressed shock, Marlene said, "What could I do, Diane? I lost mine. Stephanie Szabados sounds Spanish anyway."

Marlene was first arrested in 1978 with her then common-law husband Angel G. Miguens-Oller in Venezuela on suspicion of drug trafficking. They were held for two days and then let go. Her last known arrest was for a bad check charge a decade later, on April 7, 1988, when she was charged with a felony: uttering and delivering four false checks totalling $285.78. She has resided for various periods of time that range from a night to four months in the following institutions: the District of Columbia jail; the Alexandria, Virginia, city jail; the Manassas, Virginia, jail; the Richmond, Virginia, jail; and the Women's Federal Correctional

Institute, a minimum security penitentiary, in Alderson, West Virginia.

Cochabamba, Bolivia, a city of just over 300,000 people lies 8,392 feet above sea level.[1] It is said to be a land of eternal spring. The coldest month averages 57 degrees and the average mean temperature is 63 degrees. La Paz, the de facto capital of Bolivia, is 285 miles to the northwest by paved highway. A trip by bus, called a "flota" in Bolivia, is a ten-hour ordeal. Like Toronto, the Indian word for "land of opportunity", Cochabamba too is Indian in origin, but not as uplifting. It means, in Quechua, "swampy plain."

Located in nearly the exact center of the country, Cochabamba is famous in Bolivia for making a mean liquor from maize, called "chichi," which enables its citizens to walk around most of the day in a numb, drunken trance. The surrounding area is the bread basket of the nation, producing a variety of grains such as wheat and barley, some fruits, coffee, and coca leaves. Coca leaves, when processed, make cocaine. Bolivia is the second largest exporter of cocaine, after Colombia, among South American nations, to the United States. The drug accounts for 60 percent of the export revenues of the country.

Coca leaves grow wild in Bolivia, with the best specimens found on the sides of hills. They are also cultivated. The leaves are ready to be picked when they break on being bent. The green leaves are then spread on burlap or coarse wool and dried in the sun. A perfect finished leaf is uncurled, deep green on the upper surface, and gray-green on the lower. It has a strong odor, much like tea. The natives of Bolivia, particularly those who perform hard labor or exist in poverty, chew coca leaves for pleasure and because it enables them to withstand arduous work. When ingested by mouth, the coca leaves anesthetize the stomach so that hunger and thirst sensations are blocked. Coca stimulates the cortex of the brain, giving a feeling of increased mental power and removing any sense of fatigue. The leaf also produces euphoria and sometimes hallucinations. This stimulation is usually followed

259

by a depression of the entire nervous system. Cocaine and "crack" cocaine provide the same sensations, but intensified.

Cocaine is produced in Bolivia by soaking dried coca leaves in kerosene, then mashing them up and mixing in hydrochloric and sulfuric acids. The matter formed is a brown pulp that is dried into "Bolivian brown." To make the white "snow" that many Americans know, the brown powder is mixed with ether.

Cocaine is often sniffed and absorbed into the body through the nasal membranes. It constricts the breathing passages and has other irritating characteristics. Long, regular use causes ulcerations in the nasal cavity. Continued usage leads to a paranoid personality. Individuals addicted to the drug believe they are threatened, and thus become unpredictable in their behavior.

Bolivia is the poorest country in South America, with a reported average per capita income of $318 a year in 1987. The average life expectancy is fifty-one. It has the highest birthrate in South America; 20 percent of the population is under the age of fifteen. Bolivia is landlocked, mountainous in the west, and inundated with subtropical swamps and rainforests as it nears the eastern border. Like many South American nations it has been plagued by government after government which have sought only to enrich a few and exploit the majority. Through 1990, it had experienced 164 years of independence and 192 coups. One ruler in 1879 went so far as to go to war with Chile over deposits of bat guano and other nitrates.[2] Another dictator backed the Axis powers in World War II. He didn't change his bet until June 1943. He was later overthrown and lynched, his body hung from a lamp post in La Paz. Spanish is not the main language; the majority speak various Indian dialects, the most common being Aymara and Quechua. About 65 percent of the population is illiterate. Bolivia then, is a land to leave rather than enter.

The name Ramallo is quite common throughout Bolivia. There were just seven Ramallos in the 1989 Cochabamba phone book, but that is more an indication of the poverty of the country than the popularity of the name. Marlene was born just before Christmas 1952, shortly after Jack Kent Cooke's fortieth birthday. Her father was Roberto Andaia Ramallo and her mother was Edna Neves.

They separated soon after she was born. Later Edna gave birth to two other children, both boys.

Marlene Ramallo's childhood was quite unlike Jack Kent Cooke's. When Marlene was sixteen, she joined a Bolivian revolutionary movement for a short time. In 1970, Marlene became involved with a member of the Bolivian military, a pilot, and subsequently became pregnant and gave birth to a son, Angel Rodrigo, who was born in Bolivia on January 16, 1972. The union did not last long. Shortly after that she moved to Alexandria, Virginia, on July 10, 1972, to live with her mother and Rodrigo, as her son became known. A brother, Felix, soon followed. Another brother lived with them for a short time but moved back to South America, living in northern Chile. In mid-1991 he moved back to Alexandria.

In 1975 Marlene became involved with Angel G. Miguens-Oller, a Venezuelan. They met at a party at his country's embassy in Washington, where a distant relative of Angel's worked. He became her lover and common-law husband. In 1978, Marlene and Angel were arrested on suspicion of drug trafficking in Venezuela but both were released two days later. On July 24, 1979, Marelene and Angel produced a son, Alejandro Aaron. He is also known as Alex. Shortly afterward, Marlene was in an auto accident and her nose was broken and reconstructed, giving it a new, smoother appearance. She also had plastic surgery to remove bags under her eyes. Angel and Marlene separated in 1982 after Angel was arrested at their apartment in Alexandria for distribution of cocaine and later found guilty. Angel began serving a fifteen-year prison sentence in 1986, first at Petersburg, Virginia, where Marlene's mother, Edna, and their son Alex would visit.[3] Later he testified against a Venezuelan drug ring. Because of his testimony, it was the authorities' belief that his life was endangered and he was transferred to federal correctional institutes in Raybrook, New York; Milan, Michigan; and in late 1990, Oakdale, Louisiana.

A writer who wrote to Angel in prison and subsequently received dozens of collect telephone calls from him offered to send Angel cigarettes or other items as tokens of goodwill. Angel told the writer he had everything he needed.

"Jack Kent Cooke is very upset I'm speaking with you," he told the writer during his first phone call. "But I told Mr. Cooke he can't tell me what to do.

After Angel was moved to Louisiana, he called the writer and asked for Jack Kent Cooke's phone number. "They haven't sent my things from Michigan," he told the writer, "I know the last three digits are 4000. I just can't remember the first three." Although reluctant to talk about the details of his drug conviction over the phone, he told the writer that he had received "a Christmas card" from Jack Kent Cooke for 1990 but that he was a Miami Dolphins fan. Later he would call the writer after the Redskins' 1990 playoff win against the Philadelphia Eagles and tell the writer that he had seen Marlene on television wearing her new mink coat but that she "didn't look happy." When asked why Jack was being so friendly toward him, Angel said, "He wants to adopt my son and have full custody and I won't give it." Indeed, in the summer of 1990, Stuart Haney, Jack's in-house counsel, did send Angel an adoption agreement, on behalf of Jack, asking him to sign it and send the contract back.

After Angel was arrested, Marlene acquired a good deal of money and decided to go to Las Hadas in Manzanillo, Colima, Mexico, for a long vacation.[4] She was given the use of a one-bedroom condominium apartment in Las Hadas by its owner, a woman friend who lived at her apartment house in Alexandria. The unit was up the hill that rises from Las Hadas and commanded an excellent view of the Pacific Ocean. The friend asked Marlene to pay only the maintenance fees, which were about $60 a month. In Mexico, while partying on a cruise boat, Marlene met a sixty-five-year-old man, David Chalmers, a six-foot, six-inch tall, balding Texan who was the chief executive of a Houston oil exploration and marketing firm, Coral Petroleum. Chalmers introduced Marlene to the woman he was with, calling her his fiancée. Chalmers' girlfriend made a big fuss about the dress Marlene was wearing. Marlene told the woman which Mexican artisan had made the dress and where she could have one made like it. A few days later, Chalmers spotted Marlene and a male companion in a bar. Marlene asked if she could see his house. Chalmers was happy to give them a tour.

Chalmers lived in a Moorish-style palace he had built for $6
million. The house was named Villa Coral, after Chalmers' petro-
leum company. The Villa Coral compound was the most impressive
residence of the region and contained five guest suites in addition
to the master suite. There was a pool, servants' quarters—everything a woman who had told friends to "find me a rich husband"
could ask for. A few days later the woman Chalmers had introduced as his fiancée flew back to the United States leaving David
Chalmers alone. Marlene moved in with Chalmers shortly afterward. They were married on April 12, 1985, at the Las Hadas
resort in Manzanillo. Marlene lived two months in Houston and
then continued living in Alexandria while David stayed in Texas.
Marlene may have married David because she feared she was about
to be arrested.

Back in the late 1970s, when Angel and Marlene were flush
with cash, they purchased a new Audi sedan and a three-bedroom
condominium at Watergate at Landmark, in Alexandria, Virginia,
for $135,000, putting $37,000 down in cash and placing a $97,800
first mortgage with Perpetual Savings and Loan, a local bank.[5] The
apartment was solely in the name of Angel Miguens at first. After
Angel was arrested, Marlene had the apartment changed to her
name.

In January 1985, a Bolivian by the name of Bernardo Zabelogo, who was living at Marlene's Alexandria apartment with her,
threatened a police informant with a semiautomatic weapon. The
informant was giving information to the Arlington, Virginia, police
on Bolivian drug gangs. According to the sworn testimony of Kevin
Tamez, an agent of the U.S. Drug Enforcement Administration
(DEA), Zabelogo pointed the gun at the informant's head and told
him they were "going to take care of him" if he didn't stop talking
to drug investigators.

Two days later, four police officers knocked on Marlene's
apartment door with a search warrant. In her apartment they found
a semiautomatic weapon, 140 grams of cocaine, and triple-beam
scales, plastic bags, and other drug packaging materials.

Zabelogo was arrested, convicted, and sent to the Federal Correctional Center in Petersburg, Virginia. Marlene, who was present
in her apartment when the bust was made, was not arrested.

On February 22, 1986, Marlene Ramallo Chalmers was arrested, at National Airport in Washington, D.C., and charged with possession of cocaine with intent to distribute. She was traveling with Ariel Anaya, her lover, and one of the leaders of a large Bolivian gang of cocaine smugglers. The cocaine had been shipped from La Paz to Rio de Janeiro, where Marlene had distributed it to various couriers or "mules" and had then traveled back to the United States, stopping first at Miami International Airport before proceeding to Washington. A quantity of cocaine (10 grams) was found in the luggage that, although it had Anaya's name on it, only contained female clothing and effects. The charge, although serious, was a small one in U.S. drug annals, and Marlene and Ariel were able to post bail of $5,000 each after two days in jail.

However, the DEA presented a variety of information to the grand jury for the eastern district of Virginia that triggered a new thirteen-count indictment. A group of Bolivians—Ariel Anaya, Emilio Baccareza, Flavio Prieto and Marlene Ramallo—were charged with, among others, "bringing (at wholesale) $20 million worth of cocaine into the Washington area—51 kilograms—by the use of false-sided Samsonite-type suitcases." Anaya and Prieto fled to Bolivia; they are still at large and have never been tried. Bacarezza was caught, found guilty, and sentenced. Marlene was left to face the grand jury's indictment.

The indictment charged that Marlene and the three men conspired and agreed to import cocaine into the United States between August 1982 and March 1986. It charged her with several overt acts, specifically with smuggling a kilogram or more of cocaine into the United States from Rio De Janeiro in February 1985 and also smuggling two kilograms of cocaine into Miami from Rio De Janeiro on February 21, 1986. It also charged Marlene with bringing a kilogram or more of cocaine into the United States in November 1984. Other charges named a cocaine manufacturing plant in Laurel, Maryland. The indictment cited Emilio Bacarreza as the gang leader, Flavio Prieto as the chief contact of the source in La Paz, Bolivia, and Marlene and Ariel Anaya as the managers of the importing system that brought the drugs into the country.

An arrest order was issued on April 29, 1986, and although several attempts were made to arrest Marlene, with negotiations going back and forth between the Drug Enforcement Administration and Marlene's attorneys, Marlene failed to surrender. On June 3, 1986, DEA officers burst into her apartment. Marlene was in the shower when they entered. When the officer in charge went into the bathroom, this exchange took place:

> DEA AGENT: "You are under arrest."
> MARLENE (*cracking shower door*): "I'm not finished taking my shower." (*Marlene closed the shower door.*)
> DEA AGENT: "You are ordered to step out of the shower."

And Marlene stepped from the shower, put on a robe, and was arrested. She was taken to the Alexandria city jail.

At Marlene's bail bond hearing, on June 5, 1986, the prosecutor for the United States of America scored several points. One was that Marlene drove and kept exchanging rental cars—a frequent practice of drug people who are trying to escape detection by law enforcement investigators. Another was that Marlene had just shipped a new Jeep Cherokee to Bolivia via Arica, Chile, to the recently departed Ariel Anaya, although Marlene claimed the four-wheel-drive vehicle was sent to Ariel Anaya's uncle. And still a third was that there was good reason to believe that Marlene had two or more passports and could slip in and out of the country at will, escaping detection by the DEA's computers.

Marlene's husband of record, David Chalmers, flew in from Texas to testify for her and Marlene's attorneys placed her two sons in the front row of the courtroom. But nothing worked that day. She was ordered held without bond.

At the end of the hearing, Judge W. Harris Grimsley said, "Defendant Ramallo appears to have been engaged in a continuous pattern of drug activity over the past several years, involving trips to Rio de Janeiro and Buenos Aires, Argentina. She appears to have a constant association, including several live-in arrangements with known drug dealers, and this activity would indicate an involvement with those dealers.

"She is married to a very respectable gentleman in an executive position with an oil company, but this marriage doesn't appear to be any hindrance to her continued activity of trying to get drugs into this country."

265

Judge Grimsley continued, "Her previous companion, Anaya, is admittedly a fugitive. And frankly, but for the indictment and the arrest of this defendant, it is the opinion of the Magistrate that she would probably continue to engage in such illegal activity. For these reasons, which will be reduced in writing and put into a court order so that an appeal may be made of this decision, defendant is held without bond."

Marlene now faced a maximum ten-year prison sentence if found guilty of the charges. With the help of veteran Washington criminal attorney G. Allen Dale—he had defended Mayor Marion Barry's girlfriend Karen Johnson on her cocaine charges—Marlene cut a deal with federal drug enforcement agents and agreed to inform and help find the gang of Bolivian cocaine merchants who had fled to South America and others in exchange for a lesser sentence. The federal government then let her plead guilty on July 15, 1986, to conspiring to import less than a kilogram of cocaine. Marlene was sentenced to eighteen months in a federal penitentiary, which meant serving six months, assuming good behavior. She was also placed on two years' probation.

Before Marlene left for the Federal Correctional Institute in Alderson, West Virgina, on August 1, 1986, she spent two weeks in the Richmond, Virginia, jail and other Virginia city detention centers so that she could help law enforcement agents. She told her friends, including Suzanne Elizabeth Martin, that she was going to visit her father in Bolivia. And with that, she dropped out of sight.

The Alderson, West Virginia, Women's Federal Correctional Institute is a minimum security facility, yet it is virtually impossible to escape from it. Alderson is built into the side of the base of a steep mountain and surrounded by a quickly flowing river, the Greenbrier, which usually floods each spring. Alderson is fifteen miles from a major highway and a potential escapee would have to walk through inhospitable terrain in order to get that far. Its most famous inmate in the past decade was probably Lynette "Squeaky" Fromme, the Manson gang member who attempted to assassinate President Gerald Ford. Squeaky took, as the guards like to say, "a walk in the woods" several times, but was always brought back. Disgusted with Squeaky's behavior, the federal correctional system moved her back to a California institution.

The buildings at Alderson resemble a New England boarding school campus. In fact, the design of the compound, where 753 women prisoners were living in 1986, was copied from a college. Except for the guards, the chain link fence, and the signs that greet you equally in Spanish and English, one could imagine they were away at prep school.

Marlene took some accounting and computer courses at Alderson and studied for a high school General Equivalency Diploma. She also worked in the prison's kitchen and gained a great deal of weight.

When she returned from prison on November 15, 1986, she leveled with her friend Suzanne Martin, but said she didn't know anything about drugs and it was all a mix-up. Suzanne believed her and lent her $5,250 for cosmetic surgery. Marlene took Suzanne's check and had Csaba Magassy, a fashionable Chevy Chase, Maryland, plastic surgeon, do liposuction on her stomach and a buttocks lift at his combined clinic and offices. Susan Webster and Suzanne drove Marlene back to her apartment in Alexandria. Marlene had to crouch on the floor of Susan Webster's antiques delivery van. She was in great pain and, because of the buttocks lift, had to position herself so that she was supported on her hands and knees.

Marlene was now in danger of being deported as a result of her conviction. The wedding to David Chalmers should have kept her here permanently, but that marriage knot was about to be untied. David was filing for divorce. Marlene was arrested by U.S. Immigration authorities on November 21, 1986, and then released on $3,000 bond.

A hearing was held for Marlene on February 25, 1987, in the courtroom of Judge Joan Arrowsmith in Arlington, Virginia. Diane Martin, Suzanne's mother, testified on behalf of Marlene. According to Diane, Marlene burst into tears there and began repeating over and over, "I no want to go back to Bolivia." The case was continued. A motion for relief was later filed with Judge Arrow-smith, on April 5, 1988, by Marlene's friend Juan Chardiet. Marlene was arrested on a bad check charge two days later.

On December 6, 1987, Marlene wrote four checks that totaled $285.78 to a discount cosmetics store in Fairfax County, Virginia, on a nonexistent checking account at First Virginia Bank. Because the amount was more than $200 the charge became a felony rather than a misdemeanor. The police went to Marlene's apartment in Alexandria after she failed to show up as agreed at the cosmetics store for a handwriting sample. Marlene said she didn't write the checks. But the handwriting analysis of Marlene's signature that the police got and the signature on the checks showed that they were written by Marlene.

Marlene was then on probation from her drug conviction, but she didn't seem to take it too seriously. When her probation officer, Michael J. Meczkowski, received the news of her arrest, he revoked her probation for failing to inform him of it and failing to "file her monthly reports in a timely manner" (they were due on the third day of every month), and had her put in the Alexandria city jail.

Marlene may have written the checks because she was virtually broke. She was behind in her mortgage payments. She had put her apartment up for sale in the hope of raising money.

But Marlene's troubles were nearly over. Only a few months later she would be firmly entrenched in Jack Kent Cooke's private box at RFK stadium, just in time to greet Nancy Reagan, who was also Jack's guest. Nancy was there for a "Just Say No To Drugs" ceremony, which was to take place before the start of the game between Washington and the New York Giants on October 2, 1988.

Notes

1. In 1955, Cochabamba's population was less than 100,000. Like Mexico City, whose population is now nearly 20 million, Cochabamba has been invaded by rural poor who live in shacks of scrap wood and cardboard at the edge of the city, making a subcity or instant slum outside the established slums.
2. Guano is the excrement or droppings of various birds and other flying creatures. It is highly prized as a fertilizer.

3. The fifteen-year sentence is according to Angel. Juan Chardiet stated in Marlene's deportation relief filing that it was thirty years, but he was probably in error. Fifteen years is the most likely term, as Angel was considered eligible for parole in 1991.
4. Las Hadas, for moviegoers, is the Mexican resort where Bo Derek met Dudley Moore in the movie, "*10*", and where the famous "Bolero" love scene took place. It was developed by the Patino family, the Bolivian tin moguls, although there is no connection between Marlene and the tin kings. Las Hadas means "The Fairies" in Spanish.
5. Watergate at Landmark is a heavily secured group of high-rise buildings surrounded by a high fence, and built by the same firm that built the original Watergate apartments and offices in Washington. One needs to pass a uniformed sentry in order to enter. It offers strong protection for condominium occupants who wish to lead discreet and private lives. Marlene's apartment was on the eleventh floor of one of the buildings.

CHAPTER

20

COMING HOME

*Dreams. Rhymes with
Jean . . . Marlene . . . even Jacqueline.*

Jack Kent Cooke has lived in nine different decades of the twentieth century. He has left his mark in many ways. He has been a pioneer in sports and business. His rich, personal stamp has been attached to everything he touches.

Yet Jack may probably be remembered for everything he would like to forget. Certainly, at·least in the past decade, his many marriages and turbulent divorces have filled as many newspaper pages as his deserved business accomplishments. The building of the Forum in Los Angeles by Jack and, hopefully, the soon-to-be-built new structure, his Jack Kent Cooke Stadium in Washington, D.C., will last well past the year 2000. But historians may well focus on the temperament and outbursts he displayed inside those arenas. Saving the Chrysler Building from decay in New York City was laudatory but the puzzle of his rejecting an only daughter from birth may be discussed longer.

Jack has been a center of attention for much of his life. He will be the subject of debate long after his death.

By 1987, Jack could see death everywhere. His tax attorney, Bob Schulman, passed away on March 2 of that year. Jack did not go to the funeral. Edward Bennett Williams gave the main eulogy, and Jack's aliy of the 1970s had become an enemy by the latter part of the 1980s.

Edward Bennett Williams was dying as well. There were now

regular visits to a hospital in Boston. After seven operations, his cancer's progress could no longer be stopped. Before he died, on August 13, 1988, Jack let Ed know what he thought of him.

"He said some vile and reprehensible words to Ed when he was down," a former business associate of Jack's told a writer. "We were shocked. He could have buried the hatchet but he didn't. Before Ed Williams died, Jack had a letter sent to him revoking his tickets."

Jack let the Redskins staff know that he didn't want anyone attending Edward Bennett Williams' funeral. When it was held, on Tuesday, August 16, with more than a thousand people crowding into St. Matthews Cathedral in Washington, D.C., only one Redskin employee, Bobby Mitchell, showed up, although Williams had ruled the team for nearly fifteen years. The wife of Jack's general manager, Christine Beathard, was there and so were three former players, quarterback Sonny Jurgenson, the colorful John Riggins, and Jack Pardee, whom Williams had hired to replace George Allen. Other than that, it was a non-Redskin tribute.

At the end of the eighties, Williams had become like Jack's son Ralph at the beginning of the decade and his daughter Jacqueline at the end of it—a nonperson—at least in the eyes of the Redskins. The 1990, 260-page Redskins press guide made no mention of the existence of Edward Bennett Williams, although several paragraphs were devoted to the deaths of George Preston Marshall, Milton King, and Vince Lombardi. As a former Redskin employee put it, "Jack made Ed Williams invisible."

And then there was the tragic death of Jack Kent Cooke II.

Being given the name of Jack Kent Cooke was a heavy burden to carry. For Jack Kent Cooke II, Ralph and Carrie's son and Jack's grandson, it was a curse. He was born with a severe learning disability, saw his parents divorce at age eleven, and when he was sixteen, grandfather Jack sold what he loved most in life, the Los Angeles Kings.

By the time his peers were ready to graduate from high school and begin their adult life, Jack Kent Cooke II was through. There were jails, drugs, alcohol, and gambling binges in Las Vegas, where casinos would grant him credit because of his famous name. Later, he was reduced to hanging out near the Forum and begging tickets to Kings games from strangers. At times he would call his famous grandfather and ask for money, and Jack would ask him to come east and work for him. His namesake always refused, preferring to stay in southern California.

He died in a small apartment in Glendale, just north of Los Angeles, two days before the Super Bowl in 1989. The coroner said the cause was alcoholic liver disease and a related heart condition. He was twenty-six years old.

A small funeral was held in White Plains, New York, near the home of Carrie and Jack II's stepfather, Pete Rozelle.

Jack arrived at the funeral with Marlene Ramallo Chalmers, his now constant companion. Kathy Maxa, a reporter who was doing a profile on Jack at the time, was surprised that Jack Kent Cooke was virtually by himself.

"I thought some of his friends who sit in his box would show up," she told a writer. "But except for Marlene, he was totally alone."

Suzanne Martin Cooke had become persona non grata in Jack's mind as well. By 1988 she was only referred to as S.E.M. or "the bitch" by Jack and those who wanted to be on Jack's good side. Suzanne had given Jack her youth, and a daughter, but Jack felt she had double-crossed him on his request for a third abortion and he would never forgive her. Now, it seemed he only wanted to bring her to her knees.

In early 1987, just months out of prison, Marlene, with two children to support, needed money badly. She tried to raise some cash by putting her three-bedroom condominium in Alexandria up for sale. By now, the new-looking, neatly furnished unit had at least one lien against it. One was from the condominium owners' association. Marlene had installed a black porcelain Jacuzzi and matching bidet in a more prosperous time, but she had failed to get her condominium association's approval. It was put in poorly, with a motor that was too powerful. Still, Marlene asked $165,000 for her apartment.

The original listing by Begg Realty, an upscale Washington

firm, is written in typically gushy "realty-speak" and contains descriptions of a luxury unit with an ebony Jacuzzi, bidet, and sink in the master bedroom bath.[1] It also talks about an upgraded shower with steam jets. There is emphasis placed on the many mirrors in the apartment and the couturier curtains. The prose talks of fabric-covered walls and wood-lined closets. A woman's fantasy is the way a built-in microwave oven, special lighting, and a tiled kitchen is described. The description ends with a summary that the apartment is for those who want the ultimate in their lives.

"The unit had a flamboyant touch to it, with mostly modern furnishings," one real estate agent told a writer. "There was a white grand piano in the living room with a framed picture on it of Marlene Ramallo with President Reagan."[2] Angel Miguens, Marlene's former common-law husband, told a writer that he had purchased most of the apartment's furniture from a manufacturer in Milan, Italy.

But the apartment, even though Marlene later reduced the price to $148,500, wouldn't sell. Desperate, Marlene sold her condominium parking space for $7,000.

Next, Marlene sent word to Jack that she had information he could use in his divorce action against Suzanne. Jack said to come on out. Marlene came, renting a black Lincoln limousine for the occasion. Marlene had met Jack briefly before at the Middleburg horse steeplechase on May 2, 1987—the same meet after which Jack and Suzanne conceived Jacqueline. Suzanne had introduced them. After the introduction—Marlene had been with her beau, Fauquier County socialite Chris van Roijen—Jack had made uncomplimentary remarks about Marlene's appearance to Suzanne. Now, at Far Acres, Marlene told Jack about the baby being "her ticket" statement she said she had heard Suzanne make with Juan Chardiet present. Jack knew he had a winner. And he took a closer look at Marlene Ramallo Chalmers as well.

Although Marlene's budding romance with Jack was interrupted by her "vacation" at the Alexandria city jail for breaking probation, the bond between them was very close by the beginning of the 1988 football season. Marlene was now at Jack's side at the

Redskins' home games. And when the front office learned of her drug past, some employees gave her a cruel code name: "Mrs. Noriega."

Jack introduced Marlene around town, first as an "Italian countess" and later as his "Bolivian bombshell." He began giving her "serious" jewelry and a mink coat from Saks Fifth Avenue. He surprised friends by being far more generous with her than he had been with Suzanne. After Suzanne became pregnant, he had taken her to New York and teased her with the good life at an estate jewelry auction at Christie's. He had said to her when a twenty-carat diamond was put up for bid, "Just think. All this can be yours. All you have to do is have an abortion."

He didn't buy Suzanne any jewelry that night. He was more happy prowling through thrift shops with her, looking for bargains like wool blazers. Once Jack had presented Suzanne an old sweater that had belonged to his mother. "He made a big deal out of it," Suzanne told a writer, referring to the twelve-year-old cardigan.

Now, according to Harry Turner, his chauffeur, Jack would send to the Middleburg Bank "for $3,000 cash at a time and then send me back an hour later for another $3,000." Jack bought Marlene one piece of jewelry after another and expensive clothes that would have shocked him if Suzanne had brought them home. He gave Marlene a Visa card with the Redskins' logo and his name on it. With Suzanne, he had been a tightwad and proud of it.

Marlene, enhanced by plastic surgery, and slimmed down to 118 pounds, wearing short, above-the-knee skirts that showed off her shapely legs, was an exotic beauty. With her jet black hair pulled back and a quasi-Bolivian hat on her head, she affected regality, but with a ready laugh and a smile for all. Suzanne was incensed. Marlene, her former friend, had not only replaced her, but she was left with Jack's child, whom he wouldn't even deign to recognize. And on top of that, Jack was lavishing on Marlene many more gifts than he had ever given Suzanne. Jack also treated Marlene's two boys as if they were his own sons while continuing to ignore the daughter he had fathered. In his 1990 *Who's Who* listing there was no mention of his marriage to Suzanne or his daughter although his first two wives and sons (including a reinstated Ralph) were listed.

Jack bought Marlene a house in Las Brisas, Acapulco, Mexico, for $1.5 million and one in Washington just above Rock Creek Park near the Shoreham Hotel for $2 million. Ironically it had once belonged to George Preston Marshall, the founder of the Redskins. When he wrote out the check for the Washington house, he turned to Marlene and said, "Is this what you want, Marlene?"

And Marlene, in a diplomatic move worthy of a United Nations negotiator turned the question around. "If that's what you want, Jack," she said, "that's what I want."

When Nancy Reagan was invited to RFK Stadium on October 2, 1988, Marlene was already Jack's regular guest. The focus of Nancy's visit that day was not to see the Redskins lose to the Giants (which they did, 24–23). She was there to highlight her new antidrug campaign. Former NFL hero Bart Starr and the Redskins' all-purpose Bobby Mitchell escorted the U.S. president's wife to the center of the field just before the start of the game for a "Just Say No to Drugs" presentation. In Jack's box with the first lady was the cream of the nation's leadership—defense secretary Frank Carlucci, treasury secretary Jim Baker, former senator and potential presidential candidate Paul Laxalt. The watchdogs of the press—Lesley Stahl, Carl Rowan, and George Will—were there too. Marlene had become an eighties-style Cinderella.

By the time Vice President Dan Quayle and his wife Marilyn began attending games in Jack's box, the press had caught on. Much to-do was made about Quayle's first visit, especially when a local television station ran footage on the evening news showing Dan chatting up Marlene. But the Washington public didn't make any fuss. The Redskins were having a winning season.

When Jack married Marlene, the day of the Virginia Gold Cup steeplechase, May 5, 1990, Marlene sported a large square-cut diamond ring estimated to be at least ten carats in size. It was the second anniversary of Jack's impregnation of Suzanne. After the ceremony, the couple held court at the event, which formally begins the Virginia steeplechase season. The bride wore an off-the-shoulder, white cotton tea-length dress and a becoming brimmed straw hat. Jack was his usual natty self, in a checked shirt and a houndstooth jacket. The only damper on the day was Jack's horse, Lithograph, which Jack scratched because the gelding had a cold.

"He takes real good care of that horse," a groom told a writer.

A few days later Jack and Marlene flew to Las Hadas for a honeymoon. They had been there in January 1989. Marlene tried to get Jack to buy David Chalmer's house, Villa Coral, where she had married David five years before.

Jack went out in public much more than he had with Suzanne. There were nights out at clubs like Anton's where Jack had heckled Mel Torme and both had a raucous good time. Lloyd and Ann Hand (he was the former Reagan chief of protocol) joined the fun.

Marlene may have married Jack partly to smother her legal troubles. Her deportation worries were not over when she wed Jack. Her bulging folder at the Immigration and Naturalization Service in Arlington still had not been closed. Later it contained a photocopy of the wedding story from the *Washington Post*. And the bad check charge against Marlene had yet to be adjudicated. Technically, under those circumstances a police officer could have approached her while she was making small talk with Dan Quayle and arrested her. Less than two months after she married Jack, on June 27, 1990, Marlene's bad check charge was dropped, unprosecuted, in Virginia's Fairfax County Circuit Court. This time she was represented by John T. Hazel, a lawyer who also was one of the most powerful real estate developers in northern Virginia. Hazel, whose law firm did corporate and real estate work, had not represented anyone on criminal charges in years and gave a "no comment" when asked why he was representing Marlene. The reason given by the court for the dismissal of Marlene's charges was that she had cooperated with federal authorities and had helped them in a number of cases against major drug dealers. Marlene was home free.

On Jack and Marlene's marriage certificate, Jack completed the alterations, begun years before, of his family name. He even entered his late father's name, Ralph Ercil Cooke, as Ralph Kent Cooke. Everyone was a Kent Cooke now. Shortly after, the attractive mother of two began calling herself Marlene Kent Cooke.

After his marriage to Marlene, the salacious stories in the press about Jack Kent Cooke never seemed to end. Harry Turner, Jack's now-former chauffeur, weighed in with his memoirs in the *Washingtonian* which Jack termed "scurrilous." It was the last straw.

Jack sued the magazine in December 1989 for $30 million. That didn't stop the monthly periodical. In October 1990, the magazine's gossip columnist, Rudy Maxa, wrote that an old beau of Marlene's had nude pictures of her and was trying to sell them. But Jack got his revenge. He forced the magazine to apologize publicly and had it make a substantial donation to his favorite charity.

It seems incongruous that the final years of North America's last mogul are being spent married to a woman who grew up in one of the poorest countries in the western hemisphere. Jack Kent Cooke grew up in one of the richest nations in the world, and emigrated to the very wealthiest, settling in the most powerful city on earth. The mystery compounds when one contemplates the age difference, forty years, and the difference in wealth: one a billionaire, the other virtually bankrupt. The cultures in which each grew up are so far apart they could be on separate planets.

A writer's description of an evening in Jack Kent Cooke's present life might read like this:

The Jaguar sedan purred into the drive of the 641-acre estate Jack Kent Cooke called Far Acres. It was twenty-six miles from Redskin Park and this afternoon Jack had set a near record—forty minutes—driving the regular route like a race car driver. Tonight he would be alone, and he savored the solitude.

Marlene said she would be spending the evening with her mother in Alexandria, and that was fine—Jack had changed. Let her have some freedom. Jack opened the door of the Jaguar, slammed it, and surveyed the grounds before he went inside. He looked at the gold trees and the beginning of the Blue Ridge mountains beyond.

So much like Canada. So much like home.

It was a small house for a Middleburg squire, not more than 7,000 square feet. Its ultramodern style was a hunt country anomaly. He entered through the kitchen and couldn't resist checking his prize spice racks—every seasoning known to man, neatly alphabetized, beginning with allspice. That was part of Jack's Grand House Tour. Past the paintings by Pierre Bonnard and Mau-

277

rice Utrillo, his Postimpressionist masters. Good art, great investments. Past the closet full of Georgian silver. The snuff box collection. The Steuben glass collection. The books—the complete first editions of H. L. Mencken, all the F. Scott Fitzgerald novels—devoid of their dust covers, which Jack thought pretentious. The bronze busts of the two grandchildren that Jeannie II had done.

The living room. A perfect circle. Just like the Las Vegas house. Just like the Forum. Just like life. Half of it is glass and it faces toward the mountains. "Did I tell you it was designed by the senior disciple of the Frank Lloyd Wright school?"

No dinner tonight. Jack's menu for the week is always typed and given to the cook in advance. Some of the entrees are his own recipes. But if truth be told, Jack is a very simple man. "Business is simple really," he once said, "people try to make a mystery out of it. It's all in seeing a problem and solving it. And working hard." People were simple too. "They're ruled by greed and fear—forget everything else," he had once told a Fauquier County friend after more than one glass of wine.

The world according to Jack Kent Cooke: "If you're doing a deal never let them leave the room," he had said. "If you let them sleep on it, the deal will never get done." On lawyers: "They never make money when things are black and white. They get rich when everything is gray."

Love Is Gone. "This is the end of all our dreams," he had written. "I won't change as I've done before for love is gone." Dreams. Rhymes with Jean . . . Marlene . . . even Jacqueline. Could be a song there. Food for thought.

For all the Duke Zeibert's and '21' Clubs and Palm restaurants of the world, there was really nothing quite like a good hot dog (and wouldn't a Shopsy taste good right now?) Jack remembered when old Mo Siegel came over for Thanksgiving and they watched the Lions game. At halftime, Jack had a tray of hot dogs brought out and Morrie, dear Morrie, didn't understand.

"But Jack," Mo had groused, "this is Thanksgiving. Where's the turkey?"

And Jack had to explain to Mo.

"My God, Mo," he had said to Siegel, "Anyone can have

turkey. These aren't any hot dogs. These are Nathan's hot dogs. I had them flown in special."

But even Mo had betrayed him. He had written a column on September 17, 1990, saying the Redskins wouldn't make the playoffs and Jack had called him in the middle of the night and told him he was disloyal and that he wouldn't carry him any more. Then he had taken away Mo's tickets to the box for good measure. Nobody crossed Jack Kent Cooke.[3]

Into the bedroom. Neutral tones here. Touches of chocolate brown, his favorite color, are everywhere. His king-size electric bed awaits. There are eight newspapers he has yet to read. Three of them he owns. Bill Stryon's latest book—on depression—is at bedside. So is a gun, inside the nightstand, just in case. Push a button, the bed adjusts to a sitting position. Push a button, a servant will appear. Push a button, the lights adjust. Push a button, the television comes on.

Jack pushes a button and the television does come on. Jack's satellite dish searches the sky for sports, any sports. Stop. A Lakers game. There's Magic. Did I tell you I drafted Magic? Gave him his pro start. There he is still going strong—just like me.

On nights like this, Jack would like to hop into bed totally nude, but tonight he changes into a pajama top so that if a servant is summoned he can sit up and appear to be fully clothed. He hangs his clothes neatly in one of the dressing suites. The other is now Marlene's. Several dozen pairs of shoes are polished and displayed. Bally, Church, Peele's slippers (with embossed fox heads), and handtooled cowboy boots. There is an anteroom off the bedroom next to the dressing area, a sort of extra bedroom that one can only enter and exit by going through Jack's master suite.

Into bed, under the warm, yet light sable bedspread. It's fake sable, but a good fake—real fur. He has brought dinner with him. Kraft Cracker Barrel cheese, two slices of bread, a glass of wine, and a bowl of candy bars. He makes a very Canadian cheese sandwich and opens the *Los Angeles Daily News*, which has been flown in. These days there are nights when he can't sleep and he'll get up after midnight and roar through lonely empty country roads in the Jaguar. But not tonight. The last mogul needs to rest. Tomorrow he will be very very busy. There are deals to make and money to be made.[4]

Notes

1. In 1987, Diane Martin, selling real estate for Begg Realty, had property listings at different times for Jack Kent Cooke, the future Mrs. Jack Kent Cooke, Marlene Ramallo Chalmers, and Marlene's former husband, David Chalmers.
2. David Chalmers contributed to the George Bush vice presidential campaign. The photo with Reagan was taken during his second inaugural celebration in Washington.
3. Jack and Mo later reconciled.
4. This chapter was written prior to the November 7, 1991, press conference in which Magic Johnson announced his retirement from the NBA, following his testing positive for antibodies to HIV, the suspected AIDS virus.

AFTERWORD

Suzanne Martin Cooke and her attorney, Kathleen O'Brien, appeared before the Virginia Court of Appeals in Alexandria, Virginia, on April 8, 1991. Milton Gould and two associates were present on behalf of Jack Kent Cooke.

Before the hearing, Gould bantered and dropped names with the other attorneys in the near empty courtroom ("You must have known Mort Caplin? He made his office with Arthur Goldberg.").[1]

Three judges appeared for the commonwealth of Virginia. Again, arguments flew back and forth with Suzanne's attorney asserting that more than $29,000 was needed for annual child support and Gould claiming that any additional child support was disguised alimony.

One judge said, "Well, we can't build a palace for the child and have the mother living in a shack."

Milton Gould said, "This child will be provided for. There is a trust fund."

Kathleen O'Brien said, "The basic issue is adequate child support consistent with life-style. Cooke is the second wealthiest man in the state of Virginia."[2]

Four weeks later the court of appeals gave its verdict. There would be no additional child support or alimony. If however, funds were needed for special schooling or similar needs, Suzanne could again petition the courts. Retroactive legal fees for Suzanne's lawyers who represented her in the divorce proceedings against Jack were awarded to her attorneys.

Three months after the ruling, and four years of negotiations, Jack was on the verge of announcing that he would build a 78,600-seat stadium with luxury skyboxes in Washington, D.C. The stadium is projected to cost Jack $160 million but the District of Columbia will have to pay about $65 million in infrastructure expenses. The project was not certain and there was a slight chance the deal could fall apart.[3] The fans who sought to buy season tickets to sold-out Redskins games had grown to more than 42,000 by 1991. Thus, it is likely that there will still be a waiting list when the new structure is complete. The stadium will have a natural grass field but will be built from concrete and cold steel. It will be named for Jack Kent Cooke, a fitting monument to him.

During that same month of 1991, Marlene Kent Cooke and Jack's two new stepsons, Rodrigo and Alejandro, were spending considerable time at Jack's $2 million estate in Washington. Suzanne Martin Cooke lived with Jacqueline Kent Cooke in a rented house less than five miles away. In Los Angeles, the former Jean Carnegie Cooke continued to live at a Pacific beach community while Kay Starr lived nearby in West Los Angeles.

Jack's health, at seventy-nine years of age, is robust as of this writing. He will undoubtedly continue to seek new challenges for decades. When Jack does leave us, the author hopes he gets his expressed desire of dying after a sporting event in which his team is the winner. The wish occurred after whipping the Philadelphia Eagles on a cold Sunday afternoon. Jack looked skyward and shouted at the heavens, "If you had to die, you wouldn't mind doing it on a day like this."

Jacqueline Kent Cooke, whose life is just beginning, has met with her father once since her birth. That was at a deposition when she was one month away from her third birthday. Upon seeing her, Jack took off his dark glasses and said, "Well, there's no denying whose little girl this is." The little girl ran to him and wrapped her arms around his legs. Then Jacqueline sat on his knee for a few minutes while Jack spoke to her, his eyes filling with tears. After that, Jack began sending Jacqueline gifts—expensive Florence Eisman dresses and embroidered monogrammed towels.

Notes

1. Caplin headed the Internal Revenue Service under John F. Kennedy. Goldberg is a former justice of the U.S. Supreme Court.
2. John Kluge is the leading individual in terms of wealth, according to many financial chronicles, both in Virginia and in the United States.
3. But there was nowhere to go in the Virginia suburbs. Although land was available, the required number of traffic lanes leading into and out of such a property was nowhere to be found.

SOURCES

Chapter One. The author was present in Jack Kent Cooke's box and its environs on September 13, 1987. He was also present for dozens of other games in the owner's box between 1983 and 1988. He was not a guest of Jack Kent Cooke but of another key Redskin employee who was always given at least four seats to the enclosure.

The author interviewed Harry Turner (through his attorney), Diane Martin, and Suzanne Martin Cooke numerous times, as well as two other regular guests in the owner's box who spoke to the author on a confidential basis. He also spoke to Larry King and Chuck Conconi for this chapter. Other information in this chapter was compiled or checked using official National Football League records, and articles printed in the *Washington Post*, the *Washington Times, Washingtonian* magazine, *Reader's Digest*, and confidential sources within the Redskin front offices.

Chapter Two. The author visited Hamilton, Ontario for several days in August 1990 and in May 1991. Most of the Hamilton information was compiled with the help of a confidential source at Hamilton City Hall, the special collections department of the Hamilton Library headed by J. Brian Henley, the library of McMasters University, and Lyn Dale of the Hamilton Historical Board. The author is particularly indebted to Jerry Ormond of the *Hamilton Spectator* who took time to personally guide the author through the streets of Hamilton and who helped him locate the site where Jack Kent Cooke first lived. The author also referred to the records of the *Spectator* and the then *Toronto Mail and Empire* for more information.

The author and a key researcher visited Toronto in August and September 1990, and May 1991. The boyhood home of Jack Kent Cooke was visited by the author twice as well as other residences in which Jack lived in Toronto. The author and his researcher retraced by foot Jack's route to Malvern Collegiate and went inside Malvern, visiting the school's library and reading the archives. The author is particularly indebted to the records of the Robarts Reference Library of the University of Toronto, the Toronto Metro Reference Library, Balmy Beach Canoe Club, the librarians of Malvern Collegiate Institute, the people of Neville Park Boulevard, and to the following: Bill and Vera Brady, Joe McNulty, Al Dubin, Norman and Edna Tarver, Lloyd Nourse, Alex Barris, Jack Welch, and other sources who asked not to be named.

The author also found helpful many books which are listed in the bibliography at the end of this book as well as newspaper articles of the day in the Toronto *Globe and Mail.*

Chapter Three. The author used extensive information available in these Canadian magazines: *Saturday Night, Maclean's,* and *Canadian Business.* A confidential document was particularly helpful, as were Lloyd Nourse, Joe McNulty, and two off-the-record Canadian sources.

Chapter Four. The author interviewed Al Dubin, a representative of the Kirkland Lake Chamber of Commerce, two confidential sources, and Joe McNulty for this chapter. Other information on Roy Thomson is from various articles available at the library of the Embassy of Canada in Washington, D.C., and in the book, *The Thomson Empire,* by Susan Goldenberg. The author recommends the book to anyone wishing to learn more about Lord Thomson.

Chapter Five. The author referred to information in *Saturday Night, Canadian Business,* and *Maclean's* for this chapter as well as newspaper accounts in the *Toronto Star,* the *Globe and Mail,* and the *Evening Telegram.* Bill Brady, Al Dubin, and Bill Dalton were interviewed for this chapter as well as confidential Toronto sources.

Chapter Six. The information on this chapter was compiled from news stories that appeared between 1948 and 1960 in the *Globe and Mail, Toronto Star,* and *Evening Telegram.* Articles in the magazines *Canadian Business* and *Saturday Night* were helpful also, as were Alex Barris, Bill Brady, Margo Reid, Gloria Shan, and Rabbi David Monson. Court documents and the book *A History of Journalism in Canada* (1962) were of special use regarding the "Babies for Export" trial. The author is grateful to John Fraser, the editor of *Saturday Night*, for his help.

Besides Al Dubin, the author talked with dozens of people in Toronto about Jack Kent Cooke's relationship with Kay Starr. Everyone was aware of the Kay Starr romance.

Articles in *Maclean's* also assisted the author, as did the Oklahoma Hall of Fame in Oklahoma City. Additional information was gathered in the Library of Congress, from BMI (Broadcast Music, Inc.) in New York City, and Harry Bluestone in Studio City, California.

Chapter Seven. The author relied on news stories and editorials in the *Toronto Star, Globe and Mail, Evening Telegram,* and *Maclean's* magazine. Mary Pollock, Gloria Shan, Mary Crysdale, and a confidential source provided information, as did the Embassy of Canada, the Robarts Reference Library of the University of Toronto, and the Library of Congress in Washington. C. Stanley Allen gave technical advice on yacht racing.

Chapter Eight. The author relied on information available in the *Congressional Record, Globe and Mail, Toronto Star, Washington Post,* and *Evening Telegram* for this chapter. Articles in *Maclean's* and *Saturday Night* were of assistance. The author interviewed Al Dubin, Mary Pollock, John Monahan, and two confidential Toronto sources regarding Jack's final years in Toronto.

Chapter Nine. The author used information from articles in the *Washington Post, Globe and Mail, Toronto Star, Hamilton Spectator, New York Times, Los Angeles Times, Saturday Night* magazine, and *Washingtonian* magazine for this chapter. Jim Gustafson, David Schwartz, and Jerry Berns were interviewed for this chapter.

Chapter Ten. This chapter was written with information compiled from the *New York Times, New York Post, New York Daily News, Washington Post, Los Angeles Times, Los Angeles Herald Examiner, Hamilton Spectator, Toronto Star,* and *Globe and Mail.* Articles in *Washingtonian, Newsweek,* and *Los Angeles* magazines were helpful, as was "An Oral History," the papers of Irving Berlin Kahn (135 pages) at Pennsylvania State University's National Cable Television Center and Museum (which was visited); and the case of Cooke vs Cooke, case D 904 108, by and for the County of Los Angeles. Harry Markson, a former employee of Madison Square Garden was interviewed for this chapter, as was Dick Beddoes in Toronto and confidential sources in Los Angeles and in Washington, particularly at the

National Cable Television Association. The *Television Factbook*, an annual publication, was consulted several times.

Chapter Eleven. The author visited Los Angeles in November 1990 with a researcher and spent five days there. This chapter was compiled by talking with confidential southern California sources and using information available in the *Los Angeles Times, Los Angeles Herald Examiner, New York Times, Washington Post, Globe and Mail, Toronto Telegram, Toronto Star, Hamilton Spectator,* and *Washington Evening Star.* Magazine sources were *Los Angeles, Washingtonian, Maclean's, Saturday Night, Newsweek,* and *Sports Illustrated.*

Chapter Twelve. This chapter was written after interviews with Al Dubin, Dick Beddoes, Ken "Jiggs" McDonald, and a confidential source at the Forum in Los Angeles. Newspaper articles from the *Los Angeles Times, Los Angeles Herald-Examiner, New York Times, Washington Post* and in Toronto, the *Globe and Mail* were culled. Also information from articles in *Los Angeles, Washingtonian, Time,* and *Sports Illustrated* magazines was helpful.

Chapter Thirteen. This chapter was written from information available in the *Los Angeles Times, Los Angeles Herald-Examiner, Washington Evening Star, Washington Post, Globe and Mail, Toronto Star, New York Times,* and *Los Angeles* magazine. Kathy Maxa and Arthur Crowley, Esq. were interviewed for this chapter and the court records of Cooke vs Cooke, case D 904 108, by and for the County of Los Angeles, were used.

Chapter Fourteen. This was written with information available from case number D 904 108, Cooke vs Cooke, by and for the County of Los Angeles. Arthur J. Crowley, Esq., a former employee of the Washington Redskins, and sources at the Great Western Forum were interviewed for this chapter.

Chapter Fifteen. The author interviewed several sources who are or were employees of the Washington Redskins for this chapter. Also information was garnered from articles in the *Washington Post, Washington Evening Star, New York Times,* and *Los Angeles Times.* Articles in *Washingtonian* and Canada's *Domino* magazines were also used as sources.

Chapter Sixteen. This chapter was prepared from news articles in the *Washington Post, New York Times, Lexington Herald-Leader,* and its predecessor, the *Lexington Herald.* Public real estate records in New York City were read. Prospectuses for Cooke Media Inc. and Cardinal Productions were read at the Securities and Exchange Commission. Articles published by *Washingtonian, Forbes,* and *The Blood Horse* magazines were helpful. Jerry Berns of Club '21' and confidential sources in Lexington, Kentucky, and Phoenix, Arizona, and at Redskin Park contributed to the writing of this chapter. The author and two research assistants visited New York, Los Angeles, and Lexington for this chapter.

Chapter Seventeen. The author interviewed Suzanne Martin Cooke and her mother Diane at least twelve times for this chapter. He has talked with every member of Suzanne Martin Cooke's family with the exception of Stephanie, who lives in Scotland. He also interviewed Cathy Gilder, Susan Webster, and on a confidential basis, some "regulars" of Jack Kent Cooke's box for this chapter. Court testimony from the records of Jack Kent Cooke vs Suzanne E. Szabados Martin Cooke in the Circuit Court of Fauquier County, Virginia, was used for this chapter, as were articles in the *Washington Post, Washington Times,* and *News of the World* (Great Britain). *People* and *Washingtonian* magazines were also used as sources.

Chapter Eighteen. The primary sources for this chapter were the court records of Jack Kent Cooke vs Suzanne Szabados Martin Cooke in the Circuit Court of Fauquier County, Virginia, and multiple interviews with Suzanne Cooke and her mother Diane. The author retraced Suzanne's "long walk home" on Route 713 in Fauquier County by foot. Juan Chardiet, Cathy Gilder, Jerry Nachman, one of Suzanne Cooke's attorneys, Kathleen O'Brien, and confidential sources at Redskin Park were also interviewed. Sources included the *Washington Post, Washington Times, Fauquier County Democrat,* and *Washingtonian* and *People* magazines.

Chapter Nineteen. This chapter was compiled from Case number 86-00100-A, the United States of America vs. Ariel Anaya, Marlen Ramallo, et al., and various judgments and probation officer's reports at the United States District Court in the Eastern District of Virginia. Information acquired under the Freedom of Information Act and from the United States Immigration and Naturalization Service was also used. Suzanne Cooke, Susan Webster, Diane Martin, Angel Miguens-Oller, and confidential sources at both the Watergate at Landmark condominium and Redskin Park were interviewed for this chapter. Other sources used were the *Washington Post, Washington Times,* and *Domino* magazine. The author personally visited Alderson, West Virginia, and spoke with prison guards who work there and the warden's assistant, Faye Pollard. The author's chief researcher visited the Bolivian Embassy in Washington, D.C.

Chapter Twenty. The author interviewed Suzanne Cooke for this chapter and two other confidential sources who have spent considerable time at Far Acres. Two residents of Watergate at Landmark in Alexandria were interviewed. Other sources include an employee of Anton's, Susan Miller, Angel Miguens-Oller, and a former employee of Hazel, Thomas, Fiske PC. Sources who work at Redskin Park were also consulted. Articles from the *Washington Post* and *Washington Times* as well as Marlene Kent Cooke's probation reports were used.

BIBLIOGRAPHY

Baine, Richard. *Toronto, An Urban Study.* Toronto: Clarke, Irwin, 1972.

Berton, Pierre. *The Great Depression, 1929–1939.* Toronto: McClelland and Stewart, 1990.

Blake, Mike. *The Minor Leagues.* New York: Wynwood, 1991.

BMI Canada. *Yes, There Is Canadian Music.* Montreal, 1968.

Cole, Barry G. *FCC and the Broadcast Audience.* Boston: Addison-Wesley, 1988.

Cole, Barry G. *Reluctant Regulators.* New York: Addison-Wesley, 1978.

Cosell, Howard. *Cosell.* Chicago: Playboy Press, 1973.

Cosell, Howard. *I Never Played the Game.* New York: Morrow, 1985.

Cosell, Howard. *Like It Is.* Chicago: Playboy Press, 1974.

Fitzgerald, F. Scott. *The Great Gatsby.* New York, Scribners, 1925.

Goldenberg, Susan. *The Thomson Empire.* Toronto: Methuen, 1984.

Gould, Milton S. *The Witness Who Spoke with God.* New York: Viking, 1979.

Harris, David. *The League.* New York: Bantam, 1987.

Hauser, Thomas. *Muhammad Ali.* New York: Simon and Schuster, 1991.

King, Larry. *Tell It to the King.* New York: Putnam, 1988.

Kilbourn, William. *The Toronto Book.* Toronto: MacMillan, 1976.

Klein, Gene. *First Down and a Billion.* New York: Morrow, 1987.

Kluckner, Michael. *Toronto, The Way It Was.* Toronto: Whitecap, 1988.

Kowet, Don. *The Rich Who Own Sports.* New York: Random House, 1977.

McNeill, Bill, and Morris Wolfe. *Signing On: The Birth of Radio in Canada.* Toronto: Doubleday Canada Ltd, 1982.

McWhirter, Norris, ed. *Guinness Book of World Records.* New York: Bantam, 1981.

290

Malcolm, Andrew H. *The Canadians.* New York: Times Books, 1985.

Moldea, Dan E. *Interference.* New York: Morrow, 1989.

Nite, Norm. *Rock On.* New York: Harper and Row, 1974.

Pack, Robert. *Edward Bennett Williams for the Defense.* New York: Harper and Row, 1983.

Reader's Digest. *Heritage of Canada.* Montreal: Reader's Digest, 1978.

Sabbagh, Karl. *Skyscraper.* New York: Viking, 1989.

Salinger, J.D. *The Catcher in the Rye.* New York: Random House, 1945.

Speisman, Stephen. *The Jews of Toronto.* Toronto: McClelland and Stewart, 1979.

Stambler, Irwin. *Encyclopedia of Popular Music.* New York: St. Martin's Press, 1965.

Sutherland, Fraser. *The Monthly Epic.* Toronto: Fitzhenry and Whiteside, 1989.

Swaney, Deanna. *Bolivia, A Travel Survival Kit.* Berkeley, Calif.: Lonely Planet, 1988.

Theismann, Joe. *Theismann.* Chicago: Contemporary, 1987.

Whittingham, Richard. *Fireside Book of Pro Football.* New York: Fireside, 1989.

Young, Scott. *Hello Canada!* Toronto: Seal, 1985.

ABOUT THE AUTHOR

Adrian Havill was born in Bournemouth, England, in 1940. After the war, he moved to Canada with his mother, an entertainer, where he spent most of his childhood. As a teenager he moved to Seattle, Washington, and subsequently lived in several West Coast communities.

After serving in the U.S. military as a paratrooper in the 82nd Airborne Division, he worked at a number of occupations: newspaper editor, stand-up comedian, advertising writer, publicist, men's haberdasher, and stockbroker. His favorite accomplishments include qualifying for the Boston Marathon several times and his tenure as president of the Washington, D.C., Variety Club.

He lives with his writer-wife of twenty-seven years, and their college-age children David and Amanda, in Reston, Virginia.

He is an avid fan of the Washington Redskins.

INDEX

Abdul-Jabbar, Kareem, 161, 163, 171–73
Ackroyd, Dan, 113*n*3
Agre, Dr. Keith, 168
Ali, Muhammad, 129, 131–36, 152*n*2, 167*n*10
Allen, Etty, 167*n*12
Allen, George, 11, 165–66, 167*n*12, 169, 188, 199, 206
Allen, Perry, 120
American Cablevision, 127
Anaya, Ariel, 264, 265
Anderson, Dave, 135
Anderson, Margaret, 186, 192
Anderson, Sparky, 112
Armed Forces Radio, 131
Armstrong, James, 103
Arrowsmith, Joan, 267, 268
Arum, Bob, 135
Atkinson, Jess, 15, 16–17, 19*n*9
Auerbach, Red, 149

Baccareza, Emilio, 264
Bagby, Douglas, 183, 193
Ball, Joe, 183
Banks, Helen, 208
Barkway, Michael, 78
Barris, Alex, 51, 73, 76, 85

Barry, Marion, 6, 8, 10, 211, 252
Bass, Mike, 165
Bass, Tom, 207
Bassett, John, 107, 146
Baylor, Elgin, 149, 161, 163
Beathard, Bobby, 14, 16, 18*n*3, 19*n*9, 203–7, 209, 211*n*2, 212*n*8
Beathard, Christine, 14, 18–19*n*6, 271
Becker, Joe, 90
Beddoes, Dick, 155
Bernhard, Berl, 210
Berry, Dr. John, 237
Berton, Pierre, 104–6, 107
Berwald, Jean Carnegie. *See* Cooke, Barbara Jean Carnegie
Bidwill, Bill, 205
Bishop, Percy, 111
Blair, Janet, 143
Blanchard, C.S., 72
Block, John, 203, 239
Bonavena, Oscar, 134
Bonde, Agnetta, 209
Brady, Bill, 33, 53, 59–61, 80–82
Brady, James, 222
Brady, Vera, 33

293

Brennan, Christine, 203
Bresnan, William J. "Bill," 128
Bridgeman, Junior, 171, 172
Briggs, Walter "Spike," 95
Broadcast Equipment Corporation, 120–21
Broadcast Foundation of America, 122–23
Brown, Edmund "Pat," 146
Brown, Larry, 165
Bryan, William, 94
Burton, Charles L., 54
Buss, Dr. Jerry, 167n11, 188, 195
Byner, Earnest, 219

Cacheris, Plato, 240
California Sports, Inc., 191
Callaghan, Morley, 217–18
Campbell, Brian, 155
Campbell, Byron C., 224–25
Campbell, Clarence, 155
Canadian Aces, 34
Canadian Board of Broadcast Governors, 58, 94, 103–4, 107
Canadian Conservatives, 62, 66n7
Canadian Liberals, 62, 66n7
Canadian Social Credit party, 93
Cannon, Lou, 183, 252
Carlisle Indians, 36n3
Carlucci, Frank, 275
Carmody, John J., 118
Carnegie, Bernice (mother-in-law), 38, 175
Carnegie, Bill, 38
Carnegie, Helen, 175
Carnegie, Peter, 88, 175
Carr, Dan, 54, 81
Carter, Jimmy, 200
Cartwright, Sir Richard, 72
Casey, William, 237
Castro, Fidel, 100n2

Chalmers, David, 262–63, 265, 267, 276, 280n2
Chamberlain, Wilt, 129–30, 149, 161, 162, 163, 171
Chambers, Jerry, 161
Chance, Dean, 130
Chapman, Sidney, 85n1
Chardiet, Juan, 254, 268, 269n3, 273
Christie, Robert, 92
Chrysler Building, 214–18
Chuvalo, George, 130
CKC Group, 86n7
CKCL (radio station), 53, 65n2
CKEY (radio station), 33, 53–65, 67, 73, 74, 76, 77, 80, 84, 92, 93–94, 103, 104, 107, 109, 111
CKJB (radio station), 46, 48
CKOY (radio station), 58, 78, 103
CKRN (radio station), 50, 54
Clark, Archie, 161
Cobb, Bob, 143
Cobb, Ty, 27, 94
Coliseum Commission, 145
Combs, Leslie, II, 220
Consolidated Frybrook, 104
Consolidated Press, 77, 78, 85–86n6
Cook, Lou, 256
Cooke, Alejandro Miguens (Alex, stepson), 261, 269n3, 273, 282
Cooke, Angel Rodrigo Ramallo (stepson), 261, 282
Cooke, Barbara Jean Carnegie "Jeannie" (first wife), 36, 38–41, 51nn, 60, 62, 64, 80, 83–85, 90, 119, 138, 143, 148, 150, 151, 157, 159, 163, 166, 170–71, 174–76, 206, 282; divorce, 178–95

Cooke, Carolyn "Carrie," 140–
41. *See also* Rozelle, Carrie
Cooke, Carolyn Jean (granddaughter), 141n1, 182, 189
Cooke, Donald Ralph (brother),
25, 33, 41, 50, 119–22, 124,
141n1
Cooke, Harold Edgar "Hal"
(brother), 25, 33, 41, 50, 65,
88, 104, 141n3
Cooke, Jack Kenneth "Kent": arrest, 98; awards and honors,
76–77, 91, 97; and baseball,
87–92, 94–96, 99–100, 111–
12; and basketball, 142–64,
171–74; becomes millionaire,
50; birth, 23–25, 36n3,
37n5; and boxing, 129–36,
152n2; business relationship
with first partner sours, 78,
86n7; and celebrities, 6–8,
10–19, 132, 143, 147, 194,
202; childhood and youth,
25–37; children born, 50,
51n3, 252–54, 282; early career as salesman, 40–42,
51n4; first marriage, 36, 38–
41, 47, 83, 84, 85, 170–71,
174–76, 178–95; and foot-
ball, 5–20, 112, 117–19,
164–66, 199–212; fourth
marriage, 257–69, 272–77,
282; health, 52n8, 136, 139,
140, 151, 166, 168–71; and
hockey, 143–46, 150, 154–
59; and horse racing, 218–
23; leaves Canada for U.S.,
107–13; libel suits, 69–72,
75; magazine publishing, 67–
80; middle name changed to
"Kent," 55, 58–59, 276;

newspaper investments, 223–
28; personality, 3–4, 7, 9,
15–17, 47, 59–65, 73, 76–
77, 92, 152n6, 164; and
radio, 39, 42, 44–66, 93–94;
radio station license lost,
119–24; and real estate,
51n7, 64, 92, 119–20, 128,
132, 169–70, 177nn, 182–
83, 201–2, 213–18; romantic
interests, 65, 80, 82–85,
86n11, 209; second marriage,
206, 208; songwriting, 80–
82; and television, 58, 74–
75, 85n3, 103–7, 124, 126–
41, 143, 151, 211, 225–27;
third marriage, 4–5, 11–20,
101n4, 227, 229–56, 272,
274, 281–82; wealth, 76,
140, 145, 191, 194; yachting,
96–97, 175
Cooke, Jack Kent, II (grandson),
271–72
Cooke, Jacqueline Kent (daughter), 243n7, 252–55, 256n8,
266, 267, 272–74, 281–82
Cooke, John (grandson), 36, 170,
189, 228n9
Cooke, John (Peter) Kent, Jr.
(son), 12, 14, 36, 37n6,
51n3, 93, 127, 142, 148,
169–70, 174, 179–81, 186,
190, 211, 256n4
Cooke, Marlene Ramallo Miguens
Chalmers (fourth wife),
86n11, 218, 232, 245, 254,
256–69, 272–77, 280n1, 282
Cooke, Nancy Marion Jacobs
(mother), 24, 27–29, 31, 32,
35, 41, 51n7, 60, 147–48,
178

Cooke, Ralph (son), 50, 51*n*3, 93, 109, 140*n*1, 148, 170, 182, 186–87, 195*n*3, 222, 271
Cooke, Ralph Ercil (father), 24, 25, 28–29, 31, 32, 35, 39, 41, 51*n*7, 59, 147–48, 178, 276
Cooke, Rebecca Gilliam "Becky," 127, 170, 179, 180, 186, 190, 256*n*4
Cooke, Suzanne Szabados Martin (third wife), 4–5, 11–18, 19, 20*n*10, 86*n*11, 101*n*4, 227, 229–56
Cooke, Thelma (sister), 25, 33, 41
Cooke, Tommy (grandson), 170, 189
Copps, Vic, 135
Cornell, Katherine, 66*n*4
Costello, Sam A., 220
Coury, Dick, 207
Cox, Steve, 17
Cromwell, Oliver, 19*n*8
Crosby, Cathy Lee, 13
Crouter, Wally, 109, 110
Crowley, Arthur J., 183–84, 188, 191, 192–93, 195*n*4
Crysdale, Joe, 92, 93, 94
Curtis, Tony, 147

Dale, G. Allen, 266
Daly, John, 12
Dandy, Sam, 237, 243*n*3
Davies, Robertson, 76, 79, 80
Davis, Al, 204
Davis, Dr. Alvin E., 184–85
Davis, Bette, 143
Davis, Rev. Emlyn, 104
Davis, Ernie, 124*n*2
Davis, Marvin, 212*n*10
Davy, Ted, 59–60
Dayton, Charlie, 204

DeOrsey, C. Leo, 118, 200
Diefenbaker, John, 90
Dingman, Harold, 69, 70, 71, 72
Dionne, Marcel, 173
Dirksen, Everett, 113*n*4
Dixon, Sharon Pratt, 211
Drexel Burnham, 225, 228*n*4
Dryden, John, 15, 19*n*8
Dubin, Al, 49, 53, 54, 59, 84, 158, 159, 167*n*9
Dundee, Chris, 130
Durante, Jimmy, 158
Durham, Yank, 131, 136

Eberly, Ray, 82
Eisenhower, Dwight, 109, 110
Elizabeth, II, Queen of England, 145
Engholm, Ray, 97
Enright, C.J., 219
Essa, Abe, 60–61

Faith, Percy, 31
Farquharson, R.A., 78
Farr, Felicia, 158
Federal Communications Commission (FCC), 120–23, 140
Fernandez, Manny, 165
Fetzer, John, 95
Fine, Nate, 241
First Carolina Communications, 226
Fleming, Rhonda, 158
Ford, Gerry, 200
Ford, Rick Hunt, 4
Ford, Tennessee Ernie, 83, 125*n*5
Foreman, George, 136
Foulkes, Leon, 91
Fountain, Vera, 59
Frazier, Joe, 129, 133–36, 152*n*2
Freeman, Marvin A., 193

Frick, Ford, 100, 101n5
Fry, Christopher, 62
"Funny About a Dream" (song by JKC), 80–82, 86n8

Gaines, John R., 227n4
Gandhi, Mahatma, 68
Gardiner, Samuel, 73
Garner, Hugh, 79
Garson, Greer, 124–25n4
Gibbs, Joe, 207–9, 210
Gilder, Cathy, 252, 253
Giles, Warren, 99, 146
Gleason, Jackie, 18n1, 75
Gluck, Maxwell H., 220
Gluck, Muriel, 220
Gooderham, George, 92, 158
Gooderham, Henry S., 53–54, 65–66n
Goodrich, Gail, 163
Goodrow, George, 135
Gorme, Eydie, 18n1
Gould, Milton, 101n4, 253, 254–55, 281
Gray, Terry, 155
Greenberg, Hank, 91
Greene, Lorne, 56–57, 66n4, 132, 143, 158, 159
Greenspun, Hank, 128
Gretzky, Wayne, 36n2
Griffin, Merv, 18n1
Grimes, Burleigh, 88
Grimsley, W. Harris, 265–66
Groman, Arthur, 183–84, 186–87, 189, 193, 221, 227n5
Guild Radio Services, 67
Guinness Book of World Records, 194, 195n7
Gundy, James H., 54
Gustafson, Jim, 118
Gutierrez, Hernando, 179–81, 186–87, 190–93, 195n5

Haas, Max, 88
Haggin, James Ben Ali, 219–20
Hamilton Tiger Cats, 23–24
H&B Communications, 128
Haney, Stuart, 262
Hannum, Alex, 161
Harper, Terry, 173
Harris, Jim, 69
Harrison, Barbara, 249–50, 252, 256n3
Hawkins, Connie, 171
Hazel, John T., 276
Hearn, Chick, 147, 154, 160, 172, 179
Hearn, Marge, 179
Heintze, Dr. Achim, 242, 243n7
Hewitt, Foster, 93, 94
Hindsmith, H.C., 70
Hogarth, Gen. F. Stuart, 54
Holt, George, 195n6
Horton, Don, 50
Howard, Elston, 95
Hughes, Howie, 157
Hull, Bobby, 166n3
Hunter, Robert, 111
Hutchinson, Bruce, 73

Imhoff, Darral, 161
Imlach, Punch, 155
Imperial Transcriptions, 59, 81
International League, 89, 94, 96
Irsay, Robert, 205
Irving, John, 79
Isley, Don, 54

Jackson, Michael, 10
Jacobs, Dr. Theodore, 185
Johnson, Earvin "Magic," 173
Johnson, Lyndon B., 110, 113n4
Jolley, LeRoy, 227n3
Joyal, Ed, 155
Judis, Bernice, 56

Jurgenson, Sonny, 165, 271
Justice, Charlie "Choo Choo," 11

Kahn, Irving Berlin, 128, 136–39,
    141*nn*
Kaye, Danny, 84, 130, 174
Keiselmann, George, 224
Kelly, Hal, 93, 94
Kelly, Red, 155, 156
Kent, Duke of, 58–59
Kerlan, Robert, 168
Kiam, Victor, 205
Kilmer, Billy, 165
Kindred, Dave, 166
King, Larry (talk show host), 7,
    13
King, Larry L. (author), 7, 14,
    202, 250
King, Loyal, 125*n*5
King, Milton, 117, 165, 191, 200,
    271
Kinsey, Gwyn, 79
Klein, Gene, 204, 212*n*10
Kluge, John, 212*n*10, 283*n*2
Koppel, Ted, 6
Kornheiser, Tony, 203
KRLA (radio station), 120–23
Krupin, Mel, 210
Kunz, Charlie, 82

Labossiere, Gord, 155
Lacher, James, 128, 189, 190,
    192, 217, 244
Lamport, Allan, 62
LaRusso, Rudy, 148–49
Lawrence, Steve, 18*n*1
Lawrence Advertising, 67
Laxalt, Paul, 6, 203, 275
Leary, Al, 31
Le Cocq, Thelma, 63
Lemmon, Jack, 158
Lewis, Jerry, 143, 147

Liberty magazine, 65, 67–80
Lombardi, Vincent, 10, 200, 271
Los Angeles Blades, 145, 151*n*2,
    154
Los Angeles Daily News, 211, 223–
    28
Los Angeles "Fabulous" Forum,
    6, 32, 129, 135, 138, 145,
    153–54, 156, 158–60,
    167*nn,* 174, 188, 193, 194,
    195
Los Angeles Kings, 138, 139,
    154–59, 163, 166–67*nn,*
    171, 173–74, 188, 193–94
Los Angeles Lakers, 138–39,
    142–51, 160–64, 166*n*2,
    171–74, 188, 193–95
Los Angeles Times, 148, 193, 221,
    224
Los Angeles Zorros, 153
Lott, Honey, 90
"Love Is Gone" (song by JKC),
    81, 82, 86*n*10
Lovellette, Clyde, 142
Luckman, Charles, 153

McAree, J.V., 73
McBride, J. Boyd, 72
McCarthy, Eugene, 6, 7, 12, 16,
    252
McCausland, John, 88
McCaw Communications, 225
McCormick, John, 107
McCullagh, George, 62, 75
McDonald, Ken "Jigs," 155–56,
    167*n*5
McFadden, Bernarr, 68
McGinnis, George, 172
McHale, John, 145–46
McHardy, Norman, 78
McLuhan, Marshall, 74
MacMillan, Sir Ernest, 65

McMillian, Jim, 163
McNulty, Joe, 34, 35–36, 37n12, 51n5
MacTavish, Duncan, 58
Madden, John E., 207, 220
Magassy, Csaba, 267
Maher, Charles, 193
Maloney, Dan, 173
Mancini, Ginny, 175
Manley, Dexter, 256n6
Mann, Judy, 255–56
Maple Leaf Stadium, 88–89, 91, 100n1
Markson, Harry, 129
Marshall, George Preston, 117–19, 124n3, 271, 275
Martin, Diane Szabados (Suzanne's mother), 19n10, 230, 233, 235, 239, 242, 245, 246, 248, 252, 258, 267, 280n1
Martin, John Szabados, 230, 231
Martin, Julie, 230, 252
Martin, Stephanie Szabados, 230, 258
Marx, Leonard, 220
Matthau, Walter, 147
Maxa, Rudy, 277
Maxwell, Robert, 80, 223
Mayo, Nick, 143
Meczkowski, Michael J., 268
Mercante, Arthur, 134, 135
Meyers, Dave, 171
Microplastics, 102
Miguens-Oller, Angel G., 258, 261–62, 263
Mikan, George, 142
Milken, Michael, 225
Miller, Arthur, 13
"Mr. Jack Kent Cooke's Amazing, Mystical Conversion" (Berton), 104–6
Mitchell, Bobby, 124n2, 271, 275

Mohs, Lou, 148
Monahan, John, 107
Moncrief, Sidney, 173
Monk, Art, 15, 17
Monson, Rabbi David, 76
Monthly Epic, The (Sutherland), 79
Morton, John, 223
Multimedia deal, 4, 227n7
Murdoch, Rupert, 80, 212n10
Muskie, Edmund, 6, 7, 165, 252
Mutual Radio, 131
Muzak, 141n9

Nachman, Jerry, 250, 256n2
Nadar, Ralph, 140
National Broadcast Sales, 67
National Football League (NFL), 5, 18n1, 112
National Hockey League (NHL), 143–46, 150, 152n4, 154
National League, 97–98, 99
Neiman, Leroy, 141n5
Nelson, Admiral, 209–10, 212n9
New Liberty, 69–76, 79, 80, 85n2, 93, 111
New World, 73
New York Times, 7, 131–32, 135
Night Hank Williams Died, The (play), 14, 18n5
North American Soccer League, 150, 163
Norton, Ken, 167n10
Nourse, Lloyd, 36, 37n11

O'Brien, Kathleen, 281
O'Connor, Sandra Day, 233
O'Flaherty, Daniel, 241
O'Hara, John, 76
"Oley Kent and His Bourgeois Canadians," 30–31, 38–40, 80
O'Neill, Frank, 112

Orr, Bobby, 130
Orwell, George, 62, 76
Owen, Beverley, 69

Pack, Robert, 203
Page, Rodney, 254
Paley, William Cushing, 132, 253
Pallie, Anne, 209
Parcell, Bill, 219
Pardee, Jack, 206–7, 271
Park, James, Jr., 221
Parr, Eddie, 120, 178
Patterson, Joseph, 67, 68
Paul, Gabe, 146
Perenchio, Andrew J. "Jerry," 129–31, 133, 135, 141n3, 152n2, 181, 212n10
Perles, George, 207
Pollock, Frank, 90–91, 112
Pollock, Mary, 91, 93
Pompadour (yacht), 97, 101n3, 103
Popiel, Paul, 155
Powers, Eddie, 35
Pratt, E.J., 74, 79
Precision Dyes and Castings, 102
Prescott Proposals, The (play), 66n4
Presnell, Harve, 159
Prieto, Flavio, 264
Provan, Eddy, 63
Pulford, Bob, 173

Quarry, Jerry, 133, 134
Quayle, Dan, 275, 276

Radio Broadcast Sales, 67
Raljon Corporation, 194
Ramallo, Edna Neves, 260–61
Ramallo, Felix, 261
Ramallo, Roberto Andaia, 260
Reagan, Nancy, 252, 268, 275

Reagan, Ronald, 252
Reed, Willis, 148
Reeve, Ted, 34
Reeves, Dan, 143, 144, 151n2, 154, 163, 189
Reeves, Mary, 143, 189
Regardie, Bill, 252
Reid, Margo, 84
Rense, Paige, 177n2
Resolution Trust Corporation, 228n11
Reyburn, Wallace, 69, 70, 73, 74
Rickey, Branch, 88, 90, 99
Ricks, Jay, 127
Riefler, Don, 220
Riggins, John, 205, 209, 233, 271
Robb, Chuck, 6, 203
Robbie, Joe, 234
Robert F. Kennedy Stadium, 5–6, 10–11, 124n2, 210–11
Roberts, Leslie, 73
Robertson, W. Shore, 253–56
Robinson, John, 207
Robinson, Ray, 103
Rooney, Dan, 145
Rosenbloom, Carroll, 205
Ross, Donald, 88, 112
Rothenberg, Alan, 183, 184, 189, 193
Rouse, Randy and Michele, 239, 252
Rowan, Carl, 6, 12, 165, 202, 252, 275
Rowling, Sir Wallace, 18n3
Rozelle, Carrie (*formerly* Carolyn Cooke), 182, 271, 272
Rozelle, Pete, 141n1, 182, 237, 272
Russell, Bill, 149
Rutledge, Joe, 69
Ryan, Buddy, 5

Safire, William, 6, 202
Sahadi, Fred, 220
Sandwell, B.K., 78–79
Sandy, Keith, 56
Saturday Night, 63, 77–80, 85*n*5, 111
Sawchuk, Terry, 154–55, 156, 158
Schafer, Raymond P., 139, 141*n*8
Schaus, Fred, 148, 161
Schlafly, Hubert, 138
Schroeder, Jay, 16
Schulman, Betty, 8
Schulman, Robert "Bob," 8, 18*n*1, 135, 136, 183, 270
Scott, Barbara Ann, 90
Sedgwick, Harry, 39
Sedgwick, Joe, 70
Shabassion, Jacki, 159
Shaffer, Paul, 112–13*n*
Sharman, Bill, 163–66
Shaughnessy, Shag, 98
Shea, William "Bill," 99, 101*n*4, 107, 112, 117–18, 132, 139, 145, 167*n*7, 183, 186, 188, 246, 252, 253
Sheikh, Ali Haji, 19*n*9
Sheppard, Edmund, 78
Shirley, Jim, 193
Shopsowitz, Sam, 101*n*6, 112, 158
Shore, Eddie, 154
Short, Robert "Bob," 142, 148, 151*n*1
Siegel, Morris, 13, 14, 203, 204, 241, 250, 278–79, 280*n*3
Silbert, Martin, 54, 58
Simon, Barry, 139
Sinatra, Frank, 18*n*1, 132, 174
Sirica, John, 206, 212*n*7, 252
Skyway movie theatre chain, 67
Smith, Brian, 157

Smith, Elmore, 171
Smith, "Smoky," 112
Smythe, Conn, 156
Soloway, Howard, 183
Spanos, Alex, 18*n*1, 204–5
Stahl, Lesley, 6, 12, 13, 18*n*1, 252, 275
Starr, Bart, 275
Starr, Kay, 80, 82–85, 282
Starr, Sam, 111
Storer, George, 95
Strand Records, 119
Sullivan, Brendan, 238
Super Bowl, 4, 8, 11, 15, 19*n*7, 209, 211*n*1
Sutherland, Fraser, 79
Sutton, Mabel R., 78
Sweet, Tony, 234
Sykes, Richards, 139
Szabados, Nicholas, 230

Tamez, Kevin, 263
Tarver, Edna, 39
Taylor, Lawrence, 16, 206
TelePrompTer, 128–29, 136–40, 141*nn*, 166, 171, 188, 191, 194, 202
Tell It to The King (King), 7
Theismann, Joe, 13, 15–16, 206, 212*n*4
Thigpen, Richard, Jr., 191
Thompson, Sir John, 71
Thomson, Kenneth, 50, 59, 85*n*4
Thomson, Lord Roy, 42, 44–50, 51*n*1, 54, 67–69, 73, 75, 78, 85*n*1, 86*n*7, 126, 132, 145, 152*n*3, 158, 167*nn*, 195*n*1
Thorpe, Jim, 36*n*3
Timmins, Noah, 42
Title, Julius M., 193

Tompkins, Kenneth, 138
Toronto Argonauts, 24, 100n1, 146
Toronto *Globe and Mail*, 62, 70, 75–76, 85n4, 89, 108, 110, 127, 146, 157, 224
Toronto Harbor Commission, 89, 92, 95, 100n1
Toronto Maple Leafs (baseball team), 58, 80, 87–92, 94–96, 107, 111–12, 146
Toronto Maple Leafs (hockey team), 93, 146, 155–57
Toronto Star, 70, 90, 94, 104
Turner, Harry, 3–5, 8–9, 17, 245, 247, 249, 274, 276–77

United Soccer Association, 150
U.S. Congress, 107–10
Urquhart, Norman, 54

Vallain, Jean, 82
Van Alen, William, 215, 227n2
Van Breda Kolff, Burth, 161
Van Roijen, Christopher, 232, 273
Veale, Tinkham, II, 220
Veeck, Bill, 88, 90, 95
Verigin, Peter, 43n4
Videotape Enterprises, 194

Wagner, Robert F., 99
Wall, Bob, 155
Wallach, George, 166
Walter, Francis "Tad," 107–8
Wapner, Joseph A., 193–94
Warner, John, 203, 212n6
Washington Redskins, 3–20, 89–90, 112, 117–19, 124nn, 152n6, 164–66, 188, 194, 199–212, 238, 243n2
Webster, R. Howard, 76

Webster, Susan, 237, 245, 256n1, 267
Wedge, Virgil, 182, 183
Weiner, Arnold, 253
Wesley, Walt, 171
West, Jerry, 149, 161–63, 171
West, Jim, 41
Whitney, John Hay, 132, 220
Whitton, Dr. Charlotte, 69, 70, 72
Wilhoit, Henry, 221
Will, George F., 6, 12, 202, 275
Williams, Dick, 95
Williams, Doug, 16–17
Williams, Edward Bennett, 145, 165, 167n7, 174, 183, 187, 199–202, 211n3, 238, 270–71
Williams, Johnny, 57
Williams, William B., 56
Wilson, Jean Maxwell Williams (second wife), 190, 192, 202, 206, 208
Winters, Brian, 171
Winters, Jonathan, 205
Wiser, Wanda, 217
Wismer, Harry, 117
WNEW (radio station), 56
Wolf, Warner, 13
Wolverhampton Wanderers, 150
Woodward, Orator, 218
Wrather, Jack, 141n9

Yepremian, Garo, 165
Yorty, Sam, 145
Young, Scott, 108, 146

Zabelogo, Bernardo, 263
Ziegler, Joe, 90
Zimmerman, William K. "Bill," 54, 88